MANAGING GLOBAL ECONOMIC REFORMS

MANAGING GLOBAL ECONOMIC REFORMS

By

K.S. RAMACHANDRAN

ANMOL PUBLICATIONS PVT. LTD.
NEW DELHI - 110 002 (INDIA)

ANMOL PUBLICATIONS PVT. LTD.
4374/4B, Ansari Road, Daryaganj
New Delhi - 110 002

Managing Global Economic Reforms

First Edition, 2001

ISBN 81-261-0971-8

PRINTED IN INDIA

Published by J.L. Kumar for Anmol Publications Pvt. Ltd., New Delhi - 110 002 and Printed at Mehra Offset Press, Delhi.

CONTENTS

PART III
MACRO & MICRO ISSUES OF LIBERALISATION

PREFACE

Managing the reform effort is much more challenging than making the effort itself. Indeed, it is on the quality of reform management that the fulfilment of the various goals set by policy makers depends. I have split the book into three parts: Corporate planning, Management of intellectual property rights and the Macro and Micro issues of liberalisation. On the face of it, these are unrelated, but if we look at these closely we would find a strong link emerging. IPRs have implications that go well beyond an economy's trade performance. The manner in which the diverse players in an economy handle the IPRs largely influences their performance particularly in an increasingly open economy. Soon, our economy will be fully exposed to all kinds of trade-related pressures, with our manufacturers being threatened by nearly everybody—their immediate competitors, customers, workforce and those who supply essential raw materials and inputs to them. The consensual arrangements that are possible among all these vested interests in a largely protected environment may not work in a competitive regime that is fast emerging, courtesy the rigmarole of the WTO, the presiding deity in the global trade sector. When merit-related might becomes right, then those lacking in merit necessarily have to settle for less, which may, in extreme cases, even mean winding up. This becomes a hard reality with the mandatory removal of quantitative restrictions on imports effective April 1, 2001.

Manufacturers will be assertive in protecting their intellectual property rights and will haul up before the WTO those of their rivals whom they suspect to be living on their intellectual attainments. But, they themselves will be on the watch list of those who operate in the same product territory. Foreign investors will be even more choosy in regard to investment designations. I have cited an IFC study, which underscored the reservations of MNCs about investing in countries which offered only limited protection to the intellectual property rights of manufacturers elsewhere. The pressure increasingly mounted by WTO and the developed nations on developing countries to tighten their IPRs protection mechanisms duly reflects these reservations. Since January, 1995 when the WTO came into being, developing country governments have responded to this pressure partly by promoting an awareness among indigenous manufacturers about the patents-related perceptions of their counterparts abroad and also by strenghtening the statutory and administrative framework for patents protection. These initiatives sought to signal to the international community their readiness to accept the ground rules and norms of multilateral free trade, and not just to dispel doubts over their commitments to the new world trade order negotiated over long months of the Urguay round and finalised at Marrakech, the Moroccan resort town—better known as the robber's paradise. There is simply no going back on their part to the Uruguay deal, given the international ramifications of any default, but then, governments can always hold up things, though only up to a point. My earlier work, *"Global Trade : Challenge and Opportunity"* (1996) prepared as a project while working with ICRIER is relevant to the present work.

Managing the free trade-oriented IPRs regime should become a major corporate responsibility well before the WTO deadline to developing countries to fall in line with the ground rules of global free transfer of goods as well as services. It is this, which prompted me to address major aspects of corporate planning in the first part of the book. In this task, I have not been moved exclusively by the trade-related challenges facing service providers and manufacturers of goods. This caution is consistent with the fact that corporate managers have management of exports and imports only as one among so many aspects of organisational management. Even in corporates that are largely export and/or import-oriented, managing these activities cannot and should not be an exclusive part of corporate involvement. Neither neglect of nor undue obsession with this function is advisable.

I have dealt with this part of the book in a pragmatic—not text book style. The idea is only partly to promote easy readability and the main purpose is to view the various demands on managers from a realistic perspective. I am sure, this will be appreciated by the readers—members of the academia and practising and student managers alike.

The concluding part focuses on the cataclysmic changes that have taken place since mid-1991 when the Narasimha Rao Government bound the Indian nation and the economy to a process of liberalisation covering all areas of the regime hitherto tied to all manner of controls and regulations. As I argued forcefully in my earlier work *Development under Transition* (1998) and subsequently in my two research studies for the IMT, *Managerial Challenges of Reform* (1999) and *Corporate Preparendness for Competition* (2000), managing reform is only partly the responsibility of the Government and that those running the various manufacturing and service organisations necessarily had to accept the driver's role. The point about corporate CEOs and their teams having to drive the reform effort demands a strong reiteration at the close of the first decade of reform and at the start of what the Union Finance Minister, Mr. Yashwant Sinha, in the course of his 2000-2001 Budget speech, called the second generation reform. There is really no escape from this and more and more of industrial and business entities have got to acquire a role that would mean pushing the nation's political leadership and administrative machinery to the periphery of reform effort, confined only to an endorsement of the agenda for economic policy and related changes, itself set by the leadership of the business community.

In the first phase of liberalisation, unfortunately, the reform exercise was largely driven by political decision makers and the bureaucracy, which conveniently left the corporate captains free to blame the slow pace of reform and the impediments to full scale opening up on the apathy of those in the Government either opposed to or not very enthusiastic about pushing the Indian economy deeper and deeper into the global mainstream based entirely on free enterprise. We have moved quite a distance from the ancient regime of controls and regulations, though, obviously, not enough in terms of attitudes and systems required to ensure total freedom of enterprise. This phase has to end and the sooner the better, and for this initiatives have to come inevitably from the corporate and business sector and it would not do for a committed Government alone to push this aspect. I am hopeful that the second generation reform will be characterised by an earnestness on the part of corporate and business sector towards giving an impetus to achievement of its goals. On this note, I offer this book to the readers.

On IPRs, my work as Senior Consultant in the Indian Council for Research in International Economic Relations (ICRIER) during 1995-98 has helped considerably. I would like to thank Dr. S.P. Gupta, formerly Director & Chief Executive, ICRIER and presently Member, Planning Commission for all the assistance provided. On matters of management, my association with IMT since July 1997 has influenced my perceptions.

I have received excellent research and editorial backing from Mrs. Y. Vijayasri, who is an established research and editorial consultant currently based in Bangalore. Mr. Krishna Murari Sinha of the IMT has, for his part, provided exemplary secretarial assistance. As always, my wife, Santha has stood by me in the making of this effort. Our children, Sriram, Ravi, Vani and Viju have supported my endeavour.

K.S. Ramachandran

FOCUSSING THE WIDER ISSUES

[Given the complexity of the reform exercise, I have deemed it necessary to address certain matters which, I fear, may suffer neglect because of the liberalisation euphoria. I am sure, this apparent diversion will only help enhance the value of the book.]

—Author

A) CBI SHOULD KNOW SOME ECONOMICS

A serious effort to give CBI a deep understanding of the basic issues of ethics and accountability concerning industry and business brooks no delay. No doubt, with its involvement in the probe into match fixing by cricket players and administrators, it must learn something about cricket also. This is no joking matter, considering that serious doubts had been raised earlier about CAG's knowledge of defence-related matters when the Bofors scandal surfaced. General K. Sundarji, a key player in the decision to opt for defence supplies from Bofors in preference to its rival company, reportedly did not think that the auditing agency was competent to decide on the merits or otherwise of the choice of Bofors guns and ammunition.

The attack on "That Charlie" in both houses of Parliament was meant to strengthen the argument that defence was much too complicated an area to be dealt with satisfactorily by the acknowledged specialists in evaluation of Government and public sector accounts. CBI will face the same embarrassment when it is asked to go increasingly into areas that demand the kind of knowledge, which it cannot presently boast of given its strait jacket functioning.

Super up status

The Central Bureau of Investigation must stop viewing itself mainly as an extended arm of the police force. Its members have got to acquire a lot of professionalism rather than feel gloated with their super cop status. They must realise that the growing demands for CBI enquiry have less to do with public confidence in the organisation's competence levels and its ability to steer clear of controversies than the fact that the state level law and order machinery is widely perceived to be inefficient as well as arbitrary. Indeed, if the CBI sleuths are congratulating themselves on their own trustworthiness, this is all the more reason why they should complement their increasing work load with much more than a passing familiarity with the ground realities.

Obviously, the time has come to free the agency from Central political control and bring it on par with the offices of the CAG, Election Commission and Central Vigilance Commission. The Bofors case, in particular, has seen so much of political manipulation in respect of CBI—with its heads being changed on the basis of political whims and calculations—that the management of this particular aspect of the nation's foray into massive corruption is itself enough to demand an end to political control of its work. The gains that the Election Commission had made under Mr. Seshan and has consolidated under his successor, Mr. Gill, would appear to justify making CBI an autonomous body answerable only to the Constitution.

Yet, this will be not be the end but only the beginning of a truly professional CBI. One must remember that professionalism does not get fostered merely through enhanced authority. In fact, more power, especially where this is unfettered can come in the way of professionalism being developed. This has happened before to other agencies and could easily happen to CBI now. Still, Mr. Seshan's own ferocity only earned for the Election Commission the respect that the nation's electorate deserved. A CBI director in the shoes of Mr. Seshan can likewise make the investigating agency widely respected.

CVC's Website

The Central Vigilance Commissioner, Mr. N. Vittal has, for his part, shown what the functional autonomy of the vigilance machinery can do to put the fear of the CVC's website—if not the Constitution and the status—on the corrupt elements in the bureaucracy. Nevertheless, the Vigilance Commissioner and the CBI alike can do with a deep understanding of the nuances of banking and other specialised areas of the nation's economic activity.

Returning to CAG, despite the criticism voiced earlier that the audit teams did not always know enough of the subjects they covered, most of the CAG reports have been meticulous in dealing with complex matters. If at all there could be any complaint, this could only be that this constitutional functionary generally eschewed making statements that were even faintly suggestive of a motivated administration. Even the much-debated reports on Bofors and submarine deals only put the facts before Parliament and did not impute any motives. By tradition, the CAG maintains an air of neutrality and this approach has not changed all these years. In fact, the excessive circumspection of this functionary—in contrast to the somewhat explosive style of Mr. Seshan and the exemplary zeal presently shown by Mr. Vittal—may have led to its being sidelined, particularly when the 1991-92 securities scandal erupted, that too even after the joint parliamentary committee under Mr. R.N. Mirdha began its deliberations.

Circumspection of CVC

Nevertheless, an autonomous investigating body, obviously, stands to gain from emulating the circumspection of the CAG. While it has to be firm, it purpose would be best served by making itself clear where it stood *vis-a-vis* the politicians. It would be better still if it does not shout from the rooftops.

Rather, the thrust should be on building competence, to the point where no bank official would ever complain of members of investigating teams acting only as policemen. The CBI must get away, and as fast as it can, from the not so hollowed tradition of crime and punishment. Good bankers are perpetually on the razor's edge as it were and this is true of their counterparts in manufacturing and service industries as well. If the rule book is constantly flaunted before them, they will all be branded as criminals. True dynamism in banking and other corporates is not to be confused with proclivity to activities with criminal intent. The first lesson that any investigator or vigilance official should learn is to trust the man in business and not impute to him any criminal motive, without knowing all the facts.

In respect of the securities scandal, one reason why bank officials did not want either the CAG or the CBI to dabble in the various deals that constituted the massive act of fraudulence during 1991-92 was the fear that neither of them would know and understand the facts behind the deals in their commercial perspective. This fear necessarily has to go if investigators and auditors alike have to prevent irregularities in business and industry. After all, the essential purpose of these functions is to promote healthy entrepreneurship. Policing must be promotional and not destructive. After all, banking will come to a stop if every deal is questioned and investigators and auditors smell a rat in everything that goes on. Mangers wherever they are must be allowed room for flexibility, and dynamism thrives with freedom and not curbs. No business deal is a straightforward affair and the black and white approach of a policeman to economic activities will do more harm than good.

Under long years of regulation, dynamism was deliberately discouraged under the mistaken notion that government controls were there essentially to promote probability Yet, we all know that corruption flourished precisely because of the State being virtually everywhere. The liberalisation, supposedly, has changed the mindset but the CVC website suggests quite the opposite. In this context, the exposure of CBI officials to the day-to-day demands of business and industry has become necessary to promote facilitative investigation.

B) CVC, CAG AND CBI MUST ACT IN TANDEM

The recent CBI investigation into frauds attributed to a senior railway official based in Chennai emphasises, among other things, the element of manipulation in cost escalation of projects. Ever since we adopted the process of development planning, cost and time over-runs have become a massive regularity. The late Mr. Rajiv Gandhi had not quite exaggerated the financial magnitude of hold-ups in projects when he once blamed Yojana Bhawan for a development process characterised by the fact that just less than a sixth of the plan outlay year after year reached the intended beneficiaries. One can well imagine the extent of calculated and premeditated cheating in project delays and the escalation in costs in diverse sectors of the economy. The assets of the railway official seized by the CBI would only be the tip of the iceberg.

While all this long inefficiency has generally been blamed for over-runs in costs and time, and nothing has been done by way of corrective action on the premise that there is no remedy to gross inefficiency, now it emerges that fraud can, indeed, be a major factor. Unfortunately, however, most of the irregularities go unreported and undetected. We must take note that among various economic offences is the fraudulence aspect of cost escalation of projects ,big or small, and in the public or private sector.

An Obvious Fraud

Fraud is very obvious in over-invoicing of imports and under-invoicing of exports. A decade ago, an IMF staff report had hinted at a substantial flight of capital from India. The gains in foreign exchange from manipulative invoicing of merchandise can be substantial. False documentation of trade transactions for private benefit is an equally major economic offence. But then, this also often goes undetected. Rarely anyone gets caught and duly punished. Also, in the name of liberalisation, there is the risk of a case being made against applying too many checks on export and import transactions. Yet, it is clear that the provisions of the Foreign Exchange Management Act, 1999 in lieu of the 1970 FERA and the legislation on prevention of money laundering by themselves are not going to be enough to stop acts of fraudulence leading to a flight of capital from India. We need a strong investigative follow-up on the various provisions.

Smuggling can be actively discouraged through freer trade and removal of policy and quantitative restrictions as well as pursuit of duty liberalisation. While it is not suggested a that administrative action against smuggling should be softened, yet much of the preventive and corrective thrust should be on liberalisation in various ways.

The financial sector has considerable scope for fraudulence. The 1991-92 securities scandal and the scam involving the SBI and the nation's leading mutual fund, CRB (C.R. Bansali), underscore the dangers of very essential and entirely justifiable customer-bank contacts deteriorating into massive acts of fraudulent collusion.

Big Defence Contracts

The Bofors scandal pointed to yet another economic aberration—pay-off on big defence contracts. The submarine deal involved a similar misuse of authority for purposes of private appropriation. Despite adverse findings by the CAG, the guilt is still to be established and the guilty given the appropriate punishment on either of the deals. If every bulk purchase, whether it be of arms and ammunition or edible oil, had involved a cut to the one who placed the order, then a lot of public money should have been misappropriated under long years of control and canalisation of imports in particular.

As for the present and the future, the thrust necessarily has to be on all bulk transactions, commercial or otherwise. The CAG should conduct sample checks on a regular basis of public as well as private deals above a certain amount and refer, where warranted, the transactions to the CBI. While with deeper reform, transparency should, ideally, get promoted, one must warn against any unduly domestic assumption of probity growing because of greater openness. Rather, where significant potential gains are expected, it is prudent to monitor closely various government and non-government transactions. In this context, any distinction between public and private deals is illogical, particularly with reform, and the CAG and CBI have to be brought into the picture in regard to transactions above a certain magnitude regardless of which organisation is involved.

Such monitoring should be automatic, and should not wait for allegations to be made. For instance, any project where the time and cost over-run has been substantial should interest these two bodies as well as the Central Vigilance Commissioner. Monitoring should be swift and not leisurely. It is even advisable for the CAG and CVC to sit together to decide likely cases of fraud, instead of letting a scandal build up and intervening at that stage, and ask CBI to get into the act straight away. After all, CBI should begin to play a pre-emptive part, rather than a prolonged post mortem role. Such preparedness can be depended upon to discourage the kind of aberrations that now keep on surfacing with disquieting regularity. After all, if the three cats are jointly on the prowl, the mice would be on their guard. The CBI would also become more professional in the process.

C) MANAGERIAL CONDUCT: THE ONLY GOLDEN RULE

An interview by the Hindustan Times in October, 2000 with an industrialist, who blows up the advantage of making payments by cheque, has set me thinking on business perceptions about ethics and values. I am not making a case for corruption and permissiveness, but in business conduct flexibility scores over everything else. Ideally, under liberalisation there is no place for the kind of permit-quota raj that dominated the nation's economic scene for long years under tight regulation and control. But then, ten years after the Indian economy was put on the reform path, the Government, and all that goes with it, continue to be the hard facts of life. A sensible businessman has to go along with these forces. How best he tackles them decides the quality of management. Literature on management is free to prescribe a variety of golden rules for business conduct, but no manager with any sense would want to be tied down by inflexible parameters.

The very essence of good human resources management is the manager's responsiveness to changing situations. The industrialist who cites payment by cheque as a big advantage of the shift of his business operations from Delhi to Chennai apparently has a mindset that might let him down particularly when he needs to keep his wits. The objection is not so much to the signal he sends about his commitments to ethics as to the readiness with which he compromises on business compulsions.

Thriving on Chaos

Tom Peters was not joking when he wrote of managers having to thrive on chaos. The latter cannot succeed in the most unlikely situations if their priorities are misplaced as those of the industrialist interviewed. Let payments—wherever these can be—be made by cheque. This obviously helps in accounting and to that extent in sound financial management. But, any sensible businessman knows that he cannot make all his payments in cheque and in white. Even in this era of reform, there are politicians to woo and be bought. There are hundred and one places where palms have to be greased and those with favours to disburse are quite unlikely to take money in white and show their illegitimate gains in bank accounts.

The Central Vigilance Commissioner, Mr. N. Vittal only underscored the hard facts of corruption in this country when he wrote in IMT' s sixth research study *Industry and Business: Ethics and Accountability* of the eleventh commandment, "you can violate all the ten commandments, but thou shall not be found out." This was echoed by a key character in one of the soap serials declaring, "I am not a Mahatma, I am only a businessman." When Mr. Prabhu Chawla launched a management page in his new look *Financial Express* (where I served as senior editor in charge of the editorial page), he had a feature, "From Brats To Barons". One supposes, few brats will turn barons with all the ten commandments firmly tied to their backs.

In his lucid autobiography, the scion of the Oberoi empire. recalled the wrongful occupation of his hotel rooms by female guests of customers. He allowed them some free time before gently reminding the legitimate occupants of their excesses. This was how he built his empire. He knew more than anyone else in the business that guests were guests only and could not share the rooms of his Grand Hotel in Calcutta with their occupants. But, he also knew that a rigid enforcement of the rules of occupation would only stall his progress.

Meant to be Broken

For a good businessman, the golden rules are at times meant to be broken. This demands underscoring especially in the context of the debate over promoting corporate governance. The eleventh commandment as Mr. Vittal calls it is not always necessary. One must accept this. It must also be recognised that there are not two—and entirely unrelated—norms of ethics and accountability for businessmen and individuals. It cannot be that compliance with the written and unwritten law is only for the non-corporate citizen. Nevertheless, the demands on the business community are so hard that what is gospel to the man on the street may often turn out to be quite the country for those in business. An individual who fails to govern himself and his home will do no great damage to the community at large, but an improvident corporate entity will ruin several people—workers, investors, customers and, to some extent, the Government itself through loss of revenue. Those who preach ethics and accountability must recognise this crucial aspect of corporate responsibility.

The quality of business conduct primarily has to be dictated by its goals. A producer and a service provider must deliver and in several ways. This is the only golden rule of business conduct. Liberalisation must promote this, especially knowing that all these years of regulation, expediently bound to social, justice, only helped breed corruption. When there is a truly free market, the cause of probity will advance itself. We would not need an elaborate statutory framework to achieve this . This is no pompous rhetoric even at a time when a truly stunning example of corporate dynamism globally, Microsoft, is under tremendous pressure to break up to facilitate supposedly free competition in the infotech market.

D) RANDOM MUSINGS ON REFORM

[Mr. Sharat Kumar, Vice-President & Director, Institute of Management Technology, has raised some questions, which, I feel, are pertinent in the broader context of opening up-Author]

Looking at liberalisation only in terms of its economic aspects limits the understanding and purpose of its wider implications. Generation of wealth by itself has little meaning if divorced from the effect it has on human life, both at the individual and community level. Webester's dictionary has seven meanings given to the word liberal:

1. Befitting, or worthy of a man of free birth; free; not servile; not restricted.
2. Bestowing in a large and noble way, as a freeman; generous; bounteous; openhanded.
3. Bestowed in a large way; hence, abundant; bountiful; ample; large.
4. Free from restraint; uncontrolled; unchecked; hence, regardless of legal or moral constraints; licentious.
5. Not strict or rigorous; not confined or restricted to the literal sense; as, a liberal translation of a classic.
6. Not narrow or contracted in mind; broadminded.
7. Not bound by authority, orthodox tenets, or established opinion; not conservative.

Historical Perspective

The liberal opinion, which emerged in the political circles of early post-independence years, opted for a mixed economy so as to minimise the exploitative nature of capitalism even while avoiding the authoritarianism of the Soviet system. The patterns that developed over the years, however, overlooked the comprehensive inter-relationship of economics and politics with human freedom and values which the initial liberalism had sought to uphold. In the guise of curbing concentration and unethical use of economic power by private owners of capital, the public sector was assigned a dominant role over the 'commanding heights' of the economy.

In the late 1980s, however, it began to be widely debated that besides its inefficiency, the real problem with the public sector model was its blatant misuse (and huge expansion into areas that had nothing to do with the 'commanding heights') through a nexus between the politicians and bureaucracy. Increasingly, the politicians moved away from the pre-independence ideals of selfless public service and began to manipulate the public systems for their personal benefit. They treated their control over public property as their (short-term) inheritance. Aided and abetted by the bureaucracy (and criminals), who shared the booty, the loot of the exchequer by anyone who could became the pervasive norm, and the honest and upright men of integrity were reduced to hapless bystanders. In a recent article, Mr. Shiv Khera writes (*Times of India,* June 12, 2000): 'Societies are not destroyed by the activities of rascals, but by inactivity of good people.' It is necessary to ponder over this. Thomas Jefferson's famous statement: 'The price of liberty is eternal vigilance' needs to be acted upon.

Integrity and Governance

In substance, the essential question we are faced with is the quality of governance of the State structure, of the individual branches of its administrative units, of the economic organisations (both in private and public sectors), of local bodies and of social sector institutions. It is a question of creating an open and transparent work culture, which is efficient and corruption-free, because corruption is the biggest guzzler of the constructive energy of a society—as also of the individuals—even as its negative effects (peace of mind, health, effect on children, family etc.) may not become clear to the individual in the initial years. Dealing with corruption only at the level of economic offences represents a limited approach. The effort has to be at the source, at the inner motivational level, at the operating culture of an individual and of groups of individuals in an organisation.

Historically, societies have prospered only when they were governed by talented men of high integrity. Emperor Ashoka, committed to Buddhism during a major part of his long rule, left a lasting imprint on the Indian civilisation. For his part, Akbar (who could not read and write) had the wisdom to collect men of talent and integrity to build a prosperous and stable Mughal Empire. In the present day, the functioning culture of any large and successful corporate organisation bears out the importance of integrity and talent.

In the aftermath of the rebellion of 1857, anxious to keep intact their stranglehold on the 'Jewel in the Grown,' the British brought to bear the best of their imaginative resources to put together a grand new policy. They evolved a masterly strategy for the cultural subjugation of the Indian mind at its subconscious roots.

The British recognised that officers of the erstwhile East India Company were corrupt and that without ensuring impeccable integrity at the core levels of governance the British rule could not be sustained. Thus, came the 'heaven born' Indian Civil Service which, alongside an excellent pay, laid down a meticulous code of personal conduct and an elaborate procedure to ensure its strict compliance. With this in place, they set about creating a large group of servile junior Indian officials whose loyalty to the British Raj had to remain unquestioned. The clever device used, as opposed to the high ranking Indian Civil Service, was corruption. The objective was to corrode the moral fibre. By design, the Indian juniors were poorly paid but their corrupt actions (harassing the populace, taking bribes etc.) were deliberately overlooked. This ensured their servility to the British Raj since poorly paid junior officials (and their families) soon got accustomed to a lifestyle based on a large illegal income. They could ill afford to annoy their British superiors and could not resist any orders, no matter how anti-national or unethical these were.

The systematic inculcation of corruption continued for the full ninety years of the British Raj, enveloping several generations. The transfer of power to the Indian leaders in 1947, unfortunately, kept the system unchanged. In the face of their onerous obligations, in the aftermath of a turbulent partition and war in Kashmir, the new rulers fell back to a heavy reliance on the inherited coercive structure of the State comprising the ICS (followed by IAS, whose integrity levels have constantly been on the decline) and the corrupt junior officials. The new State overlooked the fact (notwithstanding several Commissions on Administrative reforms) that major changes in the pattern of governance were inevitable. A large number of our existing laws had been enacted in the nineteenth century under the British Raj, and even earlier, during the rule of its predecessor, the East India Company. There could be no greater proof of the inefficiency of our administrative systems than the fact that these have not been upgraded to respond to the cataclysmic changes of a century.

Colours of Maya

Physical survival is the first and the strongest instinct. Higher needs manifest themselves only after an individual comes to terms with physical survival at an internally acceptable level. Analysing the complex world of Maya, the *Arthashastra* gives a double meaning to *Artha*: 'Meaning' and 'Wealth.' Since nothing happens without action, it is the 'Meaning' perceived by an individual which propels him to action for generation of 'Wealth.' And 'Wealth' has many shades: Material, Intellectual, Aesthetic and Spiritual. Protected by parental care, a child delights in exploring the physical world around it: New toys, places, acquaintances, discoveries and mischief. As the child grows up and learns to cope with life, he has to find his own strength to protect himself. The allurements of *Maya* are great, as the Buddha saw in the course of his strivings. Desire and enjoyment are great propelling forces of life. But a sense of playful light-heartedness and fun is not a matter of uncontrolled indulgence; it requires a strong and balanced mind. The legend of Krishna reflects this essence in which the Indian civilisation had reached its zenith.

Dynamic societies, as India undoubtedly was before the Christian era, have the same attributes. For the rebirth of a strong society in India—from a new childhood in the context of the present day world to a rich adulthood—we need the same strengths. Such balance, strength and spirit cannot be created in a society by doctrinaire injections from the top, no matter how well conceived and noble these are. For such a growth, we need an atmosphere of openness and freedom in which a spirit of enquiry, initiative and opportunity pervades all levels of society.

Intellectual Bankruptcy

Actions bring about change. But, actions and strategies for effective action grow out of imagination and thought. Unless the society puts a premium on imagination and thought, constructive changes do not take place. Politicians (in power, and those trying to get there) have little time to reflect and generate ideas. But, politics and power are essentials of governance, notwithstanding their (often) unsavoury colours. For all its short comings and all the wishful thinking on philosopher-kings, it has not been possible so far to devise a system better than democracy. A politician in the democratic system necessarily has to cope with the ugliest aspects of human nature—greed, jealousy, connivance, conspiracy, back-stabbing, manipulation and insecurity—reasons that are good enough to keep 'decent' people away from the quagmire of politics. Yet, the 'good and decent' need to be involved in an action mode because the quality of governance affects everybody's life.

Unlike the affluent world, imagination, intellect and integrity are short-changed in our society. This has its consequences. It was for good reason that a senior U.N. official recently said that it was a rarity to find an intellectual of high integrity in India. There are other factors also. People in professions, whose province is imagination and intellect, should be there by conviction and inherent inclination, and not because they did not have the opportunity to get into the so-called more lucrative professions. If an intellectual seeks to ingratiate himself with politicians and bureaucrats for the sake of petty privileges instead of deriving his satisfaction from a sense of pride and value of his work, he can make little genuine contribution to generation of ideas and his voice will not be taken seriously by anyone.

Achievements originate from imagination and ideas, as the Taj Mahal did. All progress of the human civilisation, be it the theory of relativity or sending a man to the moon, Leonardo da Vinci's designs of artillery guns or the plays of Kalidasa, has emanated from this. Even in the day-to-day functioning of administrative and social systems, it is the imaginative man or woman who makes all the difference. Creativity is an amalgam of imagination and ideas put to action. While the efficiency of implementation calls for integrity, the basic question always is: what is being implemented? Whenever and wherever a premium is put on such talent, there is rapid advancement. The Government of U.S.A. bends all its tough immigration rules to grant visas to talented men. This is the American way of recognising the value of creative people. Unlike India, where a major factor for winning recognition and regard remains the contacts you have, U.S. prosperity has been built on its image as a land of opportunity for the talented. What should we do to encourage the talented persons and to create a mood and opportunity for flowering of ideas and imagination?

Action Agenda

Putting a system of effective checks and balances in place is essential for large scale decentralisation, without which no rapid forward movement is possible. Institutional systems are human artifacts. They evolve in relationship to the dynamism of a society, in proportion to the vigilance exercised by its alert citizens, who have the capacity to think imaginatively of such matters in depth. Today's free society of U.S.A. operates with a complex fabric of institutions that undergrid the freedom offered by its economic-social-legal structure. Many of its institutional frameworks—the anti-trust laws, the laws regulating the securities market and the food and drug industries, the social security legislation, the various regulations in banking, labour markets and an increasingly sophisticated employment of macro-economic tools of monetary and fiscal policy—offer safety and protection to its citizens, far above what our system of governance holds out to us. If we compare the norms and standards prescribed in the U.S. for publishing balance-sheets (which an increasing number of Indian companies have been obliged to follow) with those in India, we can observe the difference in quality, in the honesty of effort to provide truthful information for protection of investors. So much for our moribund style of governance which has continued for over 50 years as a mere change of guard, from the white Britishers to colourful Indian browns, the looting pattern changing from the organised system of stuffing the white pocket of the Raj to the disorganised lining of the pockets of a few browns. The principal institution affecting the social and economic life of a country on a daily basis is the Government. It is the Government that lays down the rules of the game under which the social and economic structures must operate. It is the quality of such institutional rules and their stability and predictability, which determines efficiency. Governments exert their influence in three major ways: (i) as being responsible for public services and goods for essential infrastructure, which private bodies cannot or will not supply; (ii) as stabliliser of economic activity through complex uncertainties of future by using requisite monetary and fiscal policies; (iii) as rule maker and enforcer.

Government must exist

As is widely believed now, the Government must move out of all other areas, the free functioning of which should be monitored and regulated by the institutional framework that itself will differ from society to society and from time to time. It has to be a dynamic process. It is necessary to be pragmatic to avoid the two extremes of an ignorant moralism, do-goodism or politically expedient populism on the one hand, which, in denying the attributes—political, legal and cultural—peculiar to a society, produces disorder and impoverishment of people and, on the other, a morally obtuse approach which, oblivious to the most important concerns of man—those that lie beyond material welfare—ends by fomenting a tide of resentment that sweeps the structure itself away (the advent of Ayatuallah Khomeine in Iran). To bell the cat—that is to build the institutional framework, which will encourage initiative at a wider base of our society, and to create a mood of recognition and regard for the talented—it will be futile to rely on the existing self-seeking bureaucratic structure of governance which has failed even to upgrade our century-old laws, as noted earlier. In the mid-1990's, when the mood was to deregulate industrial activity, a brilliant bureaucrat came up with a plan calling for 'automatic approval' of new industries. He did not even realise that the two words were mutually contradictory and his plan negated the very spirit of the intention. A change in the mind-set has to take place.

There is a rising clamour for thoughtless privatisation of the public sector as if it is one panacea for all ills. The ignored truth is that most ills of the pubic sector are created by the unimaginative and irresponsible stranglehold of the bureaucracy and politicians who exercise authority without answerability. The truth also is that the public sector has a large number of highly competent managers who, given a free hand to manage their affairs, can hold their own in a level playing field of open competition with the private sector. The proof of this also lies in the fact that fat salaries are being offered by the private sector to lure an increasing number of senior public sector managers.

In this context, it would be interesting to ponder over the remark of a highly respected and competent senior civil servant, who retired after a long career in Government with close interaction with many public sector units and spent five years on the boards of many private sector units, that by and large, managers in the public sector display a greater sense of values and the courage to stand up to their bosses. The problem, clearly, is not with the managers but with those who exercise irresponsible and inefficient control on the managers of PSUs. It is the governance—the control on the management—which is wrong. A huge amount of public money has gone to build public sector organisations. It is not at all desirable to continue with the existing system of governance of PSUs where, notwithstanding their boards, the real power is exercised by the politicians and bureaucracy without any answerability. Is privatising all PSUs the only available answer?

For a better alternative

The dismal record of performance, both ethical and financial, of a large number of private sector companies, their blatant swindling and syphoning off funds of private investors and public financial institutions, must invite a search for a better alternative. The virtual collapse of the (rigged) share prices of a horde of privately owned companies under the watchful scrutiny (of the quality of their management and financial affairs) by the FIIs and other smart investment managers should be an eye-opener for the propagandists of a thougthless privatisation. This kind of distress sale amounts to abdication of responsibility. It is also to be seen that the large amount of funds required for the privatisation of major PSUs are, broadly speaking, beyond the reach of the Indian private sector. Inevitably, they will fall into the hands of MNCs. Are we really convinced that this would be the best thing to happen? Is this the only alternative for running the PSUs efficiently?

Separation of ownership from governance is an established phenomenon with MNCs, the world over. This is bound to happen in India also, though the pace has been sluggish so far. Many of the major PSUs could leap up in performance if their ownership and governance (the back-door control and interference by politicians and bureaucrats) is genuinely separated. If the private sector can identify competent men and charge them with the responsibility of making efficient use of their investments, surely the public sector can do so.

We have a large pool of talented people of high integrity and proven record of achievement in various walks of our national life. They have a wealth of experience behind them. Such people, the silent core that keeps this country running, are not given to self-promoting manipulations and kow-towing to powers that be. Consequently, they retire and while away their time at home at the age of sixty, unsung and of no further use to society. No person of outstanding talent retires in the U.S.A. as long as he continues to make a significant contribution (and anyone, at any age, must be assumed to be retired if he fails to contribute). Peter Drucker is a full professor at the age of ninety and Stella Kramrisch, the great historian of Indian Art, continued as the curator of Indian art at the Philadelphia museum till she passed away well past the age of ninety. In India, we let, if not compel, such people to fade into oblivion (and senility) at an age, which in this era of good health and longevity leaves them fit and eminently suitable for making effective contributions based on the rich wealth of their experience. Since we have a crying need for men and women, who combine integrity with competence in all walks of our national life, this is a great national loss. There could be no better set of people to reorganise the archaic and moribund systems of managing our public services.

Such people, firm in their value system and well past the pressures of their families, do not hanker for material rewards, but need work to put their mature experience to purposeful use for giving a meaning to their lives. It is not only in the PSUs but also in large areas of public services and social sector organisations that these people can make an excellent contribution. We need to evolve a system to select such people through an open and transparent way (an imaginative version of UPSC/ PSEB). Based on their record of experience and achievement relevant to the respective institutions, they should be appointed to the board of directors or governing body of public service organisations/institutions. Such appointments for a long and stable period with a well defined code of governance will generate a deep and thoughtful commitment of the board for evolution of meaningful policy directions to the management. The replacement of the stranglehold of vested interests by an empowered group of committed individuals in governance will usher in a sea change in the efficiency of our public institutions, be they PSUs, social sector or public service organisations.

E) THE INEFFICIENCY SYNDROME MUST GO

[In a blistering attack on the anti-reform forces, Mrs. Y. Vijayasri, a reputed research & editorial consultant, wants the State to be marginalised by the business leadership as the catalyst of the development process]

Reform is essentially a process of sustained managerial excellence. Unfortunately, whatever development of the economy that is taking place in the post-reform era is largely State-driven. The business community is still looking up to the politician and the bureaucracy for guidance and support. McKinsey & Co., sometime ago, spoke of the fact that not many of the Indian industrial houses were willing to adopt the driver's role in the development process. This reluctance is a tragic aspect of what goes in the name of the reform effort that we are all boasting of. When we talk about development under reform, we should mean the development of the economy in its entirety, not just one segment, that too in very limited ways. We cannot, obviously, be satisfied with a few remarkable corporate successes within and on the international arena.

No doubt, the Indian infotech sector is winning kudos from the international community and also, a number of third generation industrial houses, have emerged strongly in the period after Government took various measures of liberalisation in mid-1991. But, this is not how one must measure the contribution of the business community to the development of the Indian economy. We must ask for a more lasting as well as comprehensive effort from business houses. Indeed, it is a big ask: The State should be effectively marginalised as the catalyst of the development process, with business barons taking upon the leadership position on matters of development. Peter Drucker once said that those who cannot and will not fight would be better off doing something other than running a business. While making this observation, the management *guru* could have hardly been thinking of India, let alone the latter's initiatives towards liberalisation. Yet, when we consider these words in the present Indian context, we can see that these were prophetic.

A corporate leadership, which cannot seriously think of taking the mantle of developmental driver, to borrow the words of Mckinsey co, is not even itching for a fight, what to speak of winning. One only hopes that this book will succeed in persuading decision-makers in the business community to make a determined bid to ease out the State from the position it had held for long years since India's independence and which, indeed, had led to the building and consolidation of the inefficiency syndrome. This syndrome must go.

PART I

CORPORATE PLANNING

1
INTRODUCTION

1. WHAT 'HOW TO' BOOKS DON'T TELL?

A lot is written of corporate planning and strategy. There are books galore that tell the students all about how the companies should be run and how they should not be. But, the best managers don't care a damn about 'how to' and 'how not to' books. They set their own rules and beat their rivals often by breaking what is gospel to them. Yet, in all this, there is a method. There is planning and whatever is done has a strong strategic base. After all, no battle is won without a plan of action. It may be unusual, non-conformist, but even in madness there is a method.

Patton won some of the best reported battles in modern history by following his own instinct. Hannibal had done that two thousand years earlier. The best generals are the ones who win. Napoleon's tactics worked as long as he respected the environment and once he defied it, he had to lose. Instincts do not always prove to be wrong but where they do it is because of neglect of the environment. Where they turn out to be right they conformed to the ground realities. While non-conformity in terms of style itself can win, the prime requisite is acceptance of the facts on the ground. Non-conformism can be in respect of tactics, but certainly this cannot be the basis on which a strategy has to be worked out. Moscow is one place that is cruel to invaders in winter. Napoleon with all his scholarship and leadership qualities could not afford to ignore this. Decades later, Hitler committed the same mistake again, only to lose the battle. Both were poor managers.

Recognise the facts

When the market is depressed, no CEO can decide unilaterally that it is quite the contrary. While optimism is the hall mark of good management, a refusal to recognise the facts on the ground and respect them is plain ridiculous. Nobody can get away with that kind of an attitude. If a corporate plan fails, it is because of wanton neglect of the first rule of good management — respect the facts. Non-conformism should not extend to this and every CEO must accept this. Excellence in management lies in using the facts — even those tantamount to chaos — to the company's advantage. If some CEOs score over others when the environment facing them all is testing, this reflects the superior quality of corporate planning and policy-making.

No manager is above the environment, business as well as a extraneous. The business environment is influenced by political and other factors and these have to be taken care of in corporate planning. This explains why CEOs have to befriend influential politicians both in and out of power and policy makers. Allies have to be cultivated in the political and bureaucratic milieu, without, however, getting involved in corrupt practices. The developments in South Korea, especially the sentence passed on the CEOs of leading *chaebols* warns against getting too close to politicians. A healthy distance has to be kept. This is a test of corporate planning. While kick-backs, are no doubt, undesirable, no company can still survive in a competitive environment without giving kick-backs to influential politicians and bureaucrats. Managing kick-backs will demand the utmost skill on the part of the CEO and his close advisors. It would be simplistic to assume that business runs on the strength of essential norms of ethics. The `to be' managers have to be told of the hard reality of running an efficient business and it would be wrong to keep them in the dark about the ways of building business and consolidating it. This was the basic thrust of a research study, *"Industry & Business: Ethics and Accountability"*, which I did for the Institute of Management Technology recently (July, 2000).

Battling Corruption

The battle against corruption and for business ethics has to be fought on a different plane and it would be quite unpragmatic to induct this in a corporate plan. This, indeed, is the task of industrial associations, themselves working in conjunction with political parties. A national consensus has to be fostered on freeing business from corruption, but this is not for individual CEOs to handle. Rather, they should keep out of this in the interests of the companies they head. For, a CEO spearheading the fight against corruption and kick-backs runs the risk of being blacklisted. This is bad for the company's business. It might lose orders when on merit it should not. When behind-the-door negotiations are the normal practice, it is not wise on the part of a single CEO to press for wholly transparent bidding. It is relevant in this context to remember that while the US law prohibits kick-backs, Enron attracted the complaint that it offered bribes suitably camouflaged to meet Indian conditions for getting the Dabhol power project. It is possible that US Companies generally do this kind of camouflaging to get round the American law. Another essential aspect of corporate planning is to look for loopholes in laws that are relevant to business. Much of the corporate success often comes from taking advantage of the infirmities in the statute. In the past, when the MRTP Act sought to control concentration of economic power, the large industrial houses had to look for escape gates in respect of substantial expansion as well as market dominance. This provides an explanation for the growth of several houses which the Act sought to keep in check. In respect of restrictive trade practices, there were what were known as the gateways of escape and these were duly capitalised on.

Profitable growth

Companies which want to succeed have to be constantly looking for opportunities for profitable growth. The emergence of zero-tax companies over a period is an excellent example of good corporate planning. For a long time, the big companies produced goods that were reserved for the small scale sector, taking advantage of the uncertain legitimacy of the 1970 administrative order by the Union Ministry of Industry, which the Government set right — much too belatedly though — by getting a Presidential ordinance issued — with the provocation being provided by the Bombay High Court's striking down in January, 1980 the 1970 order as null and void. The excise provisions have always yielded room for monetary saving, on the basis of an interpretation advantageous to producers, though in the light of the problems that the ITC has been consistently facing, no corporate planner can afford to be too clever. The CEO and his advisors must be on strong ground lest they should get caught in prolonged disputes ending only in huge tax liabilities. While CEOs usually rely on their chartered accountants and tax consultants, the responsibility is always theirs. Whether the company loses or gains, the buck is theirs. They cannot really pass it on to others.

Wooing the consumer is a key aspect of corporate planning and policy making and no CEO can let this suffer. While massive publicity and PR campaigns can be organised, the responsibility for their success remains with the top boss. (Hindustan Lever's ad spending does not match the balance sheet gains. The management rightly has not ignored this mismatch.) The number of products that have fallen on the wayside is legion globally and companies that have flopped because of product failures despite a lot of advertisement and PR spending are so many as to caution against complacency and over-optimism. Consumers are often whimsical, though they are also known to be loyal. But, even where loyalty is established, they cannot be taken for granted.

2. STRATEGY TO WIN, NOT LOSE

Managers are the ones who should be concerned about the demands of liberalisation, rather than the Government, but unfortunately they do not accept the responsibility for tackling the emerging scenario. They are still under the impression that the *Ma-baap-sarkar,* meaning the Government, will handle the situation as it develops. This is a mechanical — even destructive —

way of preparing themselves for the challenges of opening up. From what we see, the chief executive officers and their divisional heads are only thinking of parity with the salary and perks packages of the top men and women in the MNCs. They have little clue about what the unfolding scenario — globally and within — holds for the enterprises they supposely preside over. What is even more depressing is that they apparently do not even want to know about what is going to hit them a few years hence.

The softest option in the face of an MNC invasion is abject surrender and this has been exercised in some cases. Parle did it in respect of Coke and so have some manufacturers of refrigerators and washing machines *vis-a-vis* Whirlpool, the global giant. When India needs urgently to establish and promote its brands, the producers are willingly giving up brands that are well established within the country in favour of acquiring some shelter under a known MNC umbrella. This points to a defeatist attitude, the one that gives up the battle well before it has begun. This is bad market economics. Getting tied to the apron-strings of multinational producers is hardly how Indian companies should prepare for globalisation. The argument that identification with a global brand name will help secure a global presence for Indian products can sell, but only up to a point. But, even if this is true, when no effort is made to promote Indian brands, Indian companies will never become global players. As of now, with the sole exception of Bajaj two-wheelers there is really no Indian brand name that is globally — even regionally — recognised.

It is ironic that when such is the level of Indian corporate preparedness, there are management *gurus* who are asking the big Indian corporations to take the battle overseas. All talk of a level playing ground is bunkum when companies here are giving up their sphere of influence within in favour of an MNC. There are the great *gurus* willing to lecture endlessly on the merits of the market place, conveniently glossing over the fact that the marketplace is for those who will not only give battle but also win. Tom Peters wrote of thriving on chaos, and here we are quickly resigning ourselves to a frightening situation that can be averted if only we are determined to fight.

Corporate psyche

A lot obviously is wrong with the Indian corporate psyche. Otherwise, surrender to the feared MNC might could not have become the standard strategy for globalisation. On this basis, India hardly deserved becoming a full dialogue partner of the ASEAN! The companies that are big enough to give India a strong global identity over time are only deepening their presence within, ironically through tie-ups with MNCs. Did Godrej need an alliance with Procter and Gamble? What is Hindustan Lever's own record? It is going for acquisitions and mergers in the consumer goods segment but only for keeping intact its share of the domestic market. Nobody is saying that the local market should be ignored, but globalisation demands capturing a bigger share of the international market. Given their clout, the local giants can keep their domestic market share and even enhance it. But, that is not really what globalisation expects of them. The MNCs will surely try their utmost to tap the Indian market. But, preventing them from doing this is only one aspect of the Indian corporate strategy under globalisation. Pushing Indian brands overseas to establish a strong Indian identity has to be the other aspect. The sooner the giants of the Indian corporate sector realise this the better it will be for the Indian economy in the coming months. High priority should be given to boosting domestic capital formation and investment especially in the core sectors of the economy.

With the new patents law hanging in the balance for quite a while because of worries over a possible loss of the nation's economic sovereignty, things were not getting any better. There was a time-frame for getting the Patents Act amended in line with India's commitments to WTO, but until recently not many realised that, over time, the nation's economic sovereignty would stand better protected with a patents regime that offered equal protection to the intellectual property rights of foreign and Indian manufacturers. Curiously, while politicians have been pushing the sovereignty line to hold up any progress on the Patents Act amendment, they failed to look at the gains likely to accrue from enhanced protection overall to intellectual property rights.

Misusing patents

It is no doubt possible for local manufacturers to use the design of global giants specialising in fashion wear and get away with this, but, it is not going to be easy for Indian drug companies to misuse patents provisions blatantly. A large number of products, Indian as well as foreign, can still take advantage of loopholes in the IPRs regime, but this is not to argue against the essential merits of discipline all round. Ideally, the less the industry relies on politicians for protection the better it would be for their global competitiveness. Politicians can opt for throwing projects in the Arabian Sea or the Bay of Bengal and after a while decide to take them out — as the Shiv Sena-BJP Government in Maharashtra did in respect of the Enron project — but this is a course that is not open to any manufacturer, big or small. Those in industry have to be very careful lest they should hurt their credibility. They must negotiate with care from the very beginning. Partners should be chosen after the necessary ground work has been done. The kind of switching of partners that was done in the telecom sector should not be repeated. The top managers must keep their eyes and ears open all the time. They must, strategically, use one possible collaborator against another to drive a good bargain and get the best technology, equity and marketing support. But, for this it is essential that the psychosis should be one of winning, not losing. Indian corporate leaders must be aggressive, though, obviously, not to the point of being distrustful. Even where a hard bargain is made, cordiality should be the basis of negotiation.

There is really nothing like enmity in free enterprise. Indian corporate leaders have to acquire the maturity that will win lasting business contacts globally. As of now, most businessmen are adept at only one thing, cultivating the politicians and bureaucrats that matter. The tools used in this operation need no elaboration and those that are used for purposes of commercial negotiation globally are not necessarily the same. This the Indian corporate negotiators must understand. While in Third World countries these tactics may work, selling the Indian business cause elsewhere would demand other strategies. Indian managers must think globally, which means being able to communicate in languages other than English. In this area, there is a void in that most managers still do not believe that the customer has to be cultivated before a sales opportunity can be created.

2
CREATING ANIMAL SPIRITS

I. SEBI CODE ON TAKE-OVERS

The corporate sector had waited for a long time to get the kind of take-over code that came up with. The norms set have been designed to ensure orderly take-overs and promote transparency that should help bring about a vast improvement in corporate management. The take-over code focuses on ownership. This is important. Ownership — with the controlling interests having a sufficient stake that would give the requisite involvement in the company faring well — must take precedence over what passes for professional management. This is not to say that corporates need not be professionally managed, but only to underscore the fact that professionalism is usually an euphemism for the stranglehold of private sector bureaucracy. The promoters or those who are in control must have enough involvement to give the companies the requisite sense of direction. Ownership allows for risk-taking, a key part of entrepreneurship. This possibly explains why the companies taken over by the RPG group have turned around — and quite impressively — while those taken over by Chabbrias have just bled. Significantly, in the reform period, the first generation entrepreneurs (Ruias of Essar, for example) have shown greater initiative than the established industrial houses, where, obviously, the bureaucracy lacks the drive.

When we talk of entrepreneurship, the threat of take-over is more important than the assumed results of the take-over. Entrepreneurs who are threatened would fight — and take risks that they would not do otherwise — and ultimately succeed. The essence of a good competitive market is risk-taking and this is possible only with a substantial stake of the controlling interests. This offers an explanation for the loss of drive of big names in the corporate sector, with Modis, for instance, turning traders from entrepreneurs.

On a critical aspect of the SEBI code, where the controlling interests have a 10-11 per cent stake; acquisition of the same quantum of stake is enough for take-over, provided the financial institutions give their okay. They have, all this long, generally been part of the vested interests — although there are some instances of their asserting themselves to bring about a change in the management. Unless they are professional in their approach, the threat of a possible take-over may fail in the prime purpose of promoting the basis of entrepreneurship — the drive. Ordinary investors do not really matter in take-overs and must be satisfied with a better price for their scrips. The answer to this lies in growth of corporate democracy, a goal that, however, is not even distant and is only a pipe dream.

2. FIS : NO LONGER SLEEPING PARTNERS

The world over, the corporate sector is generally allowed to manage itself as best or worst as the case may be, though this does not mean that no questions are ever asked. Indeed, shareholders are an assertive lot and do not let the CEOs do what they like especially when the going is bad. Those, who get mind boggling amounts as remuneration, do have to settle for cuts when profitability nosedives. Yet, the corporate Czars who are winners behave very much like the originals dethroned by the 1917 Soviet revolution. In the United States, as long as the returns are good, the big institutional stake-holders do not bother. This, in fact, is a serious grievance of a well known management *guru,* whose work on corporate Czardom some years back caused waves. In

India, this held good all this long and holds good now under liberalisation. While the financial institutions, at times in the past, asserted themselves to change managements, generally they have gone with the controlling interests and still do. Recently, however, there has been some talk of the institutions being more professional in their approach. But then, what is, indeed, professionalism?

The big stake holders, if they go only by the return on their investment, should not think the way the trade unions and the left-of-centre politicians do. One must grant this but the other option should not be mute inaction, which, indeed, has become the institutions' standard strategy, if we can call it one. The institutions did not protest when the two managing directors of Escorts paid themselves each Rs.2.5 crore annually. Again, when the company organised the merger of a subsidiary, Escorts Tractors, with itself on terms that would boost the promoters' stake from 20 to 40 per cent at the expense of the institutions' own stake, the latter should have objected, but they kept quiet, until a tap on the back came from the Union Finance Ministry. Tata Sons did more or less the same thing at the expense of other shareholders in Tata group companies. They also asked for a fee for using the name of Tata. Now, after the event, what can the FIs do? Pretty little. No bulk investor can possibly support the governing interests on the matter of losing its clout. While sleeping partnership is not really an aberration, it becomes one when the financial institutions sleep even when their role is being deliberately marginalised. Placed as they are, obviously, they cannot do anything to protect the interests of small shareholders. This demonstration of helplessness towards safeguarding the investing public is quite as grave as letting themselves be reduced to peripheral shareholders, and knowingly.

FIs must act

When public stockholding is much too small to be assertive, it is the duty of financial institutions to do this on behalf of the investing public. This must take precedence over the track record of governing interests, unless where the latter combine a good track record with a truly investor-friendly conduct. This is not to argue against either promoters or controlling interests acquiring a stake conducive to their stability. Indeed, with impending power play by the multinational corporations, those who control different Indian companies should have a sufficient stock holding that can easily ward off destabilising efforts. The threat of destabilisation is going to get shriller. The SEBI code on take-overs focussed on orderliness and the battle against destabilisation has still to be fought by the promoters and governing interests. Significantly, the financial institutions' stake is going to be critical to how take-overs will work and even more so how the ordinary investor will be treated. How responsible, alert and assertive the institutions are is critical to the promoters and those seeking a take-over alike respecting the interests of the small investor and the ultimate goal of corporate democracy.

Thus, when the nominee director of a major stake holder initials every proposal of the governing interests without bothering to study its repercussions, that functionary is reducing to a mockery the very essence of the philosophy of shareholders functioning as watchdogs. The investing public looks to the institutions — given their stock holding and even more so the fact that they are government-owned and run — to safeguard its interests. If some inept representative of the financial institutions either does not attend a critical meeting of the board of directors of the company in which the institutions have sufficient stake to make their priorities known to the management or indulges in bonhomie at the risk of not paying enough attention to proposals that have a significant bearing on shareholders, his/her ineptness is effectively making the corporate sector infirm. One must ask in this context whether the mandarins in the Union Finance Ministry earlier had informally sounded the public financial institutions about the merits or otherwise of the issue of shares with non-voting rights and whether the institutions had subsequently protested against it before deciding in its favour.

Professional, not mechanical

Nobody is suggesting that financial institutions should keep managements constantly on tenter hooks with threats of support for efforts at destabilisation. But, their assessments should be professional, not mechanical as is the case now. They must constantly evaluate the record of governing interests and should not wait for damaging press reports to wake them up. With liberalisation, perhaps the perception about stability in corporate management should change. One may even welcome frequent threats of take-overs in the interests of corporate dynamism. More than attractive dividends, what should matter is the ability of a management to provide the required growth impetus in a competitive environment. What the earliest Narasimham Committee has said in support of the track record pertained to a different era and what held good in the context of a destabilising bid by Mr Swaraj Paul in 1983 is not so relevant now when take-over bids can boost the competitive spirit and should be welcomed for that reason alone.

As substantial stake holders, the financial institutions must exercise the utmost vigilance in regard to the performance of the units in general and simultaneously look at the capability of governing interests in coping with the emerging challenges. What was allright in a protected market may be quite inadequate in a different environment. Much of the Indian market is still protected but, surely, it is being opened up. The understanding of the track record has to change and take-overs that were suspect in a protected market could be welcome in an opened up market. The future is no longer for survivors but sure winners.

Yet, same caution is warranted on take-overs. While some destabilisation may be justified for putting the managements on the alert, financial institutions have to be wary of the tactics of professional destabilisers. They are there in good number in the United States, putting well performing companies under needless stress and strain. We have their copycats here. The institutions must first know enough of the record of the take-over bidder's own record and second, they must put their knowledge to the best use. It is essentially their responsibility to prevent a unit sliding from the frying pan into the fire. Changes in management should not be for changes' sake but for a for more viable and, of course, professional purpose.

3. CORPORATE TAKE-OVERS

The proposal for a code of conduct to promote good corporate governance had come at a time when the corporate sector was coming under tremendous pressure. In the coming months, this pressure is going to mount and managements are going to be increasingly required to demonstrate skills that hitherto were not called for. The protected market, some years hence, is going to be reduced to a thing of the past and the future can only be for the better managed companies. With financial institutions generally having a substantial stake in the corporate sector and the Government deciding how they will exercise their rights, it has become imperative for both to involve themselves seriously in matters of corporate conduct.

Beyond Cadbury Committee

The Cadbury Committee report in the United Kingdom broadly forms the basis of the code. This Committee had, among other things, recommended that the role of chairman and CEO should be different and clearly defined. But, there are other issues which the Committee had also looked into and declared itself on. While the Committee's report could be the starting point, yet given the Indian context — particularly that public financial institutions are in a position to exercise control — the code has to be reflective of the local ground realities. The institutions themselves need a code of conduct in respect of their role in the managements of companies in which they have a big stake. While the managements should generally be allowed to formulate strategies on their own, the major stock-holders should not endorse indiscriminately all the decisions taken by the managements. SEBI subsequently came with its own guidelines on governance, which cover also FIs' role.

Since SEBI has already laid down the ground rules for take-over the code of governance has to take into account these rules. Obviously, the latter must cover not only the top brass but also senior functional managers. There has to be delegation of authority to promote corporate dynamism, for no manager will be able to work properly if at every stage he or she is being pulled up by the top brass. Senior managers have to have a role in formulation of corporate strategies and reducing them to yes-men would have disastrous consequences. The Government-institutional relationship also has to be defined clearly. While the Government can legitimately claim the right to advise the institutions on how they should behave, in the emerging scenario it would be wiser on its part to let the institutions decide their own approach.

While the private corporate sector has always had a role in the performance of the Indian economy, with liberalisation this is significantly enhanced. While the public sector goes without an agenda, the opening up has been considerable in respect of the private sector. The curbs on growth of concentration of economic power under the MRTP Act have gone. The industrial licensing procedure has been substantially diluted and the capital market substantially relaxed. The foreign equity ceiling is up to 51 per cent and there has also been a significant relaxation of the procedure for clearance of foreign investment proposals. While it is difficult to establish a link between the various measures of liberalisation bearing on the private sector and the performance of the industrial sector, the fact remains that reform as of now essentially means opening up the horizon for the private corporate sector.

Equity stake

But, the reform of the capital market introduced as part of the liberalisation process has not get reflected in managements consolidating their hold over the companies through strong equity involvement. Control is still generally exercised with a low equity stake. This should explain why the SEBI code on take-overs had put the threshold level for acquisition of shares at 10 per cent.

While in the past a low stake was explained by the Government's restrictive policies, after a decade of liberalisation — particularly involving the MRTP Act and the industrial licensing framework — a possible explanation one can offer for the very limited equity holding of promoters and governing interests is that the rules for take-over are yet to be softened, though this may not be widely accepted.

Creeping share acquisitions by the controlling interests or promoters to consolidate their holdings are a difficult proposition as of now, since even when 100 shares are purchased the take-over code comes into force and promoters or controlling interests have to make a public offer for a minimum acquisition of 20 per cent of the equity capital. This leaves them with no alternative but go for preference share allotments which, obviously, are unfair to the investing public. The code formulated by SEBI sought to address that and let those in control of companies, or promoters, to acquire, without the need for an open offer, two per cent of the total equity stake annually if their stake was between 10 and 25 per cent and five per cent shares every year if their holding was between 25 and 50 per cent. The regulator, no doubt, assumed that the code would facilitate consolidation of holdings and should, over time, put an end to the low stakes with which they control companies, provided, of course, the majority stake holders — the financial institutions — stand by them against possible destabilising or take-over bids. But, in effect, the limits mooted by the capital market watchdog might work against the kind of consolidation needed in the emerging context of liberalisation.

MRTP Act

It is true, Indian companies were traditionally controlled and managed by promoters having low equity stakes, which obviously were because of the restrictions in the sphere of industrial licensing and MRTP Act provisions. Promoters found it necessary to carry on several activities instead of focusing on a few. Since resources were limited, their contribution to the equity capital of these companies was inevitably low. No wonder, the 1970 industrial policy statement by the then Union Industry Minister, Mr. C. Subramaniam mooted a programme by which the public financial institutions could use their equity stake to convert private into joint sector companies. The convertibility clause was to be used to sharpen that process.

But, the 1991 liberalisation changed all that and SEBI duly reflected that by seeking to put in black and white the absolute control level at 50 per cent by taking share acquisitions over that limit outside the purview of the code. SEBI, somewhat mechanically, acknowledged that in a competitive environment promoters had to consolidate their holdings to build their defences against possible take over threats and allowed creeping acquisitions. It, more or less let it be known that share acquisitions by promoters holding more than 50 per cent would not affect the interests of other shareholders, especially small holders.

But then, the big companies are still going to have problems considering that in their case a one per cent increase in stake would require Rs.100 crore or even more. Effectively, consolidation through fair means is not an easy proposition for the mega companies. This may be one explanation — though hardly an acceptable one — why Escorts some time ago took recourse to the merger of a group company, Escorts Tractors, that too on the basis of a dubious pricing arrangement, to push up the promoter's stake from 20 to 40 per cent, in the process causing a loss of Rs.100 crore to other shareholders, particularly the financial institutions.

Disclosure Provisions

The SEBI code formulated on the basis of the Bhagwati panel report should help promoters and governing interests by making take-overs more difficult because of the elaborate disclosure provisions on substantial acquisition of shares and other provisions like the 10 per cent upfront deposit in an escrow account. Promoters and persons holding more than five per cent in a company will have to disclose their holdings to the company within a period of two months. The company, in turn, will have to notify it to the stock exchanges. Likewise, holders of more than 10 per cent equity and promoters of companies will have to make yearly disclosures to the company and the latter, for its part, has to make yearly disclosures to stock exchanges on a continuing basis. These would help the target of an acquisition move know about an impending take-over threat.

The general feeling is that promoters may influence market prices when they want to shore up their holdings. There have to be some checks on this tendency. A counter argument to this is that if promoters do beat down their stock prices in the market for buying the permissible quantum, the lower prices may also catch the eye of a raider. Among the other major features of the code, the situations where exemptions might be granted by SEBI from the provision of the mandatory public offer were specified. The constitution of an expert panel had been suggested to consider requests for exemptions not falling under the specified situations.

Conditional Offers

SEBI has exempted preferential issues from the open offer provision but allowed conditional offers subject to certain checks. The rationale behind exempting preferential offers was that it was subject to clearance from the company's shareholders who are the best judges of the matter, it was explained. Conditional offers (those subject to a minimum level of acceptances), which were not permitted under the previous dispensation was allowed under the changed code. The proviso is that the acquirer would have to accept at least 20 per cent of shares from public shareholders (as in a normal open offer), in order to provide some comfort level to the shareholders.

While the old regime was triggered off only by acquisition of shares, the SEBI code has made an open offer mandatory for any change in management control of companies. Competitive bids have been clearly defined and the time limit for a competitive bid has been extended from 14 to 21 days.

The earlier code did not define many critical terms in play during a take-over like 'promoter', 'public shareholding', 'offer period' and 'target company'. These have been taken care of in the amended regime and terms like 'acquirer' and 'persons acting in concert' have been made more precise and widened. In the term 'persons acting in concert', financial institutions have been excluded and foreign institutional investors (FIIs) included.

Under the previous system, an acquirer could also bid for 100 per cent shares of the target company. If after the offer, the public shareholding fell to below 10 per cent, the acquirer had the option of either buying out the remaining shares and, in effect, delisting the company, or making an offer for sale so that the public shareholding of 25 per cent was achieved. Only category-I merchant bankers were allowed to manage offers and the offer announcements had to carry much more detailed information regarding funding arrangements like the highest price paid for purchase of the scrip in the last one year. Further, debt instruments had been included both for the 10 per cent amount to be deposited into the escrow account and for compensation to respondents of open offers.

Reactions to Bhagawati Panel

The SEBI had examined each and every regulation of the existing code in detail. The existing provisions were strengthened and new ones added to ensure a proper regulatory framework for take-over related activities. It is interesting in this context to recall the immediate response to the proposals submitted by the Bhagawati panel to SEBI. Reacting to the committee's recommendatons, the Torrent group, whose bidding for control of AEC had provoked the code, stated: 'The new code has more clarity than the earlier one and provisions like 100 per cent offers, delisting of companies, exemption of preferential offers, are welcome. On the whole, the interest of minority shareholders seems to be protected.'

The group, however, said that certain ambiguities needed to be addressed further. `While the code provides for control without shares, it did not clearly define control. The code decided to have the definition of control and persons acting in concert more on the lines of the definition of the MRTP Act, which, over the period, had been found to be grossly inadequate.' 'While the code had made a provision of escrow account, the option of bank guarantee or deposit of securities are areas which need further attention. For the competitive bidder, the amount to be put in the escrow account should have been higher,' Torrent pointed out. The move to revise the old take-over code had been initiated after the severe test it was put to in the celebrated case of the Ahmedabad Electricity Company (AEC), where the Ahmedabad-based Torrent group and Nusli Wadia's Bombay Dyeing fought for control of the company.

Here is a recap of the events in the AEC case as well as other cases where the take-over code had been tested: Torrent, which had picked up slightly under 10 per cent of AEC's equity capital from the market over a period of time, announced its intention to make an open offer in August 1995 to acquire upto 20 per cent of AEC's outstanding shares at a price of Rs.65 per share. Nimesh Kampani's J M Financial was the manager to the offer.

On September 15, 1995, well after the 14-day time period specified by the take over code for a competitive bid, Bombay Dyeing announced its counter bid for a minimum 50 per cent of AEC's shares at a price of Rs.90 per share. Bombay Dyeing disclosed that its current holding in AEC was less than one per cent. Udayan Bose's Lazard Creditcapital was the manager to the offer.

After seeking legal help, SEBI disqualified Bombay Dyeing's bid saying that it had not seen made within the specified 14-day limit. Undeterred, Bombay Dyeing told AEC shareholders to wait for a further announcement from it, hinting that it would come out with an offer after Torrent's offer closed. Torrent made heavy open market purchases after the announcement of the open offer. Torrent sought to revise its offer price to Rs. 105 per share.

Leading Companies with the Stake of Their Promoters

Company	*Promoter stake (in %)*
Reliance Industries	26
Tata Steel	15
Telco	13.5
Bajaj Auto	30
Mahindra & Mahindra	29
Tata Electric	20-21
Hindalco	26
Grasim	25
Gujarat Ambuja	30
Ceat	40
Great Eastern Shipping	12

as of September, 1995.

After seeking legal help, SEBI finally ruled that Torrent would have to offer the highest price paid for its open market purchases made after the announcement. SEBI determined the price as Rs 132. Torrent agreed to make the open offer at that price. During all these, AEC's share price remained well over Rs.150 on the BSE. Torrent's open offer attracted a very poor response as the AEC share price was still much higher than Rs.132. Torrent's stake in AEC already was around 26 per cent. Coming to another relevant case, NEPC and the promoters of Damania Airways entered into an agreement whereby the former would initially acquire six per cent of the latter's stake and also take over the management. SEBI, however, forced NEPC to make an open offer to Damania shareholders. NEPC made an open offer for acquiring a minimum of 50 per cent of Modiluft shares. SEBI struck down the offer saying that it was conditional in nature and not allowed under the existing code.

3

THE CORE ISSUES

1. THE LIMITED ROLE OF CONSULTANTS

With liberalisation, shouldn't the economy, particularly the industrial and services sectors, do with fewer consultants? Consultants are the ones who would not dirty their hands. In fact, the more sick an enterprise is the richer they become. Units taken up for recovery may lack several things, but they will have consultants, who, one supposes, will get their remuneration first. It is like the first claim on assets. Peter Drucker, in the *Frontiers of Management* conceded that he did not generally dirty his hands. He made his millions by writing books and newspaper columns rather than trying to revive a company. In fact, his practical experience was not only limited but also unsuccessful — for the enterprise which employed him. Consultants are the ones who proffer advice but do not take responsibility for the repercussions of the advice they give. If things turn from bad to worse, they will conveniently blame it on the shortcomings of the management. If there is a turnaround they will take the credit.

The more the consultants, the merrier it is not for the company which uses them. Yet, consultancy firms are proliferating. They have more business than they can cope with. Their prosperity, one must say, increases with more corporate failures, rather than successes. The bigger names in the profession are growing into management *gurus a la* Drucker and Tom Peters. They give lectures, hold seminars and refresher courses and are on the faculty of internationally reputed management institutions. They even help formulate strategies for coping with the challenges of multinational corporations, though in what way is a matter of speculation.

Not Totally Useless

It is not that the management *gurus* and consultants are totally useless. It would be wrong to consider the profession in its entirety a parasitical one. In fact, some of the best projects are the handiwork of dedicated consultants and behind some of the best run companies are good management experts, those who know a great deal more than giving lectures and brainwashing gullible executives. There are some in the consultancy business who just do not mind making their hands dirty but even make it a point to do this in the interests of the enterprises they serve.

Still, the fact is that parasitical attitude is growing and more and more management advisors/consultants are now convinced that what matters is their business regardless of what happens to the enterprise they are associated with. It is time someone sat down to monitor the success/failure record of the firms they work for. The millions the consultancy firms rake in should not be considered at all in this exercise. How the companies they are advising run should be the focus. While, as of now, consultants sit in judgement over how enterprises fare, someone must do this in respect of the consultants. Just as the credit rating agencies need to be rated, the contributions of management advisors and the myriad consultants have to be examined through a microscope.

Brooks no delay

This is an exercise that brooks no delay as this will lend the objectivity, that is presently missing, to use of consultants. The deployment of these professionals does not necessarily reflect on the inadequacies of the management, for in several complex areas outside expertise is needed. But, generally the management must be self-reliant and do without outside help. When an enterprise turns sick it would be wrong to assume that the pre-requisite for its turn-around is the induction of an expert who charges the heavens. While nobody can say that expertise is not necessary, accountability is always more critical to how a unit performs. A person who does not belong to an organisation and does not pay the price for his/her mistakes does not have the accountability. While a lot of passing the buck goes on in the corporate world, still when there is a crisis someone's responsibility gets fixed and often the concerned manager pays with his head. This does not happen to the *guru* from outside who submits the proposals and takes the fees. When an enterprise flops, the consultant will get the boot no doubt, but he will have other units to jump to. No consultancy firm closes down because of one unit, which it had supposedly served, pulling down its shutters. Rather, the spread of industrial sickness has led to consultants thriving, with banks undertaking revival using consultancy firms as if the fate of their efforts depended critically on the latter.

Yet, it is not always easy to fix the contribution of consultants or make a balanced assessment of what they do. Depending on the quality of consultancy provided, this can be either crucial or marginal. A committed consultant is hardly a parasite. But, unfortunately more and more of the tribe are turning parasitical — rather than dirtying their hands, they clean themselves at the cost of companies which use their services.

2. REDUCING MBAS TO GLORIFIED CLERKS

No conglomerate, however, revolutionary it is would put its materials manager as chief of HRD or vice versa. The freedom that Parliament had exercised some years back in picking two of its members who were unfamiliar with the national language for a committee specifically to monitor the use of it in India's missions in different countries no captain of industry would want to have. A chief executive can be unfamiliar with the technical aspects of the unit's operations particularly if he belongs to a dynasty. But, even in family concerns, values are changing and either the younger generation is given the engineering background or the overall charge is given to one not part of the dynasty who is technically qualified to be in the hot seat.

No sensible management would tolerate passengers but unfortunately there are umpteen cases where while the qualifications are right the job opportunities are wrong. This is particularly true of MBAs.

Young MBAs are, in fact, given the most unprofessional tasks in several enterprises in both the public and private sector. While in the universities and institutes of management, they would have, no doubt, read a great deal, not all MBAs really learn the right lessons. When they chase high salaries and good perks, they generally learn not to mind the lack of professionalism that goes with these.

One fresh MBA was told by his boss to redesign his office. This was to be done with no care for expense. When the boss came to inspect the new office, the only thing he noticed was that it was on the same floor level as that of the subordinates. He literally hit the roof at seeing that he, the big boss, was not accommodated at a level higher than those under him. He refused to consider the fact that an alteration would mean dismantling the false ceiling provided for his own comfort.

Soaked in Wealth

But, fresh MBAs cannot have the cake and eat it too. Upto a point, they can decide whether they should opt for getting soaked in wealth, *a la* General Motors, or good professional opportunities. But, they cannot do this on their own. The employers should also make it possible for them to take a decision. Whether or not the people who get out of management institutes are put in a position where they can become good managers depends largely on the perceptions of people who run an enterprise and work out the corporate strategy. Reducing the MBAs to globalised clerks is the easiest — but the most undesirable — thing to do but this happens in several places. The quality of work life inevitably suffers.

It is not also enough to have highly qualified scientists and engineers on corporate payrolls. The latter have to be treated with the respect due and have to be involved in decision making. If the idea is to make them feel subservient with the top brass taking all the decisions, then it does not really matter whether R&D and materials management are formally entrusted to qualified professionals or to administrative personnel who will carry out orders without asking any inconvenient questions. Related to this is the question of encouraging constructive dissent and discouraging yesmanship. One recalls a catchy advertisement way back on November 10, 1991. It showed the boss, the company's president, in a violent temper shouting at three standing subordinates, "I note hesitation, doubt, timidity ! Take care I will sack the whole bunch of you and get new yesmen". The men to whom this is addressed seem stunned. They simply blabber, " Yes.... Sir".

Let us take a close look at the message: "'yes" is a nice, safe word. Especially if you are saying it to the boss. 'Yes' is an even better word to hear if you are the boss. But, it is a dangerous word. It hides the hypocrite, the sycophant and the lazy minded and that is why it is dangerous. A company's finest asset is its unique collection of individual minds, people with minds of their own, who have something valuable to say. Very often that valuable something is the word 'No' to status quo. It is a big word. 'No'. It has often been the first step to the world's greatest discoveries. It would be the first step to a profitable change in your company.' 'Dissent' — encourage dissent, manage dissent — but with care, with imagination, with a sense of responsibility. With the confidence that things can be better."

"At Tata Steel we are committed to this new corporate culture. Because the one thing we should all say 'Yes' to is 'Progress'." Perhaps not everybody will be greatly impressed by this advertisement in the context of later developments — Tata Sons' demand for a fee for use of the Tata name and the tactics adopted to enhance its stake in group companies. Yet, it needs stressing that constructive dissent is the essence of good management and this symbolises the top brass's willingness to share authority and to promote alternative sources of power. When this is there, MBAs will be treated as decision-makers of the morrow and scientists and technologists as the real architects of an enterprise.

3. THE BIG RACKET DOES NOT REALLY MATTER: EMPHASISING TEAM SPIRIT

The bigger the racket, the better we can serve' screamed a cartoon on the front page of a New Delhi newspaper on June 29, 1995. It showed the BJP Chief with a mega size tennis racket — representing the UP government — offering this hope to his partymen. The time lag not withstanding this is a telling message. When we translate this into a concept of management, we can roughly say that with a big organisational structure and a superman as chief executive an enterprise can perform better than with a puny structure and a chief executive without a hero image. But, this is not really so.

With the growing popularity of tennis, using a tennis racket in an illustration makes a lot of sense. Over the years, the increasing use of rackets to give the user an awesome power, in serving as well as volleying, has led to a dimunition in the quality of play. This can happen to big companies that one would normally expect to steamroll opposition. This is a world of corporate shake-outs with transnational companies growing bigger through mergers and tie-ups. But, with size also comes a bureaucracy and with the bureaucracy also comes the risk of innovativeness getting blunted. The more worrying aspect is that faith in bigness leads to neglect of fostering team spirit.

Pioneers, one must acknowledge, are not born every day, people who set precedents for others. Ford's Petersen, Honda's Fujisawa, General Electric's Welch and Lee Iacocca of Ford were remarkable managers and men like them do not emerge just like that. This must be accepted. But, lesser mortals also have to accept the responsibilities that these super managers often turned into massive opportunities for themselves and for the companies they headed and, not only that, emulate their performance.

Giants and Pygmies

The corporate world has a place both for giants and pygmies. And it is not always the giant who wins. The mega tennis rackets cannot always win matches for those who wield them. This is why the big servers and volleyers lose to players who lack their power but have other qualities that ultimately count. Stamina and, even more so, mental strength matter at crucial moments. Giants collapse because they might lack the fighting spirit when this is most needed. One must remember that even the acknowledged corporate *gurus* did not always succeed. Iacocca's turn-around of Ford did not last all that long and Petersen, despite all the halo around him, could not keep the same company on the success route indefinitely. In the end, it is the team which wins or loses. The team is not one man but represents a group of several people of varying abilities, some very efficient and some less than par. Everyone must, however, play the assigned part and pull in the same direction. If a team stands together then it can thrive on chaos, as Tom Peters put it. The racket does not have to be huge to win matches. Neither the organisation has to be massive nor the chief executive has to have the Midas touch. A group of committed lesser mortals can turn a crisis into a winning position.

Team Spirit

In his magnum opus, *Managing on the edge — How successful companies use conflict to stay ahead,* Richard Pascale quoted Petersen to emphasise the importance of team spirit, "I want this company — Ford — to be a place where we see the best in people, and not the worst. A place where we work co-operatively, not as adversaries. To recognise and seek and trust the professionalism of others. I believe in the power of team-work. These are the lasting things about an institution — not the home run product of a particular model year, but a healthy process. It's a lot like parenting. It's not one event like a spanking or supporting your child to succeed on a particular project."

The team is always bigger than the individual, however, important he is. Success comes more to a leader who moves and is involved with the team than one who behaves as if he is born to give orders and the rest to take orders. The superiors in the heirarchy will be assured of good support if they realign processes for serving their subordinates better, as Pascale pointed out. The Japanese style management which exemplified this principle is seen by some writers as a myth. An American businessman, who spent long years watching the working of Japanese firms, some time ago came out with a book *"The Japanese management mystique—the reality behind the myth"* by Jon Woronoff (1993) that sought to explode the premises which Pascale proceeded on. But, this debate is irrelevant to the essence of team building and fostering team spirit.

4. WINNERS TAKE ALL

How much of intellectual input does a manager need? Can business do without an intellectual exercise? Here, when we talk of intellect, we do not mean academic excellence or even a familiarity with books or an association with management schools or institutes. For a manager, being intellectual, obviously, means an ability to think on his own and to be innovative. The corporate decision maker does not have to flaunt an understanding of management principles. In business, actions have to be formulated quickly and it is not going to help the manager if he sits alone and consult books by Peter Drucker or Tom Peters. A manager does not have to look academic and sport an impressive beard or be sloppy in his dress selection. What is really needed is the sharpness of mind.

Battles have to be fought and won. Winners take all. There will never be any change in this basic principle. The environment is only becoming more competitive and more challenging and is not getting any easier for managers to handle. Decisions that are mechanical are not going to win the corporate battles. So, when we talk of a manager with an intellectual bent of mind, we only mean an ability to think well and quickly. Time does not wait for man and hardly does so for the manager, regardless of what kind of an organisation he is running. The executive has to be swift in his responses and must always be ready to give battle.

Whimsical Market

Products have to be prepared that would readily sell. The market place is whimsical in its attitude and is always demanding and managers have to be alert and come up with decisions on product - mix and market techniques before their rivals can even think of them. In the global corporate community, some of the giants have become associated with certain types of marketing attitudes. But, ultimately what succeeds is not the attitude but the manner how the manager anticipates developments in the market place and acts. The market place has always been challenging and is getting more so and is meant for people who can fight, not those who either choose to wait for the opportunities to emerge or just relax.

Combining business with pleasure is all right as a way of saying, but no sensible executive will take the risk of ignoring business for the sake of pleasure. Business will come first to any competent manager. His grey cells will always be working over time. He may not really need the sagely advice of Drucker or Peters, though he may want to impress his visitors with a galaxy of well known works on management in his visiting room. The most successful managers have not been inside management schools either as students or part-time teachers. To them, education comes mainly from enterprises which they run. They learn as well as teach. This is an unique experience for those who work with them. A manager who learns and teaches sets a good example for people who work with him and he spontaneously helps groom more people like him.

No Grooming

Unfortunately, giants of management the world over have not always been good teachers and groomers. They only emerged as titans and did not bother about those who worked with them. They were conceited and egotistical and had no time or the inclination to groom good managers. This is why people like Iacocca who became heroes in their life time did not leave behind managers who could think and act as they did. Yet, intellectual superiority has to be passed on from person to person, from generation to generation. One Petersen or Welch will not do. It is also not enough for management students to read the books of Drucker and Peters. They have to be helped to become good managers. The students may get cushy jobs but may not be trained to think on their own and to find solutions for corporate problems before they emerge. After all, the essence of managerial excellence lies in an ability to visualise changes in the environment and be ready to meet them effectively before they come into the open.

5. PROOF OF THE PUDDING

The phenomenon of duplicate and bogus shares should, with reason, give rise to duplicate and bogus managements. Agreed that neither instrument can be used in excess, the fact that as many as 15 lakhs of duplicate shares of a market leader then had been in circulation since 1991-92 and for quite some time later suggested that a promoter on the fringe of losing control could throw the bogus shares that were not genuine into the market to get the holding necessary for survival. Likewise, a corporate raider is free to push in that many duplicate/bogus shares which would give the edge over the controlling interests. What had happened some years back is hardly irrelevant to the present and the future.

Both constitute a management that is either bogus or duplicate. Since it took as long as four years for anyone to know of the existence of 15 lakhs shares of the corporate in question, this is a possibility that is not hypothetical. It is not even a hypothesis to argue that recourse to bogus/duplicate shares can help stabilise a management or create one that enjoys no legitimacy strictly in terms of stake.

Finding a remedy to shares and managements that are either bogus or duplicate is not something that operating managers should concern themselves with. Trying to find out what constitutes a genuine or bogus management is outside their ambit. After all, they are not free to decide who will dictate to them and whose orders they have to take. They cannot also bother about the niceties or otherwise — often the latter — of how with bogus or duplicate shares the promoters can hold their own or some others enemical to them can dislodge them.

Managers can't dictate

For, the senior and junior managers alike have to go with those at the helm and cannot ask too many questions. They cannot say that they do not like somebody's face if the idea is to keep their position intact. How those in charge of management keep themselves strong and how they get dislodged does not really concern them. Ethics should not bother functioning managers as long as they are not asked to cheat and pay the price for it. Given the corporate ways, it is not easy for managers to declare what kind of a top brass they would want. Nor can they set the agenda for those who lead. They can either take and or leave it. They cannot dictate. In practice, the legitimacy of the management in terms of stock holding does not always decide how well or poorly an organisation functions. There are umpteen units which have performed abysmally despite the controlling interests having a stock holding largely on the basis of genuine transactions. There are an equal number of companies which have scored over their rivals despite recourse by them to unfair tactics to secure a controlling interest.

When we say unfair, a clarification is due. There is really nothing like fairness in business. Successful businessmen have to do several things that as individuals they would not want to and should not. While social responsibility of business has to be fostered, this cannot and will never be the exclusive goal of any business. Most successful businessmen will accept social responsibility only insofar as it does not come into conflict with their essential profit motive. For a more focussed debate on business ethics, I suggest a close look at my sixth research study for IMT, "*Industry Business*: *Ethics and Accountability*" (July, 2000)

So, what if the management is either bogus or duplicate as long as it delivers the goods? Everything is fair in love and war, goes the adage, and commercial practice often goes literally on the extended principle that everything is unfair in love and war. This is not to say that unfairness is essential to successful enterprise. Indeed, a good businessman has to camouflage his tactics and strategies in such a way that even a blatantly unfair means of achieving impressive results has to appear as one that is based on the long forgotten code of *Manu*!

Tarnishing the Image

One is not being funny in saying this. While only the achievers matter at the market place, the public perception of cheating can tarnish the corporate image. The stock market can be played up and down depending on what the listed company wants, so long as it has on its side brokers with a lot of clout. But, when it comes to selling goods and services, there is something like customer satisfaction. This is no illusion. When a product is spurious or the service provided is indifferent, the customer will be lost.

The bourses operate on principles different from those, which apply to the real market place where goods and services are sold and bought. In the stock market, bogus and duplicate shares can be traded in without doing any great harm to how the customer in the other market reacts. A company can play havoc with the stock market and capital market and play with all the instruments open to it but as long as its goods and services are held in esteem, it will command good custom. While this cannot be offered as a justification for manipulation of the capital market and bourses, yet for any business the proof of the pudding lies in the eating — how well or badly the product or service sells.

6. HRM SHOULD NOT BE HMV

Human resource management (HRM) should not deteriorate into his master's voice (HMV). But, unfortunately, this happens more often than warranted by the imperative of sound management. In the process, manpower management suffers and the unit is unable to get the most out of the resources at its disposal, human as well as otherwise. The human resource manager is in a testing situation, having to satisfy the top brass and workers simultaneously. The unions generally would think that he is the *chamcha* (disciple) of the top management and the latter, especially when it is under pressure, would assume that he is pro-worker. A good management depends critically on how deftly this particular executive performs his duties.

Not all managements recognise the value of an independent human resource manager. Yet, since this functionary has to be flexible in his approach, it is necessary to give him a lot of leaway and not tie his hands behind his back. He must have considerable negotiating authority and be able to make commitments to workers, which he can subsequently honour. If the top brass treats him as a whipping boy, his credibility with workers declines and the unit's productivity overall suffers ultimately.

Unfortunately, it is easier making prescriptions and submitting proposals than being on the spot and taking decisions quickly. On the floor, there is always a lot of tension and the human resource manager needs to be innovative as well as courageous if he is to avert an escalation of differences in perceptions. A small dispute can grow into a serious agitation leading to suspension of work and even lock-outs. This is where the role of this executive will count a great deal. He must be able to sort out personnel problems without losing his face and for him to be able to do this he needs the strong support of top management as well as workers.

The human resource manager always has problems waiting to be resolved. With the growing affluence of senior executives, friction is inevitable and he has to ensure that this does not get reflected in loss of productivity. In a competitive environment, the unit, whatever its operations are, has to perform very efficiently. Presently, with the strong winds of change, more and more undertakings have to address themselves to rationalisation of workforce to give themselves a competitive edge, not only globally but also within.

Loss of Productivity

It is not easy for the human resource manager to propose rationalisation of workforce when top managers give themselves liberal perks and salaries which they believe is necessary in the context of globalisation. But, it is for him to tell the top brass what the tolerance limit of workers is. He will always be required to anticipate the feelings of workers and never should he let himself be shocked. It is hazardous for a manager to cope with the situation that has emerged from a lack of preparedness to meet a feeling among workers that they have been left in the cold while managers soaked themselves in extreme wealth. Ultimately, the burden falls on the human resource manager. Essentially, his task will be to prevent a feeling of discontent leading to a loss of productivity.

The top brass has to be sensitive to the problems of the man on the hot seat. It must listen to what he has to say on the perceptions of workers. Here, a clarification is due. Workers should not be equated with the unions, meaning their leaders. Often, it happens that those who lead the unions do not seek to serve the interests of the people whom they represent and support instead the management. Trade union activity in this country reflects in some way this phenomenon. The human resource manager should tell the unions how they should behave. But, never should he be identified with union leaders. If he does so, he stands the risk of his motives being mistaken by both the management and workers. He has to keep a distance not only from the unions but also from the top brass. He has to be independent and must show himself to be so.

Such independence, obviously, cannot be established by the human resource manager acting by himself. He needs the cooperation of the top brass as well as workers. He should not even suggest that he is speaking his master's voice. He must be open to suggestions from the staff and must be willing to risk putting these across to the management. He must also be prepared when necessary to support proposals that in his assessment are in the long-term interests of the unit.

Not a Sanyasi

Unfortunately, the independence of the human resource manager does not always receive the attention necessary. Generally, it is assumed that the human resource manager is just part of the managerial cadre and he will go with the other executives. For, he also is soaked in wealth and gets the perks and salaries that others in the executive cadre get. Nobody is suggesting that the human resource manager should become a *sanyasi* (ascetic). But, being treated as an executive does not mean that he can behave like one especially when he has to deal with a touchy workforce.

Who is to lay down the guidelines for human resource management? These guidelines, obviously, the manager cannot himself formulate. These have to be part of the corporate culture. One would expect the management associations to fix the norms of conduct of the human resource manager *vis-a-vis* the top brass and workers. There has to be a debate and the associations must get a general consensus in favour of a human resource manager, who does not speak his master's voice but prefers to speak his own. An independent functionary is a key aspect of sound personnel management and the management associations have to take upon themselves the responsibility for promoting an ethos that give the manager in charge of human resources a quiet authority in dealing with the top management as well as workers.

7. YESTERDAY'S PIONEERS AND TODAY'S BRATS

By focussing on business brats, management writers are, in a way, making the point that the rags-to-riches story does not belong to the distant past. The qualification is warranted by the fact that unlike Jamshedji Tata, G.D. Birla, Oberoi, Nanda and Rabinder Nath, today's brats are not really starting from scratch. While they start their business and build it up, they have access to the kind of financial support that the pioneers of the past just did not have. This is not to say that there are no brats standing on their own feet but a good look at their profiles would show that they did not start as babes in the wood.

The pioneers of yesterday and brats of today still have a lot in common. They have to fight to succeed and success does not come easily. The format is similar but there are differences in the required responses. The ones who had built up empires from virtually nothing had a virgin territory before them. They could really do anything they wanted. Jamsedji did not have to go for India's first steel plant. He could have done something else. G.D. Birla also was free to put up a steel plant. In fact, it emerges from B.M. Birla's biography that he was keen to enter the petroleum sector in the immediate post-Independence period.

No Virgin Land

But, today for anyone who wants to go on his own there is nothing like a virgin land. If there are diverse opportunities, this has largely to do with the dynamism of the industrial and services sectors. The problem is to make the right decision and go for a product or service that will sell well. In the twenties, mistakes could be made and the promoter can recover, but presently no brat can afford to make a mistake, whether it be with his product mix, the scale of investment or the market strategy. Every mistake can prove very costly and recovery is not easy. Brats, thus, cannot wine and dine most of the time and expect their product or service to take care of itself. They are free to pursue mod ways but business has to be fostered and this needs a lot of doing. Nothing comes on a plate. Opportunities are greater because there are more needs and more entrepreneurs. Anyone who is aiming for the heavens must have a solid platform and this comes from creating opportunities where there are none.

Tata could make steel because nobody else was doing that. He would have had problems getting the technology, the workmen and the orders. But, mind you, Tata Steel reigned supreme for several years and the public sector steel plants did not start commercial production till the early sixties. Not so now and anything you produce today, someone will do tomorrow at a competitive price and quality. This is the market. Nobody really dominates the market. There are exceptions though, but not enough that can make the first producer feel very sure of selling what all he turns out. Eagles thought — it proved a costly mistake — that nobody dare challenge them, but today there are others in the fray. Melaware had convinced itself that nobody could beat them, but it took only a few years for strong competitors to emerge, who produced the stuff that suited the lower middle class, the one segment that looked at the price tag before taking a decision whether to buy or not to.

Under Greater Threat

Thus, today's brats are under greater threat than the pioneers of the twenties and thirties. They have to constantly innovate and interact with the consumer. Indeed, writers on management should, after a while, go back to the same people who were seen to be at the top sometime ago. In the past, while there were rags - to - riches stories, there were few that turned the other way round. But, in the fiercely competitive environment of the present, there may be at least a few riches-to-rags stories.

A survey recommends itself. A brat ceases to be one once he crashes down the ladder. One of the tennis greats, John Mc Kenroe was known as the brat, but this was only as long as he was winning on the courts. Once the decline came, nobody described him so.

Even granting that most corporate brats survive the initial test, how many of them progress to the level of barons? Barons, no doubt, are not born and only brats grow into barons. But, many of the entrepreneurs who start in spectacular fashion could wither away, unable to stand up to the challenge. Progress has to be sustained and one victory will not do. Battles at the market place come when you least expect them and an entrepreneur who is not ready to win is as good as not being there. It is important for brats and barons alike to remember this, more so the former. For, the barons have an army to fight their battles, which few brats can boast of having. After all, barons head empires, with vast resources and crisis managers to help them at different levels. But, the brats have to fall back only on their limited resources when there is a crisis. In fact, their capacity to become barons is severely tested in such a situation.

8. STYLE DOESN'T MATTER

The world over, each corporate giant is identified with a particular style. For long years, Proctor and Gamble was linked with what was known as the Proctor way of marketing, which involved exhaustive pre-launch product and market testing. This had two implications. While the focus of the company's managers was on system fulfilment rather than meeting consumer needs, as for the company's competitors, they were helped to launch competitive products. Top managers who operated globally also had distinctive styles of functioning. While Petersen made informality a way of life, there were others who spread an air of egocentrism.

What is style? Does it really matter to managerial performance and how a unit functions, whether it succeeds or fails? Style represents the manner in which a unit or an individual behaves and responds to a certain situtation. Till an American manager who — after long years of doing business in Japan — (Jon Woronoff), exploded the myth of the Japanese style of management it was generally assumed that the focus on motivating workers was the ideal way of running an organisation. Peterson of Ford was, in fact, known as the Japanese style manager, though, after what Woronoff wrote of the uninspiring ways of Japanese companies, the former chief executive of Ford and architect of its turn - around at one time might not have wanted to be described in that fashion!

But, the point is whether what a manager or a management does by way of a response to a particular situation should be classified as a style and duly recommended for emulation by someone else. For, the moment a style is bandied about, then a signal gets sent out that what a company or manager has practised successfully recommends itself all too readily to another unit or manager. Style then becomes a staitjacket and is marketed. This is a wrong approach as corporate dynamism thrives on the ability to grapple with emerging challenges and this means that managers and managements must devise remedies and corrective measures as they go along and not go on the basis of remedies that worked for some others.

No dressing up

One is free to dress in the way someone else does, but managing a company is not the same as dressing up. Management is much more than aping or emulating. After all, what did wonders for one manager or company may fail dismally for another. While certain principles hold good for all people and for all times, this cannot be said of operational techniques and strategies. These vary from company to company depending on the situation and how well or badly the management tackles it.

Indeed, there could be mayhem if a senior manager decided, very foolishly, that a miracle that occurred in one company could be repeated to give him the halo of success he is looking for. The environment can vary between one outfit and another and the macro fundamentals that are depressing may hurt one but may benefit another. When the economy overall is booming, again a manufacturer may have problems meeting both ends meet while another may be doing wonderfully.

Remarkable things happen because of managerial innovativeness and a chief executive officer choosing to go his way, not sticking to the beaten path. The managers who lag behind may call it style if they want to but it would be quite unwise — even downright foolish — to emulate it without a close look at the particular undertaking's potential and its capacity to achieve things, even more so its inadequacies. An indifferent worker or manager has nothing to gain or lose from some one else's style or lack of it. Ultimately, what matters is the ability to thrive in the face of heavy odds. Achievers do not need the style of someone to set the goals as well as to give an agenda that would succeed. They would rather pursue their ways and get the best of everything.

Big conglomerates can risk trying out several strategies but not so the small companies with very limited resources. While the giants can launch and pull out a product that fails at the market place, this is an option that is not open to several small companies. For the latter, everything must work and very well. There is nothing like trying out different products and strategies. Whatever they do must do wonders. No corporate entity can afford to lose. This is a world of winners taking all and losers losing all. Emulating somebody's style should not, thus, be on the agenda at all. Pushing a product and getting orders do not need anything but good commercial sense, which cannot be syndicated.

9. SUCCESS IS OFTEN BY INSTINCT

Management today is much more challenging than it was some years ago. Several developments in recent years have combined to turn it into a hazardous one. What managers know as the virtual revolution — the evolution of products and services before several producers and consumers have even thought of them — underscores the magnitude of the task that today's corporate decision makers face. The only receipe for success is dynamism, and dynamism is spread over several disciplines. Obviously, what a good manager needs is a mix of market - friendly economics — friendly to the corporates, the market and the producing unit —: a lot of common sense, a commitment to cost cutting and, above all, a sense of accountability — to the users of products and services that the company provides as well as to those who are involved in turning out the products and services.

While theories and concepts do matter, based as these are on first-hand experiences, what finally sells is a pragmatic response to the ground realities — to the extent that the latter cannot be changed to suit the suppliers' needs and to promote the latter's gains. And where this can be done, the success must be traced to the ability of managers to do this. Pricing on the basis of marginal cost does generally make sense, but where markets can bear more why should any supplier go by this principle? Yet, falling to the temptation of making the market pay more than what it should may fail in the long run as a corporate strategy. The loyalty of consumers is something that should not be trifled with. One must remember that the strong consumer preference remains even if prices go up at a later stage, once the loyalty is established. This is demonstrated by the success of certain brands in the country and elsewhere and the failure of others.

Essential lessons

Managers, obviously, have to learn the very essential lessons of wooing the market and keeping its support intact. These do not come in textbooks and in classrooms. While those who attend management schools or institutes should know about the problems that managers face every day and also solve, often they do not. Theories and concepts have to be tested against the developments in the marketplace and those that do not work have to be rejected. But, the question is whether those who teach management - related subjects are prepared to do this. Unfortunately, this is not done, with the result that the products of management courses are not prepared for the challenges of the profession they have taken up.

In this context, one must recognise that after long years under the protected market not many enterprises operate with a sense of urgency. The attitude is one of *sub chalta hai* (everything goes). Here, it is possible for young managers to take things easy, with no great damage done either to their careers or to the companies which employ them. What producers have to do is to revise prices by a certain margin annually and let the market take whatever is put out.

But then, the nineties were different from past years and the new millennium is going to be even more so because of liberalisation. Complacency has to be replaced by dynamism, which means that the students and the professors alike must expose themselves to the demands of the free market. Basically, there has to be an attitudinal change, but this has to be backed by appropriate inputs, constituting an ability to cope with the challenges as they emerge. Whether prices should be hiked or cut, what kind of marketing strategies need to be adopted and whether inputs should be changed and what remedies are open in the sphere of cost management are some of the strategies that have to be carefully examined.

Beyond Textbooks

In these areas, clearly, text books are not going to be of any great help and the faculty of management institutes has to look beyond the eminently respectable discourses of Peter Drucker and Tom Peters and go instead into the nitty gritty of management. In this respect, the involvement of professionals in teaching becomes useful, though in this there is always the risk of the latter either exaggerating their successes or under-stating their failures. There is besides the tendency to see teaching as a pleasant diversion, an extra - curricular activity that is also seen to give them an advantage over their rivals who prepare to attend to their chores rather than seek these diversions.

Senior managers and chief executives may tend to view lectures to management students as an escape valve from their day-to-day drill that is often taxing. Ultimately, the students may not gain from their exposure to managers coming as members of the guest faculty, although the institutions may want to boast of their association with successful men and women in business, industry and Government.

Peter Drucker's candid admission that he did not dirty his hands is a warning against the assumption being made that regular visits by senior executives will make the students better equipped for the challenges of the morrow.

There are successful managers who do not bother too much about what the books on management say. Even where they have gone to the best management institutions, they often act on the basis of their survival and success instincts. Instinct is not something that can be taught or inculcated. It just comes by hindsight and this is out of bounds to others. This explains why either the most successful managers are not always the best qualified professionally or that success has only peripherally to do with academic achievements.

Don't Ignore basics

But, this does not mean that managers of the morrow should be prepared without any focus on the basics. For the arithmetic to turn allright, managers have to know how prices should be fixed and must be more than familiar with the essence of input-output ratio. The rules of marketing, likewise, must be understood even if some CEOs have been known to take the non-conformist route and succeed handsomely. Outrageous behaviour by astute CEOs has paid dividends in the past and might do so in future. But, this cannot be held up as gospel. Young managers must learn the ropes first before they can start experimenting.

Obviously, management teaching and learning must be strong on theory to start with. Exposure to the challenges in management must come next. A sound approach would be to mix theory with practice, although the student should not be encouraged to believe that someone's success or failure will necessarily be his/hers. Pascale's warning against being influenced unduly by the successes of CEOs like Peterson must be heeded, though with the rider about failures as well.

4

STRATEGIC PLANNING

1. PLANNING IS BETTER THAN INTERVENTION

In matters of corporate planning and policy, it is important that the top brass has a clear perception of the environment and is neither too optimistic nor unduly pessimistic. After all, nobody can change the environment. Even big monopolies cannot play with the market in the way they like, given the market regulators. A company is better placed to make the environment work to its advantage with the management accepting the power and strength of the situation that it is facing rather than assuming that it can be won over.

It makes sense to crawl your way up instead of trying to break a stone and failing in the process and going into oblivion. This has happened before in respect of several companies and producers. Today's top managers would do well to remember how Hindustan Lever had failed in the Sixties to push the Pepsodent tooth paste as well as a beverage called Astra and also how both were pulled out within a short while. Pepsodent is back now, but nobody remembers Astra. Then, the company had bowed to the market realities. But, in retrospect, the manufacturers should have avoided getting into the production of the two goods that the consumer clearly did not want. Good corporate planning is characterised by success at every step. Strategic intervention to correct a mistake is not the same as formulation of a plan that works from the start.

This is explained better with a retrospective appraisal of the steel casting industry in the mid sixties. The author was then the Secretary of the Steel Furnace Association of India, the representative body of the industry, and was closely involved in the working of the industry under conditions of recession then prevailing. How different constituents of the industry reacted to the recessionary conditions in the railway wagon industry offers an important lesson in corporate planning and strategy making. Mukand Iron and Steel was the premier electric steel maker then but chose to enter the more complex area of alloy and special steels. Such a diversification was a response to the phenomenon of recession in the wagon industry.

No Fancy Programmes

Very clearly, it was not the company's size that helped it cope with a sharp fall in demand for steel castings and, not only that, also come up on top. Its emergence as a top engineering company had more to do with its corporate dynamism. At that time, the perception in the industry was that its steel re-rolling capability — in terms of technology and engineering expertise — was not the best but it is important to remember that the company did not let this constrain its overall performance. It surged ahead. It did not go for fancy programmes, but stuck to the conventional route.

There was one other arc steel producer in the late sixties that succeeded despite all odds, Bhartia Electric Steel. This company showed a different kind of dynamism. It also diversified. It added one more plant at Faridabad to the one that was already there in Calcutta. Its strategies were different from Mukand's but these also succeeded. The fact that its Managing Director had a hot line with the Railways in New Delhi demonstrated a kind of preparedness that was non-existent elsewhere in the steel casting industry then.

The non-performance of others tells its own story. What happened to Kumardhubi Engineering Company was very significant, but in a different way from Mukund and Bharatia. Every aspect of its management then was a lesson on how a steel foundry — and, for that matter, any industry — should not be run. It was managed by the Bird-Heilgers group, which had by then seen its better days. The stress was more on style and flamboyance rather than getting into the basics. A decision — to call it corporate would be to make a mockery of the expression itself — was taken to set up a 7.5 tonne arc furnace — the biggest then — precisely when steel castings had few buyers. The irony was compounded by the management deciding to run a fully air-conditioned train from the Howrah railway station near Calcutta to Kumardhubi in Bihar to take the honoured guests to the factory for the formal inauguration of the furnace. The cost and general extravagance that the inaugural functioning involved were consistent with the total want of pragmatism in the setting up of a new big steel furnace. How the company's banker, the Allahabad Bank, provided the credit for the purpose defies a rational explanation.

No Takers

There is more. Those who were managing Kumardhubi Engineering decided on a diversification that made no commercial sense. The Central Mechanical Engineering Research Institute under CSIR had, indeed, developed cable and paper making machinery, but to take up their manufacture was commercially inadvisable then. Inevitably, there were no takers for what Kumardhhubi offered and the public sector cable making unit in Rupnarainpur near Calcutta did not want to go beyond sample checks. The less said the better about paper producers. The one captive buyer, Titaghur Paper Mills, then part of the Bird-Heilgers group, was already sick — hardly a situation where it could invest in machinery, that too one that had to establish itself. With such grave managerial inadequacies, it was but inevitable that the company should fold up and seek the helping hand of the Government. Then, of course, it could be nationalised, a course that cannot, however, be seriously considered in the present context of liberalisation when sickness would be deemed to invite liquidation, especially in a case like Kumardhubi Engineering Company.

There were other steel producers quite as badly run. There was one, National Iron & Steel Company, again a reasonably big name. This was ruined by mismanagement of a different kind. While in Kumardhubi there were no underhand dealings, these were the core of National Iron's management or whatever you may call it. The senior personnel saw to it that they handled the supply of all the essential inputs that the company needed. Effectively, they were squeezing the company so that they could profit. The price of imported graphite electrodes had to be hiked every now and then so that the controlling interests could earn an extra rupee. In regard to scrap, while at the industry level the company was fighting for better terms from the scrap suppliers, at the company level what mattered was the personal interest of its director, who dealt in scrap and whose personal profit depended on the company being exploited. There was another in the industry, Hindustan Iron & Steel Company, whose proprietors preferred an investment in a five star hotel in Calcutta to making the foundry a viable proposition. Good corporate planning and policy depends critically on responsibility and accountability. The moment these are seen to be ignorable, than trouble begins for the unit in question. But, this is something that text books cannot teach nor can professorial sermons help.

2. CHOOSING THE BEST STRATEGIES

The quality of corporate planning is tested severely when an enterprise is under considerable strain. It is often immaterial what the reasons are for the tight situation that top managers are having to grapple with. Financial ratios and performance norms get reduced to total irrelevance when the going is bad and is only turning worse. While there is always room for manipulation of the norms that are gospel to finance managers and those who pass off as experts, the real test of performance lies in the unit in question being physically able to get out of the trap in which it is caught or has got itself into.

When business prospects overall are bad, the firm with some cushion — this may be in the financial sphere or in others — is better placed than another without such a facility. But then, cushion is not everything. At best, it is a temporary support mechanism and too much should not be made of this. Reserves provided the kind of cushion that helped bail out a firm facing a liquidity crunch and the cash flow being constrained by recessionary conditions outside. But then, reserves and other cushions are intended to be used only as such and not as the basis of sound management.

No easy place

Ultimately, it must be realised that the market is not an easy place for non-performers. Those who succeed, at times, may have factors other than good performance to help them out, but it is not always so. In fact, it would be foolish, even downright disastrous, to assume that something or the other will always help them out. Managers have to fight most of the time even to stay in the same place. How successful managers push their firms up when going downhill seems an inevitable prospect is the story of resolution and hard labour, with some good luck thrown in. Petersen of Ford was different in temperament and character from Lee Iacocca. But, there was no doubt whatsoever that their remarkable success at the helm was largely due to these factors. Their unique leadership qualities are not sought to be downplayed by emphasising these aspects, but only to underscore the priorities in good management and warn against glossing over these.

An ideal structure of corporate planning has to be focussed strongly on dynamic decision-making. There has to be room for consultation between the top brass and senior and even junior managers. Petersen relied on this process. Indeed, he wanted suggestions to come from workers, so much so that he was called a Japanese style chief executive. That the myth of motivational Japanese style management was later exploded is not relevant to the fact that a chief executive officer of Ford took the entire team along to lead the premier American automobile producer to success at one point of times.

But then, we would do well to remember that while Petersen did bring about a revival of Ford's fortunes, this was not to last. Obviously, one man and his ways of inspiring workers and managers could not keep Ford on the success path all the time. If this was not divine intervention. it must have been something else. Markets are no respecters of big names and men and women with a halo around their necks. This needs underscoring in the present context of liberalisation, when first generation entrepreneurs are outpacing the established houses. Obviously, this phenomenon has a lot to do with the ways of management. Essar is a first generation company and see where it has gone and where it wants to go. It would have even entered the banking sector and would have had the Tamil Nadu Mercantile Bank in its pocket, but for RBI's act of intervention and for the wrong reason. Despite the set-back this house suffered subsequently nobody could dispute the dynamism of the Ruia group.

Big names don't help

Big names do not really help when the challenge is a tough one. The best run companies are those that have the best strategies. Strategic planning is critical to how different companies fare in the market place. Some time ago a benchmark study of strategic planning practices was conducted under the aegis of the International Bench Marketing Clearing House (IBC), which is a unit of the American Productivity and Quality Centre. The study covered six large and successful companies, which were identified as the best in the area of strategic planning. The six companies were Alcoa, John Deere, Frito-Lay, Shell International, Whirlpool and Zerox.

Indian companies do not have to try to get into this exclusive club, but they can certainly pay some attention to strategic planning. They have long been suspected of doing a lot of aping and the global corporate perception is that Indian manufacturers cannot be trusted to respect the intellectual property rights of others.

This we will come to in the second part. One aspect of the six highly rated companies was that their planning process was continually evaluated and improved upon. How many Indian companies can boast of this? The IBC study virtually asks other lesser placed companies to emulate their ways, notwithstanding all the concern over violations of intellectual property rights.

In this context, the question that must be faced is: How professional are the Indian companies? When we talk of professionalism this must not be equated with issues of control. Family controlled businesses were generally considered unprofessional and the only exception was the Tata group. However, in recent years one had to change that perception. Tata Industries have been sought to be reduced to a family group with the controlling interests, Tata sons, charging a brand fee for the use of the name of Tata, and not only that, giving Tata Sons a bigger stake in the group companies at the expense of the general investor and, of course, financial institutions. After all this, Tatas, one might venture to say, have ceased to be identified with professional management. When promoters have only a very limited stake, they cannot behave as if they owned the companies which they controlled. Control should not be equated with ownership, an equation that is, however, becoming quite common. This is a virtual repudiation of professionalism. Indeed, not making such an equation is the first lesson in professional management. But, how many corporate czars will eschew this? Given the stake holding pattern of promoters and controlling interests, the case for an end to family control makes itself strongly. But, who will let this happen?

True Professionalism

But then, one is not saying that either family control is necessarily unprofessional or that a large stock holding gives a free licence for totally unprofessional conduct. Professionalism ultimately does not have anything to do with the level of stake holding. True professionalism not only demands involvement of senior managers in decision-making but also the taking of measures that are designed to foster the general interests of the companies in question. Neither the Tata Sons nor those at the helm of Escorts did that when the controlling stake was enlarged through an operation that was against the interests of other shareholders. Even if all the senior managers of the two companies had been involved in the formulation of this particular strategy, it would not have given it the professional tag. For, if managers can only say yes and can dare say no to what the top brass wants only at the risk of losing their positions, such corporate planning is far from the ideal. It is not enough for management students to understand and the management *gurus* to preach this. The top brass must understand this.

5

TOTAL QUALITY MANAGEMENT

Quality of production is a critical aspect of corporate planning under increasing liberalisation. TQM has been in practice for quite a while in Indian industry even under conditions of control and regulation. This has to acquire a sharper thrust with the second generation reform.

1. THE BASIC PRINCIPLES

Total quality management (TQM) is a process of change and has the following characteristics:

Focus on customer expectations.

Prevention of problems.

Building commitment to quality in the workforce.

Open decision making.

T Q M represents self-improvement and group improvement through team building to improve working practices. It epitomises a gradual change in people's behaviour towards the tasks they perform and their attitude towards other people. The process must run slowly and in small steps and allow plenty of time for peopie to change their behaviour.

In the new millennium, the competitiveness of any organisation will depend largely on continuous quality improvement using TQM methods and procedures that cover all functions, all activities and all members of staff. We in India and elsewhere are moving from an industrial society to an information society; from hierarchies to networks and from representative democracy to a participative democracy. Some of us might want to call this "the new communism" or "communalism". It is certainly more effective than the adversarial business methods earlier used because TQM involves all the people in the decision making process. In this, management personnel become responsible for managing change and not for deciding everything.

There are three basic types of the quality model—process analysis, integrated and charismatic. Each of the processes focuses on the customer in order to determine what actions the organisation should take to improve itself. However, the structure and organisation of the TQM processes used to achieve these actions differ substantially.

Several aspects of each of the three processes are similar and all merge into one when excellence has been achieved.

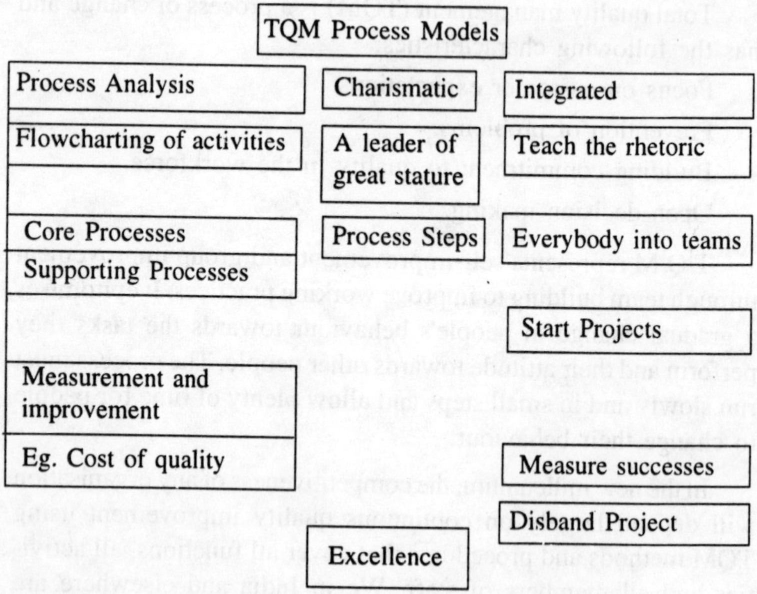

2. PROCESS ANALYSIS TQM

Process analysis stands for analysing the activities of the various processes of business for a better understanding of where improvements can be made. The core and supporting processes of the business should be identified and flow charts prepared showing the interlinks between them. Process analysis is essentially a 'top-down' process of improvement with reviews from the 'bottom-up'. Identifying the process owner is an essential requirement and nothing of value is likely to happen until the process owner is found. The owner, however, is often an elusive character and initially may well deny responsibility for his own process, though this person may lay claim to somebody else's process!

3. CHARISMATIC TQM

Charismatic TQM is less structured. This is typified by the local shop keeper! He is there, with his staff, all day, every day, and serving his customers. He doesn't need a fancy manual to describe his quality policy, vision and mission in life. He shows it all day and every day to his people and his customers. The question is, can he infuse the same sense of continuous excellence in his operations if he has five or six shops spread around the town? This is not irrlevent since under reforms consumer goods ourlets should develop in a chain formation.

4. INTEGRATED TQM

Integrated TQM is an `all fronts' process based upon teams at all levels. The focus remains on the customers' expectations and the prevention of problems, but with this type of TQM process model, the method of accomplishing the actions is to organise people into teams from the top to the bottom of the organisation. These include steering teams, quality circles, facilitator networks and various types of project teams.

The involvement in teams and team-work is highly motivating and builds commitment to quality in the workforce.

5. MANAGEMENT COMMITMENT

Commitment is simply deciding that we will do something and leadership is about doing it. Commitment cannot be faked; either we are or aren't committed. It describes an emotional state which is deeply rooted in the beliefs and conscience of people. Unfortunately, commitment to issues and people is often vague and half-hearted and compromise can come as result. This will not do for an effective TQM process. We must understand this. The commitment of management to TQM cannot be delegated and we have to show our commitment by our actions. If we are a profitable organisation and are committed to TQM, the CEO may deem it enough to commit the resources to TQM and delegate the rest. But, this will turn out to be a waste of money, because it will not work. Quality must be a commitment of management, not just the job of the quality control department. Little or nothing will happen until the top brass gets involved. Those in the organisation will automatically look for evidence that it is committed to the process of improvement.

Management has to develop a vision for the future of the organisation. The necessary resources have to be committed in the form of time and money; usually it happens that the people do not demand much money, particularly in the early stages. The greatest barrier is the availability of time. When solutions to problems are found, these should be promptly implemented. It's no good saying, "Yes, remind me about that next week, I am a bit busy with the 5-year plan at present". The formation of problem solving teams and giving them the time and resources to deal with the problems are not enough. Does the CEO attend problem-solving team meetings from time to time? Dismantling barriers between departments and listening to suggestions for improvement from anyone who cares to make them is equally important.

Quality processes go through phases. After 1 to 2 years from the start, the process usually gets stalled. When this occurs, evidence must be available of management revitalising the process. TQM demands that organisations move away from `management by control' to `management by commitment'. One does not have to be the immediate supervisor or boss of people to get things done. Effectively organised companies have managers who get their own way when they are right, and don't when they are not, irrespective of whether the people they are asking to change work directly for them or not. Politicians are generally quite clear about words like commitment. This is what know as populism; obviously, the politician's interpretation of commitment will not do for organisations that badly need to improve their quality of goods and services.

6. LEADERSHIP

There's more to leadership than autocracy or democracy. One needs to become a `situation' leader by `contracting' with the staff about what kind of leadership it needs through a `diagnostic' process of analysing its needs. The leader becomes `flexible' and manages the staff according to the contract he or she has worked out with it. This is situation leadership and it needs practice because one does not have to be a situational leader; the leader has to learn to behave like one. Leadership is that quality in a person that induces others to follow. John Harvey-Jones called it `Making things Happen'. And remember, these people are both customers and suppliers and not just the people who work for the managers.

The leader cannot delegate leadership. If a subject is important, then the leader should be personally involved, seen and heard by his or her people. At times, this means getting his/her hands dirty, unlike Peter Drucker, with the details of what he or she is trying to accomplish. The difference between the boss and his/her subordinates is that the boss doesn't get dirty as often as they do and when he or she does, he or she may as well arrange for the cameras to be on him/her. We must not confuse leadership with a mere show of authority, a tasty morsel that feeds upon itself for self-gratification.

Modern Leader Job Description	
Mentor	Coach
Facilitator	Teacher
Innovator	
Broker	
Producer	
Director	
Coordinator	
Monitor	

Involvement and Participation

Participation by management in TQM is not enough. Only total involvement will show the staff that the CEO is committed to quality improvement. But, what is the difference between involvement and participation? Deepening reforms demands that we all should get involved, get our hands dirty occasionally and demonstrate our commitment by our actions.

Styles of Leadership

When a manager is leading a quality process, he or she must be an educator, a communicator and the person with the vision of where he or she is going and how he/she is going to get there and how he/she is going to measure the collective progress. There are many types of managers, which depend to some extent on their personality and the job they are doing. Michael Macoby described them differently as jungle fighter, company man, and gamesman. But, what about the possible styles that can be adopted to be a "situational leader'? Macoby describes these styles as 'directing', 'coaching', 'supporting' and 'delegating'. The type of leadership we use for each person we manage depends on the situation. It is neither democratic nor autocratic but simply practical. People are not equal. We should not believe that we are at *Animal Farm* where everybody is equal, but some are more equal than others. That would be dishonest and lacking in sensitivity as well.

We need to know what the overall goal is and the daily needs and guidance that each of the staff requires. Some need one style of leadership and others a different one. It all depends on the `potential' of the subordinate. Some things can be managed, others delegated and yet others supervised. We should not delegate the responsibility for quality and at the same time we should not confuse leadership with supervision. These are not the same thing at all because quality improvement is a management function, not a technical one.

7. QUALITY IMPROVEMENT TOOLS

These do not come in a box from a `do it yourself shop' and do not include a hammer. Indian managers must begin telling this to themselves instead of asking the Government to protect them from overseas competitors through stringent curbs on dumping.

This is no joke. Quality improvement and measurement tools are sensitive instruments and are used to help identify uses, problems and sources of improvement as well as to present the solution to a problem or to show the plan to be used to tackle the problem. There are many tools used in effective quality processes, but many are well beyond the scope of this book. However, the main tools are shown below and can help considerably to improve business:

* Flow Charts
* Cause and Effect Diagram
* Scatter Diagrams
* Functional Analysis
* Failure Model Effect Analysis
* Normal Group Technique
* Simple Statistical Process Control
* Gantt Charts
* Pareto Analysis
* Line Diagrams
* Control Charts
* Histograms
* Brainstorming

We should not forget common sense and general knowledge, although common sense is rather uncommon and general knowledge is hardly ever general. To illustrate the use of most of these quality measurement and problem solving tools, let us look at the baking of some loaves of bread. This is not 'Elementary, Watson' stuff, although under-graduates should be quite familiar with the role of the petty baker in the intricacies of management.

The Baker's Dough

Bakers make bread from flour, water, yeast and, no doubt, a few other things like air. When the dough has `risen', it is cut into pieces so that it can be baked into bread. The size of the lumps needs to be carefully controlled. The easiest way to find out how `consistent' the lumps of dough are is to weigh them. The baker knows that the correct weight of the `perfect' lump of dough is 495 grams.

He wants to find out if the dough cutting machine is accurate enough to meet the size specification of the finished loaf of bread. So he allowed the machine to do its job and then accurately weighed (grams) the lumps on a calibrated scale with the results as shown in the foregoing table for 50 lumps of dough. He wrote down the consecutive values on a table. Unfortunately, putting the values into this table gives no clear picture but at least he has recorded the data. The baker rearranged the 50 values from the table into an ascending order and placed them in a second table. The data already look better, but further improvements are, no doubt, possible.

The Baker's Gantt Chart

The baker realised that to conduct his investigation properly, he needed to do things in the right order; so he prepared a time chart, usually called a Gantt chart. A Gantt chart can be used as an aid in the planning of work. Primarily, it shows that the time planning has gone awry. Further, a Gantt chart shows where activities need to be started and finished in relation to other activities. A Gantt chart is a time-based chart showing the start and end points of various time-based tasks.

Flow Chart

To ensure that the team of people assembled to address the baker's problems are fully involved and can make their maximum

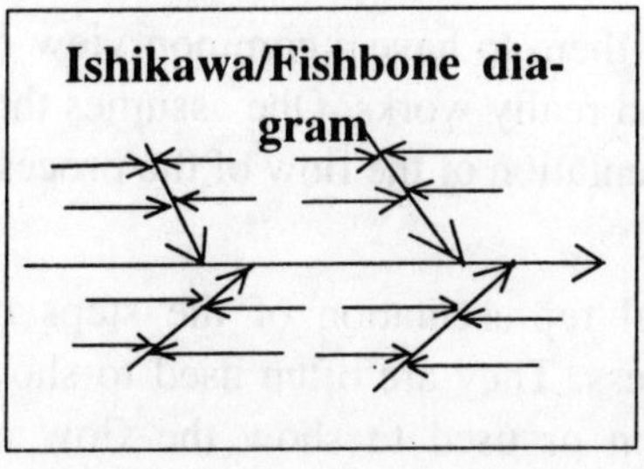
Ishikawa/Fishbone diagram

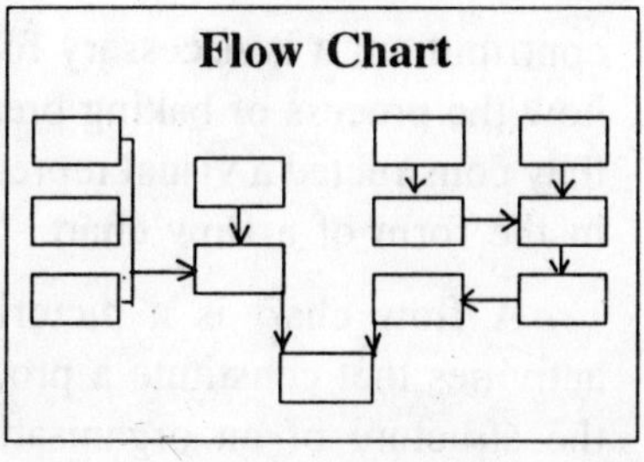
Flow Chart

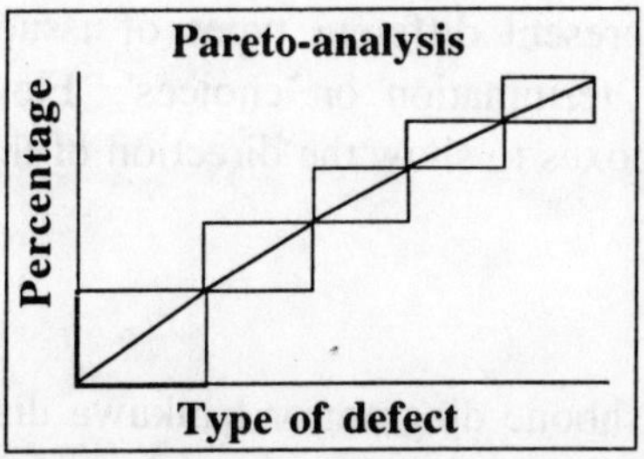
Pareto-analysis
Percentage
Type of defect

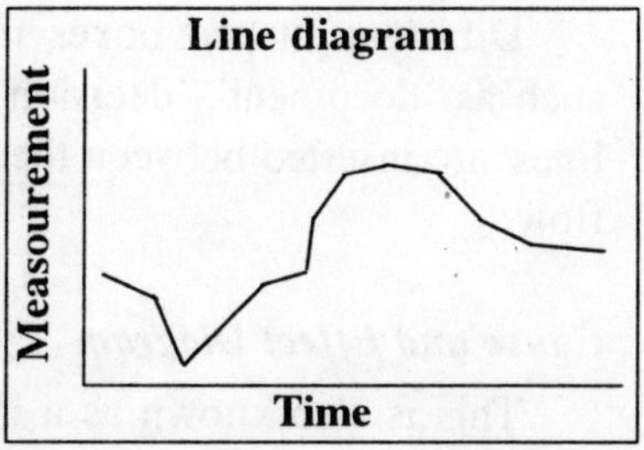
Line diagram
Measurement
Time

contribution, it is necessary for them to have a common view of how the process of baking bread really works. One assumes that they constructed a visual representation of the flow of the process in the form of a flow chart.

A flow chart is a pictorial representation of the steps or activities that constitute a process. They are often used to show the structure of an organisation or used to show the flow of computer programmes.

Different shaped boxes represent different types of issues such as `document', `decision', `termination' or `choices'. `Flow lines' are inserted between the boxes to show the direction of the flow.

Cause and Effect Diagram

This is also known as a Fishbone diagram or Ishikawa diagram after its inventor. This quality measurement tool has often proved to be a great help in brainstorming sessions because it displays the possible causes of a specific problem or condition. Let us put the goal or idea at the head of the fish and divide the contributing factors to the achievement of the goal into categories such as the 4M's, men, machines, materials and methods.

There are several other M's, such as maintenance, measurement, markets and money. However, the four M's in the diagram

496	499	491	488	484
491	481	491	495	494
494	487	492	487	511
506	496	496	494	496
489	496	499	495	488
489	496	499	495	488
494	496	499	503	496
494	486	496	490	496
495	496	492	492	503
497	496	488	511	492

are the classical ones and sufficient for most purposes of thinking about issues to be considered. The contributing factors that affect each of the 4M's can then be filled in by the problem solving team. The ribs fit to the backbone and sub-ribs to the ribs and so on until we are satisfied that we have captured all the issues.

Before the baker's team went on to try to solve the problems they had, one presumes that, they decided to list all the issues. They used a fishbone diagram for this, because it helped to show

480	489	494	496	497
481	489	494	496	499
484	490	494	496	499
486	491	494	496	499
487	491	494	496	499
487	491	495	496	503
488	492	495	496	503
488	492	495	496	506
488	492	495	496	511
488	492	496	496	511

Checkpoints for Baking Experiments

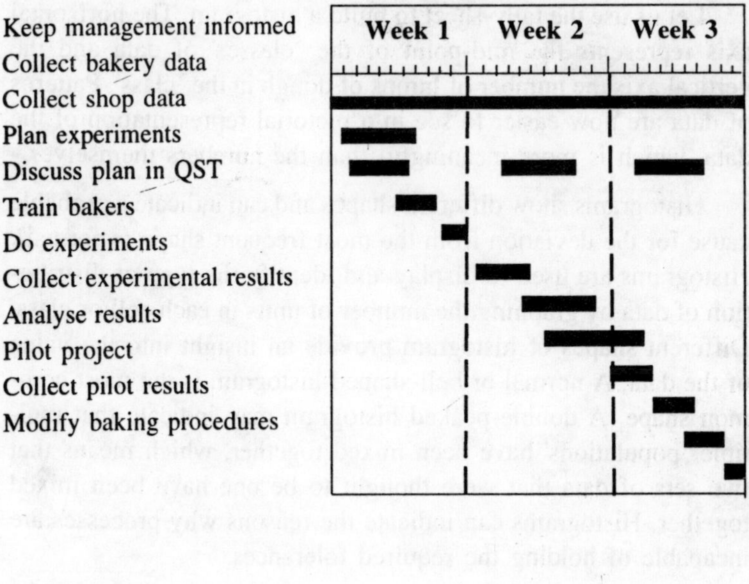

where the relationships existed between one issue and another. It was also a very stimulating way of getting the ideas to flow from people. The use of fishbone diagram in conjunction with the nominal group technique has proved to be a very effective way to identify possible solutions to problems. The finished diagrams look rather like a fishbone, hence the name, and can be very comprehensive. Cause and effect diagrams are useful to show the relationship between one issue or contributing factor and another. Obviously, they do not tell us about priorities, which are best tackled using other quality representation and measurement tools. This proved nothing other than that there was a wide variation of weight and that the process of weighing consecutive lumps of dough did not show any meaningful pattern. But, suppose the weight had been rising with consecutive lumps weighed. It would have allowed a completely different conclusion to be drawn. Anyway, this was not the case; the relationship between consecutive lumps weighed and the weight of the lumps showed a random relationship.

The Baker's Histogram

Let us use the tally-sheet to build a histogram. The horizontal axis represents the mid-point of the `classes' of data and the vertical axis the number of lumps of dough in the `class'. Patterns of data are now easier to see in a pictorial representation of the data, which is more meaningful than the numbers themselves.

Histograms show different shapes and can indicate a probable cause for the deviation from the most frequent shape (=normal). Histograms are used to display and identify the type of distribution of data by graphing the number of units in each cell or class. Different shapes of histogram provide an insight into the value of the data. A normal or bell-shaped histogram is the most common shape. A double-peaked histogram may indicate that multiple `populations' have been mixed together, which means that two sets of data that were thought to be one have been mixed together. Histograms can indicate the reasons why processes are incapable of holding the required tolerances.

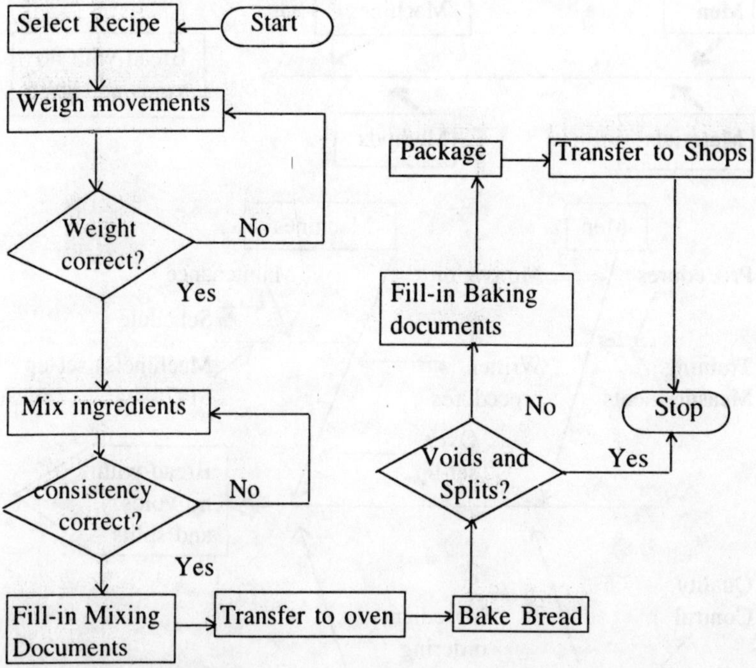

The Pareto Principle

The Pareto principle was invented by Ishikawa and is used to divide the `vital few' from the `important many'. It is particularly useful where it is necessary to decide on the priorities for critical quality costs. There is little point in fighting the battle where it isn't raging. Working on an aspect of quality problems, that is small and of low impact, is obviously going to bear less fruit than one which has a greater impact. A few examples of Pareto type statements serve to illustrate the point.

* 80% of quality costs come from 20% of the problems.
* 80% of sales go to 20% of the customers.
* 80% of the performance of people comes from 20% of their activities.
* 80% of the talking is done by 20% of the people.

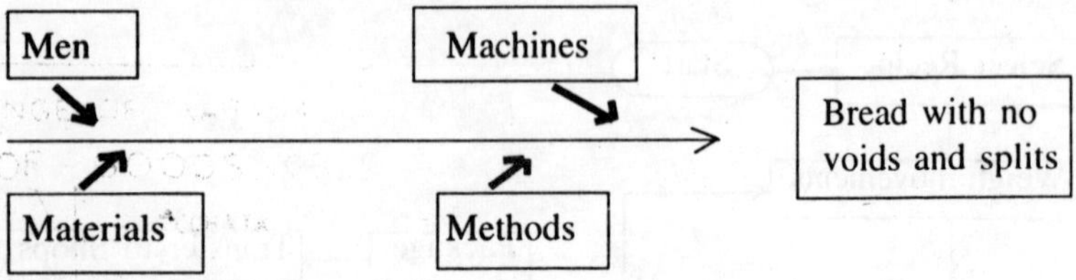

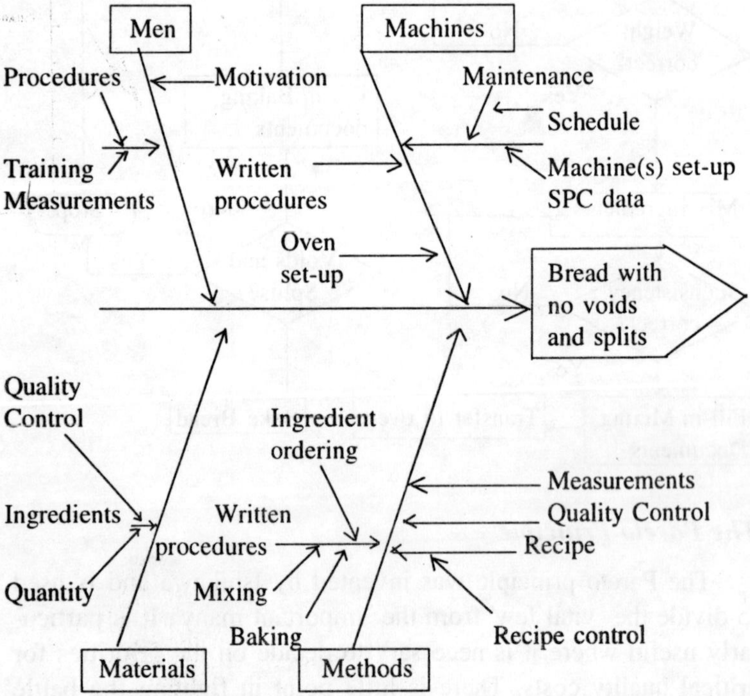

* 85% of problems are caused by management and 15% are caused by subordinates.

The Pareto Principle is used to catch the big fish and to leave the little fish in the pond for attention at some future time.

The Baker's Pareto Table

Apart from getting the weight wrong, the baker is also having trouble with a few other things.

He listed all his quality defect troubles in a table and counted the number of times that the defect occurred and then rearranged the data in the order of frequency into a Pareto table. This table was then used to construct the Baker's Pareto diagram.

The Baker's Pareto Diagram

A Pareto diagram is a method of showing the causes of

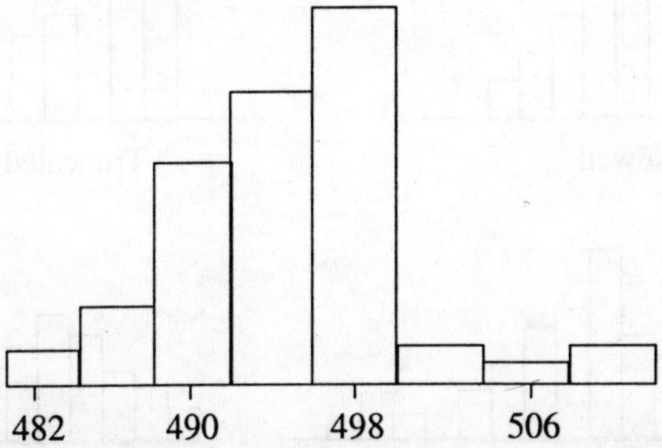

defects which are the most important. It divides the vital few from the important many. The data from the Pareto table is used to construct this Pareto diagram using the Pareto principle. This representation of the data is yet another method of `viewing a picture' of the data and can help in predicting the effectiveness

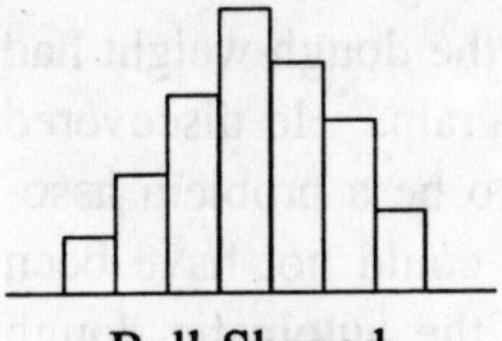
Bell-Shaped

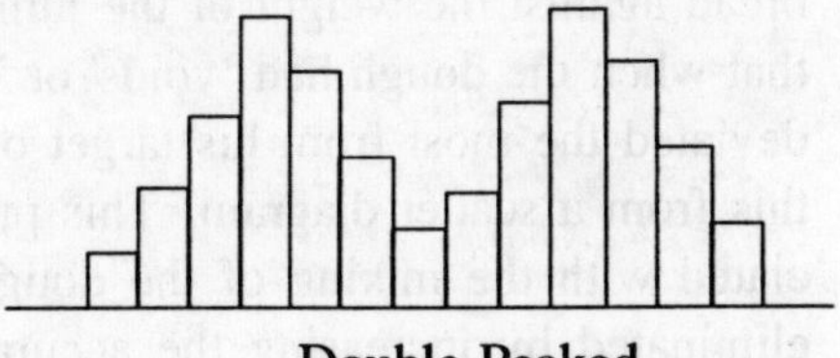
Double-Peaked

of improvements and enable an understanding of problems and their seriousness at a glance.

The Baker's Scatter Diagram

Since the baker so far found no relationship between the weight of the lumps and the consecutive batches, he went looking

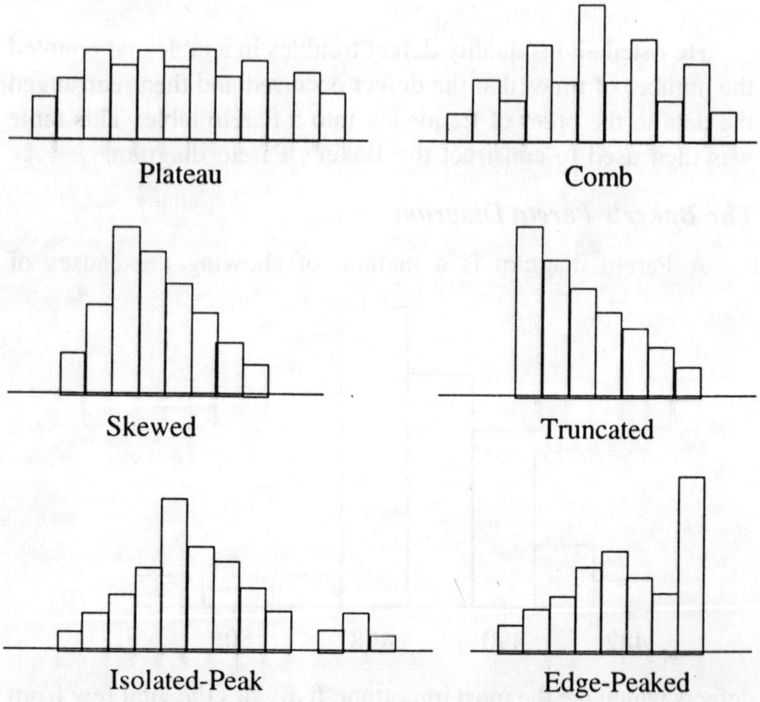

for other variables that might explain the variations. He made a table of the weight of dough lumps against the incidence of different defect types.

Then, he plotted the various different defects in the baked bread against the weight of the lumps of dough and discovered that when the dough had `voids' or `split', the dough weight had deviated the most from his target of 495 grams. He discovered this from a scatter diagram. This proved to be a problem associated with the mixing of the dough that could not have been eliminated by increasing the accuracy of the automatic dough cutting machine. Scatter diagrams show the relationship between two variables and each point represents a pair of variables.

The Baker's Control Chart

After a great deal of effort the baker began to really get his act together and discovered that the weight of dough lumps had little to do with the accuracy of the dough cutting machine, but the weight did alert him to all sorts of other problems related to protential defects in the baked bread. He was able to control his process using the weight of dough lumps. He plotted his weights on a control chart. The dough lump weight accuracy improved to such an extent that he could use the average of five lumps for plotting purposes. This is represented as x(pronounced, bar x). UAL means the upper action limit, UWL, upper warning limit, LAL, lower action limit, and LWL stands for the lower warning limit. Statistical analysis shows for a process under control that 95.4% of the values are between the warning limits and 99.7% of the values between the action limits.

Measurement of Quality

Money is the usual system of measurement. It helps to manage the business, but traditional balance sheets rarely tell us much about quality. When someone buys a washing machine, and it doesn't work, he or she would want it fixed. Whether or not the supplier makes a profit in the end is not the buyer's concern. Conversely, saying `we increased profits last month by 10 per cent' gives little indication about customer satisfaction. Certain costs are related to quality, and these measurements show us how the quality improvement process is performing and help the management identify critical issues which need addressing.

Globally, the transnational Company, ICI Paints is known to use the following criteria as measurements of customer satisfaction:

* Deliver accuracy
* Invoice errors
* Right first time
* Lead times
* Telephone responses
* Suppliers deliveries
* Customer complaints/queries
* Bills of material accuracy
* Inventory record accuracy
* Forecasting accuracy
* Adjustments per batch

If a manager is in production management, he or she will certainly understand and use the concept of `yield'. The concept

Name of Defect	*Number of Occurrences*	*Cumulative Number*
Wrong Weight	128	128
Wrong Shape	91	128+91=219
Too Crusty	36	219+36=255
Underdone	23	255+23=278
Voids	15	278+15=293
Splits	9	293+9=302
Others	12	302+12=314
Total	314	314

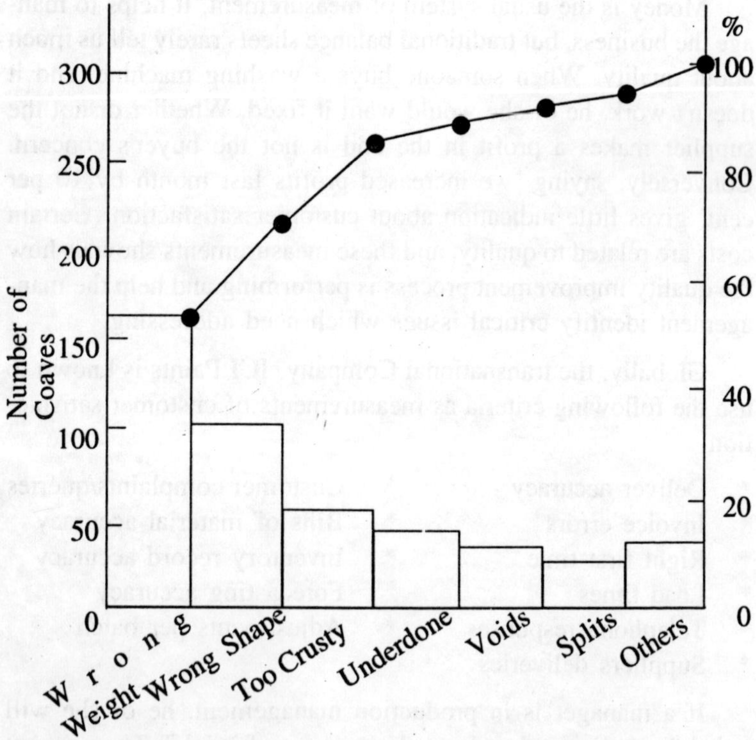

Wt. (g)	No. Voids/ Splits	Wt. (g)	No. Voids/ Splits	Wt. (g)	No. Voids/ Splits	Wt. (g)	No. Voids/ Splits	Wt. (g)	No. Voids/ Splits
480	10	489	6	494	2	496	3	497	5
481	9	489	5	494	1	496	3	499	6
484	8	490	5	494	3	496	2	499	7
486	8	491	5	494	2	496	3	499	6
487	8	491	5	494	2	496	2	499	7
487	7	491	4	495	0	496	4	503	8
488	7	492	3	495	1	496	3	503	7
488	7	492	4	495	0	496	3	506	8
488	6	492	3	495	1	496	3	511	9
488	6	492	4	496	2	496	3	511	10

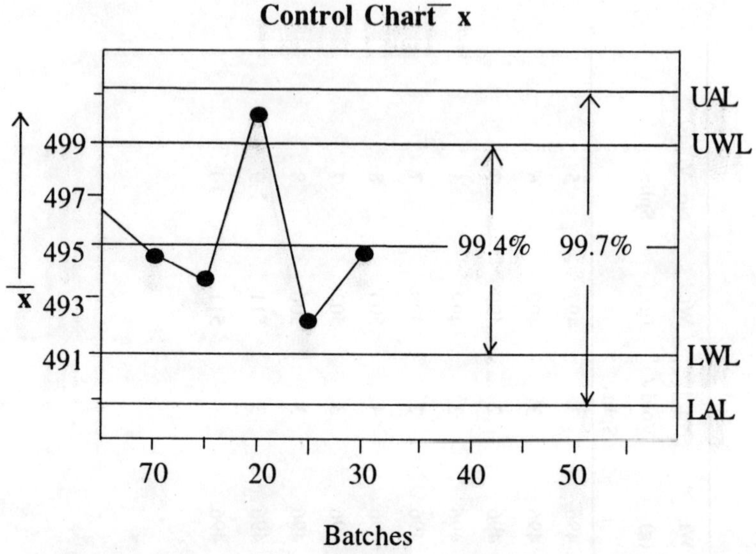

of yield can be applied to customer satisfaction as well as production. It simply undercores the need to define what the 100 per cent yield is and seek to achieve that.

Of greater significance to the quality improvement process than issues such as cost or quality are the thousands of small measurements, which often are not expressed in financial terms. For example, we have to look at the number of times the photocopier jams, the number of complaints, the number of credit notes, missed deadlines, customer surveys, paperwork errors, delays in meetings, missed deliveries, overtime worked, training defi-

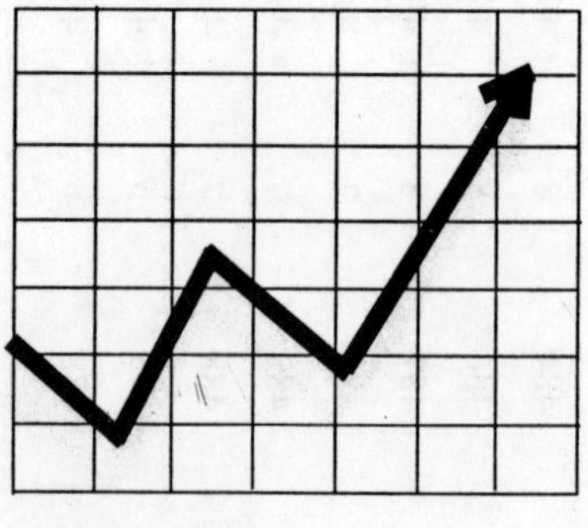

ciencies, computer down-time, volume of effluent, adverse (and good) press reports, and so on.

The manager must ask the subordinates to do their own measurements. That must in turn stick charts on the walls for all to see. It helps to make the quality improvement process more visible. Workers tend to set themselves goals when they see measured trends in the form of simple-to-understand graphs and charts. Everyone concerned wants to see the line of the graph go in the right direction. This part of the book necessarily had to be bookish. But, there are important lessons in this treatment for the corporate top brass and the managers below. The quality of reform, to some extent, gains or loses on the strength or weakness of TQM. We must understand this.

6

ESSENCE OF MARKETING

1. CREATING A MARKET PLAN

The business plan is usually what is provided to the banks, FIs and investors and outlines what the product or service is, how it would be produced and distributed, the type of research and development procedures and funds needed to succeed, the size and composition of the potential market and cost and profit projections over a given period. Based on this, banks, FIs and investors determine that the business does or does not have a chance of succeeding in difficult times. Once funded, the business plan moves to the left side of the desk and the marketing plan to the centre. This cannot be any different in the present context of growing international competition.

The American Marketing Association defines marketing as "the performance of business to consumer or user." In his book, *Marketing*, Prof. Robert D. Hisrich expands on this a bit. He says, "marketing is the process in which decisions are made in a totally inter-related changing business environment on all the activities that facilitate exchange in order that the targeted customers are satisfied and the defined objectives accomplished."

Perhaps, something that is a bit more concise will suffice. I suppose, we should define marketing as the packaging, positioning, pricing, promotion, distribution, and selling of product or service. The marketing plan is the outline for accomplishing this. Sometimes, it is strategic in nature and is as brief as this definition. Sometimes, it is hundreds of pages long and as deep and rambling as Prof. Hisrich's definition. Too often, the really weighty marketing plans seem as if these were created to satisfy either someone's ego or someone's boss. These are painstakingly written, copied and bound — and placed in a drawer never to be looked at again, the response these deserve, particularly now when quick reflexes are the prime need of competitive business.

The best marketing plan is a map, a guide or a checklist that, when viewed as such, should never be so complicated as to discourage its use. While research is a major component, both in formulating the marketing plan and in evaluating its correctness, research must never be used as a justification for inflexibility or even failure. Indeed, in recognising that market factors can change in a day or in a moment, a marketing plan must be flexible enough to accommodate change without becoming either obsolete or irrelevant. Too often, trained marketers rely on research alone as a justification for their decision or, worse, their lack of decisions, to be responsive to changes in the market climate.

In *Contemporary American Marketing,* Harper W.Boyd, Jr., and Richard M. Clewitt quote Alvin Toffler's 1961 *Fortune magazine* article in which he discusses Pepsi Cola's never-ending, intense rivalry with Coca Cola, "while the product varied wildly from franchise to franchise, even more serious was the fact that it was tied to an out-of-date market strategy." This warns the manager not to allow himself to be locked into an inflexible plan.

For structure, yet maximum flexibility, the marketing plan, I suppose, should, ideally, take this form:

a) Situation analysis

What do we know about the product, the market, the customer and the competition? This is the place to utilise the research. Consider the history, standing, regulatory considerations, future prospects — pros and cons.

b) Objectives

What does one expect the marketing plan to accomplish? Increase sales? Market share? Name awareness? Change public opinion? Win recognition from regulators or critics?

c) Strategy

What approach should one take to achieve the objectives? To some, the marketing plan itself represents a strategy — a strategic approach to doing business.

d) Tactics

What will the strategy require one to do? Advertising, public relations, research, promotions, lobbying — all are separate functions, vehicles, and disciplines. These can work together, separately, or compete and contradict each other. Managers must determine which tactics best apply to the strategic plan, identify them and coordinate their implementation.

e) Evaluation

We must measure the results and determine if our tactics are working and on schedule. If not, we must determine if new tactics need to be employed or if the strategy is flawed. Or both. Or neither. At this point we should again consider if the objectives were realistic or if market factors changed along the way. At each deadline we have set, we re-evaluate the plan and, finally, we must be flexible. Yes, flexibility is a key aspect of managerial excellence.

What about time? The period of time typically covered by a marketing plan is usually tied to budgets. Since advertising, public relations, investor relations and other components of the plan will be costly, the plan should be subject to review and revision annually — as are most budgets. Funds should be allocated for contingencies. Planning is important and evaluation critical. In evaluating the results, we must have the funding necessary to alter the course if justified. Should the advertising strategy need to move in another direction, for example, media, creative and production expenses can be costly. We must allow for possibilities of such changes during the budgeted period. Hindustan Lever must be thinking on these lines in the light of reported concern over the impact of the company's ad plans.

2. REVIEWING THE PLAN

If the goal is to achieve certain objectives over, say a five year period, we must budget realistically, anticipating changes and also inflation. We must review the plan and ask what changes will be necessary if it succeeds or falls short and make projections accordingly. Given below are the basic elements addressed by a well-defined marketing plan:

Packaging

Is the name and/or logo and signature familiar? Inviting? Suggestive of security and stability? Warm or brightly coloured? Boring or bland? Has the most readily identifiable characteristic been merged with the background? What can we do about this? What do we want to do about this? Some companies use corporate colours extensively as a means to identifying themselves. Cards, order forms, cartons, delivery trucks and service vehicles, uniforms and envelopes all sport the uniform the company colour. How much is enough to make the packaging familiar and friendly and a part of the lives of present and future customers?

Pricing

How do managers determine the pricing of a product or service? Regulated? Fair trade? Well-promoted discounting? How is the price perceived in relation to that of a major competitor? Is the value of product obvious? Is the value reflective of the cost? In the case of drug companies, research, development and manufacturing costs force the product to be priced high as compared to what the public feels the product should cost. The price isn't too high, it is only perceived as too high. The challenge to the marketing team is to establish the value to the customers beyond what they would like to pay. People would always be willing to get into debt, much less just pay the fee, for the best doctor, the best lawyer, the best stereo system or car. Quality — or perceived quality — would consistently win out over cheaper or generic brands.This holds good everywhere and in every economy.

Promotion

Within the broad definition of marketing, there is a variety of disciplines that are distinct, but inter-related, including:

advertising;
public relations;
education; and
publicity.

Many people believe that public relations (PR) and publicity are the same thing. This is not so. Publicity is `publicising' something. It may be an item planted in a column in a magazine or a local paper or it may be a sky writer, a handbill or stunt. Public relations is a much larger activity that includes investor relations, government relations, scholarship funds, recognition and awards programmes, informational lectures, concerts or other performances — live or via tape or media — or any of a myriad of other projects. A company's annual report is a legal and financial document, but to many companies it is also the centrepiece of a PR programme. Education includes literature, seminar courses, research studies, white papers, and the hybrid "advertorial," part education/information and part advertising, often with as much impact as the boldest product ad.

Advertising alone or as a component of the marketing plan is perhaps the most persuasive, effective, immediate and expensive avenue to influence, recognition and success. The effectiveness of an ad programme can be maximised in the following ways:

1. Let us define the market. Let us know who we are talking to in terms of age, sex, marital and family status; business/profession; and income/geographic influence.
2. Identify the competition, present and likely.
3. Prepare a competitive analysis.
4. Determine how much our customer knows about the company and product—alone and relative to the competition.
5. Identify the customer, main source of information about the product.

6. Let us know why the business gets better or worse—seasonality, discounts advertising, rebates and news stories.
7. We should know what we want advertising to accomplish—increase awareness, reverse a negative image, expand markets, or increase sales or market share.
8. Let us merchandise research.
9. Establish benchmarks for results.

Positioning

Does the public know what the firm is and what it does? Alone and relative to the competition? How do they think of the company? What do they think of it? Is the firm a good neighbour or a less well-regarded corporate citizen? Way back in 1981, marketing consultants Al Rise and Jack Trout in their book, *Positioning: The Battle for Your Mind*, had coined the word positioning to describe the process of putting the brand or company into the mind of the prospect. The word and its usage carry so much power that it is often at the centre of every marketing plan. How a product is "positioned" will affect its pricing (bargain/low-cost/mass market or top-line/big ticket/upscale), its distribution (discount warehouse stores/the shop at the mall/home shopping TV network or personally shown by appointment/limited quantity/exclusive franchise) and its packaging (generic/commercial or private label).

No management should confuse image advertising with corporate advertising, the two terms, which are frequently, incorrectly though, used synonymously. Corporate advertising is used to get the target audience to know the name to make them aware of the presence in the market place— to make them think of the firm. Image advertising is to influence how they think of it. To this end, positioning may be a factor in corporate comparisons. In a corporate sense, a company or product may be "number one in the world." In an image campaign, the company would be known as the "oldest, largest, and most trusted name dedicated to your family's health and safety." The difference in the approach is between the market just thinking of the company and how it is thinking of the company. As Rise and Trout noted, "the basic approach ... is not to create something new and different, but to manipulate what's already up there in the mind, to retie the connections that already exist."

The marketing plan, through packaging, pricing, promotion and positioning, will determine, to a very large degree, that the people constituting the target audience thinks of the firm, that they know it is out there and how it fits into their lives. A phrase like "The world's most trusted" is the product not of quality or efficiency, but marketing. Media selection is important in advertising because the best ad is a waste of time if no onc sees it. Similarly, the best company, service or product is doomed to failure if it isn't correctly marketed (packaged, priced, promoted and positioned). This demands underscoring in the context of Hindustan Lever's somewhat casual distribution recently of a new variety of Modern bread in New Delhi, with marketing failing to support the ad on free supply of one loaf. Some of these points seem obvious and logical. Yet, so many efforts fail because the obvious is overlooked.

3) SUMMING UP

Let us do well to remember that the business plan tells the bank, FIs or investors what the firm proposes to do, how it proposes to do it, what it expects to achieve in terms of sales and market share, and how much it will need to do it. The marketing plan, however, is the strategic map for achieving the goals.

* The firm must be flexible enough in the marketing plan to be responsive to changes in market climate.
* It must consider the elements of an effective marketing plan: the situation analysis, objectives, strategy, tactics and evaluation.
* It must remember that the basic elements of the marketing plan should consider packaging, pricing, promotion, and positioning as well as distribution and sales.

7

STRATEGIC ALLIANCES: WHERE ARE THE INDIAN DAVIDS?

In recent years, there have been several global corporate shake outs and strategic alliances. There were instances of giants either breaking up or coming together to form mega giants as a response to the global market challenges. This is despite the fact that there is a strong anti-monopoly law in the United States and elsewhere in the western world and in some of the developing countries as well. The South Koreans have adopted a deliberate policy of cutting down the local giants, the *chaebols*. Pressure is being applied on them to restructure themselves and, some time ago, criticism of this policy quickly led to massive raids on the offices of some of the *chaebols*. In the United States, historically, there has been a public distrust of monopolies and the Sherman Anti-Trust Act was the earliest legislative response to fears of a possible domination of economic activity arising out of an unbridled growth of large corporate groups. This was duly reflected in the sustained essorts to dilute the supposedly monopoly character of Microsoft.

This explains why while the obvious gains of strategic alliances have prompted mega groupings care has been taken to ensure that the companies involved did not fall foul of the anti-monopoly machinery in different countries. Mergers and acquisitions have a significant role in efficiency arising from economies of scale and this has been duly acknowledged by the regulators, though the latter, whether it be in the United States or members of the European Community, have been very careful to prevent economically justified mergers and acquisitions deteriorating into unholy monopolies capable of acquiring a stranglehold on vast segments of domestic economies and using the clout even to control or influence global events.

1. U.S. BUSINESS LOBBY

American MNCs have long been suspected and even accused of triggering the fall of popular governments in Latin America. Presently, the business lobby in Washington is sufficiently powerful to force White House to follow policies that are beneficial to the big U.S. corporate entities — mark how the latter have influenced the US approach to Chinese trade and IPRs violations. What the MNCs do outside the reach of their domestic monopoly regulating agencies does not obviously concern the latter. But, their counterparts in the countries where the MNCs operate are unlikely to let monopolistic activities pass by unnoticed.

Obviously, the MNCs have to take the utmost care to see that the strategic alliances do not violate anti-monopoly laws. Indeed, they must be doing this, judging by the proliferation of such alliances. When trade globally is being liberalised, obviously, there will be more of these alliances and there is not much that developing country manufacturers can do by of way counter-action. The South Koreans are breaking up the *chaebols* for a different reason. Their main goal is to force the giants to specialise, not diversify indiscriminately. In a way, this is the correct response to the emerging global trade challenges, but what about the Indian effort to foster *swadeshi* strategic alliances against MNCs?

2. THE INDIA CLUB

The Indian corporate sector is now focused on the India Club being promoted, ostensibly to fight the emerging MNC threat. After the Bombay Club, now, there is a lot of talk about this club. But then, this is not going to help when the Indian groups have nothing to boast of by way of globalisation. There is before us the success of Bajaj Auto against Honda, Yamaha and Piaggio, but what else is there to demonstrate the growth of indigenous Davids against global Goliaths? There are really no Indian MNCs, if we go by the definition of an MNC as a corporate entity with not just a diverse but also a significant global presence. A few joint ventures here and there do not give any of the Indian collaborators the MNC status. Nobody is saying that Indian corporates should try to influence local political regimes, but when they are not able to play a crucial part in economic activity both within the country and abroad, all this talk of countering MNCs is bunkum. On Indian territory the locals are better placed as they can sell cheap but this advantage will go once the consumers realise that cheapness goes with poor or indifferent quality. Kelloggs cornflake is priced so high that domestic supplies are price competitive, but once consumers begin to feel the difference in quality and also develop a taste for what the MNC offers, then there will be few takers for the indigenous substitute.

Nevertheless, an inferiority complex is not how the Indian corporates should respond to the challenges of liberalisation. After establishing industrial capacity in diverse areas over successive five year plans, we should not declare our helplessness all too quickly. It is true that our producers have operated for long in a protected market and that has made them less efficient compared to their global rivals. But, given a certain dynamism and shedding of the flab, they can become cost and quality competitive. The protected market has, over time, given them a lot of cushion and this will come handy in the effort to develop a competitive edge.

Unfortunately, almost everyone in industry thinks that the only way to survive under opening up is to tie up with an MNC. Mr Rahul Bajaj, the Chairman of Bajaj Auto, was not exaggerating when he declared at a panel discussion organised some years back by the Indian Merchants Chamber in Bombay that in the automobile segment of indigenous industry there were actually no Indian corporates and most joint ventures for production of passenger cars were owned by MNCs. No wonder, the locals in this area have pressed for measures by Government to prevent MNC dominance.

3. GETTING AN MNC TAG

Nevertheless, generally the view is beginning to prevail that multi-national support is the essentile basis of business success. The open admission that no venture can succeed unless there is an MNC tag is self-defeating, but then we can see that this is entirely consistent with the approach that declares that mergers and acquisitions will be directed only against small local players. The tie-up between Proctor and Gamble and Godrej and the merger of Hindustan Lever with Brooke Bond have nothing to do with the tall talk about Indian corporates bracing up to MNCs.

Nobody can argue against foreign investment and technology flow but both must be sought on the basis that Indian collaborators can succeed on their own. What comes from overseas must be perceived to be supportive, not displacing. Even in respect of foreign technology, the wiser course would be to seek transfer from the Asian MNCs, rather than their Western counterparts. The Japanese and South Korean corporates are no mean performers compared to those in the United States and United Kingdom. Rather, American companies have problems holding their own against their rivals from Japan and the Asian tigers. Yet, here we are going out of our way to seek technology and equity from the American multinationals. If somebody thinks that Western enterprise is necessarily a passport to globalisation, then let the first option be exercised in favour of German companies. This is not to argue against strengthening Indo-U.S. economic co-operation, but only to stress on a balanced approach to this aspect of globalisation.

The first step towards strategic alliances is to set the agenda and to define its goal. Our corporate barons have yet to focus their grey cells on this. They cannot wait indefinitely to do this. Time does not wait for man and this has to be true of Indian CEOs. They have to set about forming strategic alliances among locals specifically against MNCs, not only within Indian territory but also abroad.

REFERENCES

1. K.S. Ramachandran, *Power of Motivation.*
2. Richard Pascale, *Managing on the Edge — How Successful Companies Use Conflict to Stay Ahead.*
3. Peter Drucker, *Frontiers of Management.*
4. Tom Peters, *Thriving on Chaos.*
5. Joe Marconi, *Crisis Marketing.*
6. John Gilbert, *Total Quality Management.*
7. Robert D. Histrich, *Marketing.*
8. Harper W. Boyd. Jr. & Richard M. Clewitt, *Contemporary American Marketing.*

ISSUES FOR DEBATE

I. Introduction

1. Explain how a CEO should deal with issues of corporate planning and practice.
2. How should Indian corporates react to the MNC challenge?
3. What should be the corporate approach to corruption?

II. Creating Animal Spirits

1. What do you understand by take-overs?
2. What does the SEBI take-over code lay down?
3. What should be the role of financial institutions?
4. How will you promote good corporate governance?
5. Would you say that take-over is necessarily good or bad?

III. The Core Issues

1. What role can consultants play?

2. What role would you envisage for MBAs?
3. How important is team spirit?
4. What should be the essence of good human resources management?
5. What is the essence of corporate dynamism?
6. What, in your view, are the managerial challenges of liberalisation?

IV. Strategic Planning

1. Explain what you understand by strategic planning?

V. Total Quality Management

1. What are the basic principles of TQM?
2. How should management commit itself to TQM?
3. Explain the styles of leadership?
4. Explain the quality improvement tools?

VI. Essence of Marketing

1. How will you define marketing?
2. What should the ideal marketing plan be?
3. How will you maximise the impact of an ad programme?

VI. Essence of Marketing

1. How will you define marketing?
2. What should the ideal marketing plan be ?
3. How will you maximise the impact of an ad programme?

PART - II

MANAGEMENT OF INTELLECTUAL PROPERTY RIGHTS

1

INTRODUCTION

Intellectual property rights (IPRs) are going to be an area of considerable debate and controversy in the coming years. While governments will discourse and negotiate on various issues, it is the domestic manufacturer that is going to face the music. IPRs management, thus, is quite as important — may be even more so — as diplomacy. It is time Indian industry realised that the Government will not do the management for its different constituents. This is essentially the latter's responsibility and they have to prepare themselves for it rather than want to be spoon-fed. Indeed, how well they are able to withstand the pressures of MNCs will depend on the preparedness for the global framework on IPRs.

Obviously, the rules will be stringently applied and where there is room for manipulation this will also be done. The manufacturers have to protect their hold of the domestic market and simultaneously fight hard to capture the overseas market. The agenda is a tough one and expecting the mandarins in the Commerce Ministry to sort out these problems can prove to be a recipe for disaster. Dialectics are also not going to help and getting into an ideological debate will do no good either. Selling abroad has always been hazardous and with the IPRs provisions in force, Indian marketing skills would be severely tested. The soft option of avoiding the foreign market and concentrating more on capturing local consumers is going to disappear — sooner rather than later — again with the IPRs rules in place, and the MNCs using these to force themselves on Indian consumers.

A clear understanding of the provisions alone will not do — though this is a must and should not be neglected in favour of grandiose ideas or schemes. Indian manufacturers and providers of services have to look for loopholes or opportunities to exploit and simultaneously be able to cite provisions to hold up MNC invasion of the domestic market. The local market will cease to be a protected one any longer and at every stage rivals operating globally will cite patents violations or infringements to discourage domestic enterprise and flaunt their own patents to push their ware hard.

1. REGISTERING PATENTS

The first step would, no doubt, be to register patents and in a manner that is globally indisputable. There have been suggestions that even such articles of daily use as neem stick should be patented. The fact that several articles have been used since time immemorial will cease to hold any water and the immediate task for any manufacturer would be to legitimise use of all inputs and processes whose exclusively indigenous nature has been taken for granted all this long.

Intellectual property rights have acquired a global dimension with the Marrakech accord and use of every input and process will be questioned unless there are supporting patents. While there is a growing awareness of the emerging challenges in international trade, not much attention has been paid to IPRs management. In respect of drugs and pharmaceuticals — the area where Indian producers face the toughest challenge — and an effort is on to plug the areas of possible MNC pressure, but the general apprehension of drugs getting globally priced — thus becoming out of reach to most consumers — and foreign suppliers swamping the local market is threatening to cloud a meaningful strategy to prevent drug prices within the country from hitting the roof and denying the sick access to essential medicines as well as pressure being brought on Indian drug exporters to reduce exports in a big way because of problems over patents.

How well equipped are our manufacturers to check possible IPRs violations well in time before disaster strikes them? Countries like South Korea which are in the IPRs hit list have set up a strong monitoring and deterrence framework and here we have been dithering on getting the Patents Act amended in line with the demands of the global IPRs regime. Hitherto, India was able to prevent the US threat of punitive action under 301 provisions of the US Trade Act from getting translated into crippling sanctions partly because of the fact that intellectual property rights were not sufficiently protected. Now, such protection is available and will be enforced and India will have to be and to be seen to be adhering to the IPRs framework..

We have wasted a lot of time in recapitulating instances of Western acquisition of intellectual property rights by deception or arm-twisting. This monologue has to stop and both policy makers and administrators have to focus on formulating an effective mechanism that will avert such possible MNC tactics in respect of known Indian herbs like *tulsi* and *neem*. The sensible course would be to establish patents on the basis of global recognition. South Koreans have acted decisively and with a sense of purpose, knowing fully well that they would be among the first to be pounced upon for IPRs violations or infringements. If South Korea has come close to being recognised as a nation with First World potential, despite the strains that have emerged recently it is because that country is constantly awake and does not have to be woken up. In India's case, it would not be an exaggeration to say that it is refusing to be woken up.

2. ACCEPTING THE REALITIES

The Presidential ordinance on patents was forced to lapse because the Opposition then was determined to resist India's shift to the global regime of free trade, conveniently glossing over the fact that keeping out of the regime was not an option at all. If China can resist US pressure that it should be treated as a developed country for trade purposes, it has both economic and political clout. India does not have this. India should have accepted the realities and not claim parity with a superior power.

Acceptance of the game rules is a must for a country situated as India is. This does not mean that Indian trade negotiators have to give up the responsibility for protecting the nation's economic sovereignty. Despite all the Third World rhetoric about the Marrakech accord having been unfair to the developing countries, the agreement reached at this Moroccan resort town—known to travellers as the robber's paradise--gives them greater access to the global market in lieu of an opening up of their own economies.

The IPRs agenda does facilitate increased penetration of the Third World market by First World producers and simultaneously sets rules that developing country manufacturers all this long did not bother about. But, to say that MNCs will be all over the place and industry in the developing countries faces liquidation is plain nonsense. Patenting is critical to making the best of the IPRs regime and refusing to do this is not how countries like India should fight their battle. When we have capacity to produce, why not formalise this? This capacity really sums up the IPRs of any country. Granted that global majors will go all out to flaunt their superior capacity — this is after all one aspect of truly free trade — still for developing countries to complain of recolonisation is to surrender well before the battle begins.

2

THE TRIPs AGREEMENT

1. THE RUN DOWN

During the Uruguay Round negotiations, the industrial countries, particularly the USA, insisted that the final accord should include an agreement on the protection of intellectual property rights. A strengthening of IPRs protection was necessary, it was claimed, because insufficient protection reduced investment in cost-intensive R&D activities, especially basic research. This, in turn, reduced innovation, which itself is the main source of global development and progress, as recent developments in both trade theory and growth theory had clearly demonstrated. This was the reasoning.

However, the insistence of industrial countries on the inclusion of IPRs protection was fundamentally due to a major shift in the pattern of world trade during recent years and the resulting adjustment challenges. For more than a decade now, world trade has grown faster than world production, which has intensified competition significantly. The adoption of an export-oriented economic policy in a large number of developing countries had given North-South trade a new dynamism based on a different structure of exchange. Apart from most African countries, LDCs are no longer predominantly exporters of primary products, but they also export in a big way manufactured goods. Unlike in the past North and South trade largely consists of similar goods. This has increased the adjustment pressure of all parties concerned and could provoke large-scale displacements in the industrial countries.

The production of a large number of industries, especially standardised manufactured goods, where technology is geographically highly mobile, has been shifted from the old industrial countries to developing countries in general and the South East and East Asian NICs in particular. This process has resulted — perhaps for the first time in the history of North-South trade — in a trade pattern characterised by the standard textbook exchange of ubiquitous goods leading to massive adjustment problems in the old industrial countries, which, in turn, constitute the prime reason for the increasing trend of neo-protectionism observed from the eighties onwards.

Simultaneously, both in a reaction to this development and due to technological progress, the importance of knowledge-based, high-technology industries has grown dramatically for the developed countries. It was estimated that, by 1986, more than 27 per cent of U.S. exports contained intellectual property components while the rate was less than 10 per cent when the GATT was negotiated. Due to the special characteristics of knowledge — as opposed to capital and labour — as a factor of production, this development led to new sources in the determination of comparative advantages and, thus, radically altered the nature of competition. No wonder, the NICs gained in international competitiveness. The familiar phenomenon was that the comparative advantage in producing one good or the other shifted from the old industrial countries to the developing countries in a later stage of the production cycle. In contrast, in recent years by combining their comparative advantages and their capabilities of imitation, the NICs entered the markets for innovative products faster. This up-grading of NIC exports based on a strategy of imitation shortened product cycles immensely.

The interest of industrial countries in the strengthening of IPRs protection is that it improves and facilitates the development and production of knowledge-intensive goods, so that the industrial countries' comparative advantage in the production of those goods will be maintained. Firms, workers and policy-makers need to adjust to these changes in the global economy. At the same time, the global trade system has to be adapted to the challenges of increased globalisation, enhanced international competition and the resulting adjustment problems.

2. THE AGREEMENT: AN OUTLINE

The Agreement on Trade-Related Aspects of Intellectual Property Rights, including Trade in Counterfeit Goods, is based on the existing multilateral conventions on IPRs protection, most of which are administered and supervised by the UN World Intellectual Property Organisation (WIPO). The TRIPs agreement integrates the existing systems of IPRs protection and complements these in those areas, where — for various reasons — no international consensus existed so far.

As its basis, the TRIPs agreement stipulates that all WTO members adhere to the existing conventions on IPRs protection, such as the Berne Convention for the Protection of Literary and Artistic Works, the Paris Convention for the Protection of Industrial Property and the International Convention for the Protection of Performers, Producers of Phonograms and Broadcasting Organisations. Considering that IPRs protection follows the territorial principle, i.e. the extent of protection is subject to the respective national law, differences in the level and enforcement of protection effectively constitute a non-tariff barrier. Therefore, one of the main elements of the TRIPs agreement is the call for harmonisation of national rules.

The TRIPs agreement requires WTO members to treat nationals of trading partners on the same basis (the most-favoured-nation principle) and to provide for national treatment with regard to protection of intellectual property. All norms of the agreement are minimum standards. The agreement covers a wide range of IPRs. This includes the improved protection of copyrights, which is especially important to computer programmes. The provisions on trademarks closely follow the 1988 EC trademark directive including the right to hold and transfer trademarks without actually operating the business concerned.

Most important, however, are the provisions regarding patents, where the industrial countries' conception of patent protection prevailed. This applies to the length, where the agreement requires that 20 years' patent protection be available for all inventions in almost all fields of technology. It also applies to the criteria of inventions eligible for patent protection, the exceptions from patent protection as well as the rights of the patent holder and the regulations concerning process patents. It must be regarded as one of the great successes of the Uruguay Round trade negotiations that such a high standard of protection could be achieved. This includes strict limits on compulsory licensing or similar infringements of the exclusive rights of the patent holders.

LLDCs were granted a transition period of eleven years for the full implementation of the agreement and developing countries and transitional economies a period of five years. Recognising that IPRs are only insufficiently institutionalised or even completely unknown in some LDCs, these exceptions were granted to soften the blow of stronger IPRs protection. To pharmaceutical and agro-chemical products, the transitional period applied only in part. Moreover, the agreement contains provisions regarding trade secrets, which was especially demanded by the chemical industry. Finally, new, internationally binding rules on the enforcement of IPRs protection have been agreed upon. These provisions cover civil judicial procedures and remedies, including provisional measures, procedures involving customs authorities in preventing the import of counterfeit and pirated goods and criminal procedures in cases of piracy carried out on a commercial scale. In regard to provisional and border measures in particular, detailed requirements are laid down to safeguard against abuse.

3. DYNAMIC TRADE THEORY

The importance of TRIPs in the context of North-South trade is a natural corollary of the dynamic trade theory. Drawing on Schumpeter's growth theory, this postulate explains foreign trade by the existence of dynamic competition. An innovation grants a temporary monopoly to the pioneer entrepreneur, which in due time will be eroded by competitors by means of imitation. Due to the introduction of new products and production processes, old markets are destroyed while new markets and competitive positions are created. Dynamic competition is based on the premise that a country's comparative advantages are not, as is commonly assumed, exogenously given, but result from a process of searching and learning, which itself is determined by incentives for competition and the institutional setting. Consequently, comparative advantages are partly endogenous. In this conceptual framework, foreign trade is primarily determined by technological progress, which in turn raises the question of the necessary and different conditions for technological progress.

If we go by the technological gap model of international trade, it is the different availability of technological knowledge in industrial and developing countries respectively that explains a good part of North-South trade. Innovating firms and countries enjoy a temporary monopoly, enabling them to avoid pure price competition to a certain extent. The possession of comparative advantage based on technological leadership is, however, limited by scope for imitation. Once the technological edge is lost, the direction and structure of trade is determined by traditional explanations of foreign trade, such as different factor proportions.

In this model, the structure of international trade depends on the imitation lag. The duration of the lag is, indeed, the decisive factor of competition. On the one hand, it decides how long innovators can draw super-normal profits from their innovations and, thus, how big the incentive for innovation is. On the other, the lag decides when those who follow begin to participate in the benefits stemming from the innovation. The imitation lag represents the temporal dimension of the adjustment process and is of particular interest from the point of view of competition. The duration of the imitation lag is not exogenously given, but is itself the result of entrepreneurial activity and economic policy. The relevance of TRIPs is, thus, easily explained.

Traditional trade theory assumes perfect markets, a well-functioning price mechanism and perfect factor mobility. As a consequence, adjustment occurs instantly and without costs. In contrast, models of dynamic competition trade theory concede the existence of far-reaching adjustment processes, which are neither instantaneous nor costless. From the point of view of competition, international trade is a process of constant searching and learning riddled with uncertainty. The specialisation of firms in certain countries not only reflects their own adjustment behaviour, but also corresponds to that of their trading partners, which again in a way provides both the framework and the impulse for their own adjustment.

Two dimensions of adjustment are of particular relevance: the costs and the time taken. The former include those of new investment, retraining, relocation and social costs. As to the necessity of developing new technologies to replace those imitated by the followers, it has to be realised that technical innovations do not fall from heaven and require efforts and these impose costs.

The adjustment time is relevant in respect of the dynamic game of innovation and imitation. After all, innovations follow an extensive research effort and both innovation and introduction of new products take time to emerge.

4. BENEFITS FROM TRIPS

If technological progress is endogenous and if the distribution of technological knowledge is decisive for the pattern of international trade then what motivates firms to devote resources to research efforts? It is primarily the prospect of super-normal profits that pushes firms into research. Indeed, the expectation of super-normal or "pioneer" profits is a pre-condition for technological progress. The idea of enforcing the right to intellectual property is built around the assumption that the process of innovation depends on a system of incentives. To that extent, the IPRs constitute a decisive factor in ensuring that incentives play an important role in the adjustment process.

In this context, it must be noted that a large number of developing countries — following the example set by Japan — have made the imitation of industrial countries' advanced technologies a cornerstone of their catching-up strategy. The imitator usually saves the high cost of innovation and most imitating countries are competitive largely due to their low wage levels. Yet, competition is the main force behind technological progress. The efficiency of technological development is greatly enhanced by competitive pressures and the constant threat of losing the temporary monopoly. Stronger competition does not, however, necessarily translate into technological progress and welfare gains for all. Rather, this may well impede the dynamics of technological progress, if the amount of super-normal ("pioneer") profits accruing to the innovator is insufficient.

In this sense, TRIPs share certain aspects with the contestable market theory. The competitive pressures of international trade are sought to be maintained by keeping market entry barriers low, while preserving incentives for innovation by securing super-normal profits. TRIPs are, thus, an element of the policy on international competition.

Developing countries tend to regard TRIPs primarily as an attempt by the industrial countries to evade stronger competition from imitating LDCs. TRIPs seem to be in conflict with the development necessary to open industrial countries' markets for LDC exports. Equally important, developing countries, obviously, have a strong interest in gaining a share of the high profits accruing in the early phases of the product cycle as soon as possible.

There are a number of reasons, however, why developing countries, too, may benefit from stronger IPRs protection. The strategy of catching up by imitation depends on the existence of sufficient incentives for innovation: no imitation without innovation! By using the public good, "technological knowledge", for their imitation strategy without sharing in the R&D costs needed for the production or, rather, generation of this good, developing countries take a free-rider position, which will not be tolerated indefinitely by industrial countries. LDCs will benefit from a clear and stable system of international competition rules. TRIPs will remove the uncertainty about the extent of IPRs protection; they will also make technological developments more transparent: to protect intellectual property is to make it public! To sum up, a uniform, well institutionalised system of TRIPs is an important step towards a system of transparent and unequivocal rules for international competition, which also supports developing countries in their catching-up process.

Thus, while TRIPs may impose considerable short-term costs on developing countries as far as trade in knowledge-intensive goods is concerned, seen in the dynamic context of North-South trade the preservation of a rules-based international trading system will yield considerable long term benefits for both industrial and developing countries. Even from the point of view of development economics, the debate should not be about whether to introduce TRIPs at all but about the `right' specification.

5. TRIPS AND INTERNATIONAL COMPETITION

Increased competition in both standardised and high-tech goods has altered the world economy to an extent which calls for a completely new set of competition rules. The successful catching-up of developing countries, especially the NICs, based on a strategy of imitation, has affected the industrial countries' capacity and willingness to adjust. The acceleration of imitation has not only enhanced adjustment pressures and costs, but also the protectionist instincts of innovating countries. The crucial point for industrial countries is that given the possibility of imitation and, thus, a shift of production from the North to the South, a constant innovation in the North is necessary not just to grow, but also to maintain real incomes in the North.

To maintain their technological leadership, innovating countries do not only resort to protectionism. Without pushing the idea of an "acceleration trap" too far, it is certainly evident that increased international competition compels firms to ever greater R&D efforts. Trying to alleviate the pressure, firms tend to try to "nationalise" those costs by shifting the burden to the general public. Thus, national industrial policies targeted at high-tech industries become increasingly important. The growing budgets of national industrial policies are part of the attempt to lessen the pressure on firms suffering from a shortening of the imitation lag. Whether this strategy lessens the costs to society too is, however, debatable. The rat race to enhance national competitiveness clearly demonstrates that stronger international competition is not exclusively advantageous. Stronger technological competition certainly results in higher R&D efficiency and a greater effort to improve locational advantages in general. It also leads, however, to more frequent recourse to mercantilist instruments. It is in the field of competition policy that TRIPs have a role to play but not as one might want to assume—TRIPs are not there to manage the intensity of world-wide competition.

TRIPs are, obviously, not a first-best text-book recipe for equitable international trade. Rather, these can hinder international competition and the up-grading of developing countries. However, when perceived not as a protectionist device of industrial countries, but more as a calculated, fixed-term adjustment mechanism, these are certainly superior to a technological competition sustained armoury. Strengthening international IPRs protection helps raise incentives for R&D and secures pioneer profits for innovators. This strategy is more rewarding and less costly than trying to push ahead by means of national industrial policies. By guaranteeing a world-wide reward for technological advance, TRIPs can be said to contribute to keeping Schumpeter's dynamics alive.

However, if the temporary protection provided by TRIPs is not used efficiently, it will turn out to be a pyrrhic victory for developed countries. For, without the willingness and flexibility of firms in the industrial countries to constantly improve upon their innovative and productive capabilities, the TRIPs agreement merely affords them an opportunity to rest on their already withering laurels for a few more years.

3

WHAT IS INTELLECTUAL PROPERTY?

Countries with innovative local industries almost invariably have laws to foster innovation by regulating the copying of inventions, identifying symbols and creative expressions. These laws encompass four separate and distinct types of intangible property, namely, patents, trademarks, copyrights and trade secrets, which are collectively referred to as "intellectual property." Intellectual property shares many of the same characteristics associated with real and personal property. For example, intellectual property is an asset and as such can bought, sold, licensed, exchanged or gratuitously given away like many other forms of property. Further, the intellectual property owner has the right to prevent unauthorised use or sale of the property. The most noticeable difference between intellectual property and other forms of property, however, is that intellectual property is intangible, i.e., it cannot be defined or identified by its own physical parameters. It must be expressed in some discernible way to be protectable.

1. WHAT IS A PATENT?

Patent systems are designed to encourage the disclosure of information to the public by rewarding inventors for their endeavours. One might say that a patent is a contract between society as a whole and the individual inventor. Under the terms of this social contract, the inventor is given the exclusive right to prevent others from making, using and selling the patented invention for a fixed period of time in return for the inventor disclosing details of the invention to the public.

Although the word "patent" finds its origins from documents issued by the Sovereign of England in the Middle Ages for granting a privilege, today the word patent is synonymously linked with this exclusive right granted to inventors. The duration of patent exclusively varies from country to country. However, under all patent systems, once this period has expired, people are free to use the invention as they wish.

The benefits of an effective patent system can be partially illustrated as follows: A patent rewards the investment of time, money and effort associated with research; it stimulates further research as competitors invent alternatives to patented inventions; and it encourages innovation and investment in patented inventions by permitting companies to recover their research and development costs during the period of exclusive rights. The limited term of a patent also furthers public interest by encouraging quick commercialisation of inventions, therefore making them available to the public sooner rather than later. Patents also allow for greater latitude in the exchange of information between research groups, help avoid duplicative research, and most importantly, increase the general pool of public knowledge.

A comparison of the number of inventions developed in countries with adequate patent protection with the number of countries without it demonstrates that patent systems stimulate investment in research and development. A look at the pharmaceutical industry in Italy before and after patent protection for pharmaceuticals became available in that country provides a good illustration. Prior to granting protection, there was significantly less capital invested in Italian pharmaceutical research and development when compared to the amount of money invested in the research and development of other technologies. Following Italy's enactment of patent laws protecting pharmaceuticals, the relative investment in the pharmaceutical industry in Italy rose significantly.

As stated before, the right conferred by a patent is a right to exclude others from making, using or selling the patented invention during the terms of the patent. It is important to understand that a patent does not necessarily give the patent owner the right to make, use or sell the invention himself. For example, the owner of a patent for an improved method of producing a chemical compound would not be free to sell the compound made using the patented methods if the compound is itself patented by someone else.

Patents are granted under national laws and, therefore, the rights are also national in scope. Thus, a United States patent can be asserted only against infringing in the United States. In most countries, these rights are enforceable by civil, rather than criminal, proceedings. Accordingly, enforcement falls solely to the patent owner. In general, any act of making, using or selling the patented invention without permission infringes that patent, whether it be by the State, a corporation or an individual. Any such infringing act will give rise to liability, regardless of the infringer's intent or lack of knowledge of the patent.

Remedies for patent infringement can include injunctions, orders to deliver up or destroy infringing articles and compensation for damages suffered by the patentee or profits made through the infringement. An issued patent remains open to attack for invalidity, and it is a common defence for an alleged infringer to assert that the patent is invalid. Typically, patents are challenged on the ground that the claimed invention was invented by someone other than the named inventor or that the inventor would have been obvious to persons skilled in the relevant technology.

2. WHAT IS A TRADEMARK AND A SERVICE MARK?

Trademarks and service marks are primarily intended to indicate the source of goods and services and to distinguish those goods and services from those of others. They also symbolise the quality of the goods or services with which they are used. Most trademarks and service marks (called "marks") are words, but they can be almost anything that can distinguish one product or service from another, such as symbols, logos, sounds, designs or even distinctive non-functional product configurations. While virtually all countries recognise and offer protection for trademarks, many—but not all— countries recognise and protect service marks. In some countries, protection for a mark is acquired by using the mark on goods or services. In others, the owner must register the mark with the national trademark office before protection in that country is granted.

The duration of protection afforded to a mark varies greatly from country to country. Registrations are issued for finite periods of time. However, because of the fundamental purposes of these marks — avoiding public confusion, encouraging competition and protecting the owners' goodwill — registrations may be renewed and, thus, extend indefinitely as long as the marks are used. The owner of a mark may preclude others from using a similar mark if such use is likely to cause confusion in the minds of purchasers. Determining whether two marks are so similar as to be confusing usually involves a multi-factor analysis that compares the parties' marks, their goods or services, their advertising and trade channels, the defendant's intent in choosing its mark, and the presence or absence of actual confusion.

3. WHAT IS A COPYRIGHT?

A copyright is an exclusive right to reproduce an original work of authorship fixed in any tangible medium of expression; to prepare derivative works based upon the original work; and to perform or display the work in the case of musical, dramatic, choreographic and sculptural works. Copyright protection does not extend to any idea, procedure, process, system, method of operation, concept principle or discovery, regardless of the form in which it is described, explained or embodied. Rather, copyright protection is limited only to an author's particular expression of the idea, process, and concept, in a tangible medium.

Copyright protection automatically subsists in all works of authorship from the moment of creation. The duration of copyright protection varies from country to country and can be dependent on such factors as the subject matter of the work, whether the work was made for hire and whether the work is published. In the United States, the copyright for a work of an individual author lasts for his or her lifetime plus 50 years. However, if the work is made for hire, the copyright lasts for 100 years from the time of creation or 75 years from first publication.

The exclusive rights granted to the copyright owner do not include the right to prevent others from making fair use of the owner's work. Such fair use may include use of the work for purposes of criticism, comment, news reporting, teaching or education, scholarship or research. The nature of the work, the extent of the work copied and the impact of copying on the work's commercial value are all considered in determining whether an unauthorised use constitutes a "fair use."

4. WHAT IS A TRADE SECRET?

A trade secret represents information that is secret or not generally known in the relevant industry and that gives its owner an advantage over the competitors. Trade secret protection exists as long as the information is kept secret or confidential by its owner and is not lawfully and independently obtained by others. Examples of trade secrets include formula, patterns, methods, programmes, techniques, processes or compilations of information that provide one's business with a competitive advantage. The owner of a trade secret may recover damages resulting from improper disclosure or use of its secret by another.

5. TYPES OF INTELLECTUAL PROPERTY COMPARED AND CONTRASTED

A product may be protected by one or more of the four types of intellectual property protection discussed above. A common example is a household lamp with a sculptured base. The functional electric components of the lamp and the light bulb may be protected by a patent. The label on the lamp may contain a trademark identifying the source of the lamp that distinguished it from other manufacturers' lamps. The sculptured lamp base may be considered a work of art and therefore be subject to copyright protection. Finally, the manufacturer may have compiled a list of customers who are known to buy such lamps or a list of preferred parts suppliers. If these lists have been kept confidential and secret, these should be deemed trade secrets.

6. ECONOMIC BENEFITS TO COUNTRIES AND COMPANIES

Countries that provide for the protection of intellectual property benefit in many ways. In addition to increasing the general pool of information and knowledge, adequate legal protection fosters investment and trade. When looking for new markets or countries in which to expand manufacturing or distribution facilities, companies often look to countries that will protect their intellectual property. Companies that are active internationally often will not allow certain technologies or other intellectual property to be sold in countries that will not protect the property owner's rights. Where the owner's rights are not protected, third parties may use the property and, therefore, unfairly reap the rewards of the owner's investment in developing and marketing the property. Thus, inadequate legal protection for intellectual property acts as a trade barrier.

Companies benefit from the protection of intellectual property through the exclusive rights granted by such protection. Companies, therefore, often build extensive portfolios of patents, marks, copyrights and trade secrets. Such portfolios are important for both the "offensive" and "defensive" goals of the company. Patents, marks, copyrights and trade secrets have an independent value as a business asset. This value may be actively exploited for commercial gain. Because an owner of intellectual property has exclusive rights in that property, the owner may allow others to use the property for a fee. Such licensing arrangements are quite common and lucrative. Cross-licensing is another technique used by companies to benefit from their intellectual property portfolios. When one company desires to use the intellectual property of another company, the companies may "exchange" or cross- licence the right to use certain intellectual properties owned by the respective companies. A large portfolio of intellectual property will aid a company in negotiating a cross-licence with another company. Finally, because intellectual property has independent value, the property may be used to secure financing in some countries.

7. REQUIREMENT AND OBSTACLES IN OBTAINING PROTECTION

Intellectual property is protected on a national basis. Thus, the specific scope of protection and the requirements for obtaining protection will vary from country to country. There are, however, similarities among national legal arrangements. Moreover, the current worldwide trend is towards harmonising the national laws.

Patents

Even though patentability is governed by national laws, most countries have adopted similar requirements. In general, to be patentable, an invention must be novel, useful and non-obvious. It is a prerequisite to patentability that the invention be capable of some practical application. This emphasises the importance the patent system puts on usefulness. Although this principle remains constant, the phraseology used within the legislation of particular countries varies, e.g., in the United States the patentable subject matter must be "useful," whereas in the United Kingdom it must be capable of "industrial application."

The invention must be new, that is to say, the subject matter of the invention is not or cannot be inferred to be part of what is already known. This is commonly referred to as the "novelty" requirement. New or novel in this context means "new to the public." Therefore, something that has previously been used or known but has not been made available to the public (for instance, if it has been kept a secret) is not a bar to patentability. The invention must also be non-obvious. This prevents someone from taking advantage of the patent system and obtaining protection for something that is a mere extension or trivial variation of what is known. Generally, the test for inventiveness or "non-obviousness" is based on what a reasonable person skilled in the field to which the invention was made, would consider to be so. For reasons of public policy some countries do not allow the patenting of chemical compounds, but instead allow only the patenting of the processes for preparing them.

It is particularly difficult to enforce a process patent as the burden of proof is on the patent owner to show that the patent has been infringed, i.e. "copied." The patent owner must prove that a particular manufacturing process (i.e., that covered by the patent) was used to manufacture the particular chemical. This can be very difficult to show where there are many possible process variants and where access to the potential infringer's facility is not available. In practice, this is done by looking for trace impurities that are characteristic of the manufacturing process. One can imagine how complex the issues can become if, for instance, a patent protects a pharmaceutical and the pharmaceutical is made in Turkey, where there is no protection for pharmaceuticals, and exported to Finland, which provides protection only for manufacturing processes.

Over the past 15 years, many countries have changed from "process" to "product" patenting, and this trend is continuing with more countries expected to upgrade their patent laws within the next few years. Not only are the utilitarian aspects of new and useful inventions patentable, but many countries also extend patent protection to novel, ornamental industrial designs. In the United States, this form of protection is known as a design patent, while in many European countries, the property right in an industrial design is referred to as a design model. In addition to the usual subjects of patent protection such as devices, chemical compositions and processes, some countries provide patent protection for living matter. For example, sexually reproduced varieties of plants, excluding bacteria, uncultured plants and tuber propogated plants can be protected as can sexually reproduced plants (by seed), excluding bacterial, fungi and first generation hybrids.

Trademarks and Service Marks

As with all intellectual property, trademark and service mark laws are national in origin. Some countries grant rights to the first person to use the mark in the course of business, while other countries grant rights to the first person to obtain a registration in that country . In "first-to-use" countries, rights may subsist without registering the mark with the national trademark office. However, registration is still desirable because it is presumptive evidence of the validity of the mark and the owner's right to use that mark. It also appears on the national register of marks providing notice to the world of the owner's use and claim to ownership. Some countries require that the mark be used in commerce prior to the issuance of a registration, while other countries permit registration based on the intent of the applicant to use the mark in the future. Following the use or registration of a trademark, the owner must use the mark or it may become subject to attack by others on the ground that the owner has abandoned it.

At the minimum, most countries require that a mark be distinctive, i.e., capable of distinguishing the goods or services of the owner of the mark from the goods or services of others. To determine whether a mark meets this test, one must determine the "strength" of the mark. A mark's strength is usually measured across a spectrum. This spectrum includes, from the weakest to the strongest, terms that are generic, descriptive, suggestive, arbitrary and fanciful. At the weakest end of the spectrum lie words, symbols or devices that are not capable of distinguishing goods because these are common terms used to identify the goods themselves, e.g., books, table, chair. Such terms are called generic terms and are not protectable as trademarks. The next category comprises descriptive terms. A mark is descriptive if it describes the intended purpose, function, physical characteristic, laudatory quality or end use of the product.

Copyrights

To secure copyright protection, the work in question must be an "original" work of authorship fixed in a tangible medium of expression. Works of authorship that fall within this definition may include:

- literary work (including computer programmes);
- musical work and accompanying lyrics;
- dramatic work and dialogue;
- pantomimes and choreographic work;
- pictorial, graphic and sculptural work;
- motion pictures and other audiovisual work; and
- sound recordings.

It is important to note that the laws of many countries do not limit the type or form of work because authors are continuing to invent new ways of expressing themselves. The test for the originality of a work is usually two pronged. First, the work of authorship must originate from the author, in the sense that it must have actually been independently created by the author and not copied from other works. Secondly, the work must contain a sufficient originality so as to be more than a trivial variation over pre-existing work.

To be copyrightable, a work must be "fixed in a tangible medium of expression." A work is "fixed" when its embodiment in a tangible medium is sufficiently permanent or stable as to permit it to be perceived, reproduced or otherwise communicated for a period of time that is not transitory. This means that the manner or medium of fixation is irrelevant. Copyright registration in most countries is relatively straightforward and inexpensive. Although copyright protection subsists from the moment the work is fixed in a tangible expression, copyright registration confers additional important benefits in some countries. In those countries with a registration system, registration may be a pre-requisite to initiating legal action to stop others from infringing a copyright, and /or for recouping the costs, including attorney's fees, of enforcing those rights. In addition, in some countries, a copyright registration constitutes *prima facie* evidence of the validity and ownership of the copyright.

Trade Secrets

Trade secrets are not registered like other forms of intellectual property and are not creatures of statutes. Instead, the judicial systems of each country determine the requirements for obtaining trade secret protection. Some of the factors commonly considered include:

- the extent to which the information is known outside the business,
- the extent to which the information is known by employees and others involved in the trade secret owner's business.
- the extent of the measures taken to guard the trade secrets,
- the value of the information to the owner and his competitors,
- the amount of money or effort expended by the trade secret owner in developing the secret, and
- the effort required by others to acquire or duplicate (through reverse engineering) the information.

The "secrecy" of an alleged trade secret is the most important factor to be considered. If the information claimed to be a trade secret is available through any legitimate means and is obtained in this way, then the information is no longer 'secret' and may become ineligible for protection. However, if the owner has taken reasonable steps to protect the information, but the trade `secret' information nonetheless is publicly disclosed, the courts in many countries may still grant protection. Such `reasonable' steps may include requiring those persons, who encounter the information as the result of normal business ventures, to sign confidentiality and non-disclosure agreements.

Costs vs. Benefits

As with all business-related activities, economics plays a big role in the determination of whether to protect intellectual property. Companies must weigh the potential value of an intellectual property right against both the probability of realising that value and the costs of securing, enforcing and maintaining that right. There are no hard and fast rules that determine the potential value of a given intellectual property right. What is valuable to one individual or company may be worthless to another. There are certain obvious factors that contribute to the potential value of the intellectual property, including the potential value of exclusive or other rights, assignments or licences, cross-licences enforcement against infringers, and as collateral for securing financing.

A trademark or service mark may be a very valuable asset. For example, the German automobile manufacturer "BMW" purchased the British automobile manufacturer "Rover" primarily to obtain its portfolio of desirable trademarks including `Land Rover,' `Range Rover,' `Triumph,' `Austin,' and `MGB.' On the other hand, a trademark will be virtually worthless if consumers associate it with poor quality.

National Policy and International Accords

Countries that protect intellectual property — copyrights, patents, trademarks and other forms of intangible property — provide an incentive for capital investment in research and may aid the ability to develop new products. Adequate legal protection also fosters investment and trade. Companies looking for new markets or locations for manufacturing or distribution facilities often look to countries that will protect their intellectual property.

Yet, where the owner's rights are not protected, third parties may use the property and unfairly reap the rewards. The damage resulting from such unauthorised use includes lost domestic and export sales and royalties, other financial losses, and harm to producers' reputation. Many countries have national laws aimed at protecting intellectual property, but little or no international law exists in this area. Several multinational treaties and conventions have been negotiated that oblige member countries to provide a minimum standard of intellectual property protection to foreign nationals. The last of these is the TRIPs agreement and this we know is the most comprehensive.

United States Policy and the USTR Report

The United States encourages all countries to eliminate trade barriers that affect U.S. exports of goods and services and direct investment by U.S. citizens (including corporations) in other countries. According to U.S. policy, the inadequate protection of intellectual property rights is a significant trade barrier. An annual report on significant foreign trade barriers is prepared by the United States Trade Representative (USTR) and is submitted to the President, the Senate Finance Committee and appropriate committees in the House of Representatives. If warranted, the United States will impose trade barriers against particular countries under what is known as a `Special 301' or 'Super 301' action.

International Cooperation

There is very little international law governing intellectual property. However, there is remarkable transnational uniformity, which results from treaties and international conventions that usually oblige member countries to provide minimum norms of intellectual property protection and to extend the protection for the benefit of foreign nationals. Several of the more important treaties and conventions are discussed below.

The Paris Convention

The International Convention for the Protection of Intellectual Property is probably the single most important multilateral treaty on intellectual property, and is better known as the `Paris

Convention'. Most industrialised nations and many developing countries are parties to this convention and are referred to collectively as the Paris Union. To date, 56 countries have ratified the latest revision of the text, which covers a wide range of intellectual property rights including patents, industrial designs, trademark, trade names, service marks, collective marks and unfair competition. The Paris Convention grants foreign nationals the same protection and benefits accorded to nationals of any other member country, without discrimination.

One of the most important provisions of the Paris Convention relates to "Convention Priority." An applicant's priority date is the date on which an application is first filed in the applicant's home country. The convention allows the applicant to claim this date as the effective one on which an application for the same patent, industrial design, utility mark or trademark was filed in any other member country, provided that the application is filed within 12 months (for patents and utility marks) or six months (for industrial design and trademarks) from the claimed priority date. This removes the need and cost to file all the separate country applications at the same time to obtain effective protection. Under the conventional priority filing system, intervening third party applications cannot act as bars to the owner's application if the owner files within the prescribed time.

The Berne Convention

The Berne Convention, established in 1886, is the principal transnational convention relating purely to copyright protection. The Berne Convention is based on national treatment, and imposes minimum norms of copyright protection. Like the Paris Convention, the Berne Convention grants foreign nationals the same protection and advantages as those granted to nationals of any member country, without discrimination. The membership of the Berne Convention has increased from an initial membership of 10 to over 90 countries including nearly all leading economic countries. Under the Berne Convention, and its six subsequent amendments, copyright protection is automatic throughout all member countries without the need to comply with any formalities.

International Filing Systems

There is currently no single way to obtain truly international protection of intellectual property. The closest current approaches to such international protection are those provided by the following conventions establishing international application filing systems:

European Patent Convention

The European Patent Convention (EPC) created the European Patent Office (EPO), which is based in Germany. The convention currently applies to most European Economic Community member states and to several other European countries. The EPC provides for a single application in English, German or French, on which a central search followed by an examination is carried out. Once the patent is accepted for grant, and the appropriate fees and translations are submitted, the single application is converted into a bundle of individual national patents. The system also allows an objection to the grant to be lodged at the EPO within nine months from the patent grant. Subsequent issues of validity, however, must be dealt with on a country-by-country basis by individual national courts.

Patent Cooperation Treaty (PCT)

This system, which includes many countries in addition to European countries, similarly provides for the filing of a single application designating the member countries from which patents are desired. Although the single filing takes place under the auspices of the World Intellectual Property Organisation (WIPO), a specialised agency of the United Nations system that seeks to promote international cooperation in the protection of international property, the actual filing is made either in the United States or the EPO. The single application is searched, and it is possible to request a non-binding opinion on patentability. After payment of appropriate fees and the filing of appropriate translations, the application is converted into a bundle of individual national applications, which are then subject to examination by national patent offices.

The Madrid Agreement

The Madrid Agreement concerns the international filing of registration applications for trademarks. It enables registration of a trademark in WIPO's International Bureau in Geneva, in much the same way as the PCT provides for international filing of patent applications. WIPO acts as the administering agency for action taken under the Paris Convention. Once registered with WIPO, the trademark is protected in each member country. Therefore, the protection obtained is governed by the national laws of individual member countries and is limited by national laws.

The Madrid Protocol

Signatories to the Madrid Agreement and other countries have negotiated a new agreement referred to as the Madrid Protocol. The Madrid Protocol seeds to obtain protection for trademarks through international recognition and is to be policed by the WIPO, which will maintain records of all applications. Each registration will be effective for 10 years, although this period would be indefinitely extendable on request for additional 10 year terms.

NAFTA

The North American Free Trade Agreement (NAFTA) is a general trade agreement between Canada, Mexico and the United States that imposes general requirements for both the domestic and international treatment and enforcement of intellectual property rights. NAFTA 'significantly' advances protection of intellectual property in Mexico. However, it also requires that the United States and Canada make certain changes. The agreement recognises the need, at a minimum, to accede and give effect to the main international conventions relating to intellectual property, i.e., the Paris Convention (intellectual property), the Berne Convention (copyrights), the Geneva Convention (protects phonograms or audio works), and the Union for the Protection of New Varieties of Plants (UPOV). Under the UPOV, protection is given to plant varieties that:

- belong to one of the botanical species on the national list;
- are distinct from commonly known varieties;
- are sufficiently homogeneous; and
- are stable. In essence, NAFTA requires each member country to extend protection to foreign nationals equivalent to the protection granted to domestic rights holders.

GATT/TRIPs

The Uruguay Round of international trade negotiations, launched under the auspices of the General Agreement to Tariffs and Trade (GATT) in Punta del Este, Uruguay, in September 1986, concluded seven years later on December 15, 1993. The result of the negotiations was a comprehensive set of agreements, including one on Trade-Related Aspects of Intellectual Property Rights (TRIPs). This has been discussed at the outset.

European Union

The European Union has formulated certain agreements, leading to creation of Community patents and trademarks. The Community Patent Convention (CPC) has led to the creation of a Community patent that covers the entire European Union and is subject to common legislation on validity, enforcement, etc. The convention requires that disputes be litigated in national courts at the first instance. The final appeal, however, would be to the Community Patent Appeal Court. Similarly, the Community Trademark Convention proposes the creation of a Community Trademark, which would cover all European Union member states.

The U.S. Patent System

The patent system in the United States differs in several ways from what may be considered to be the worldwide "norm," if such a "norm" really exists. Currently, a U.S. patent has a term of 17 years from the time of grant, which is to say that the patent term does not begin while the application is pending; it begins only when the patent is actually granted. It can be a matter of years before a patent is granted from the time the patent application is first filed.

In compliance with the GATT, after June 8, 1995, a U.S. patent will have a term of 20 years from the date of the first filing of the application. Most other patent systems already have patent terms that run for a fixed term from the date the patent application was first filed. For instance, the United Kingdom, Germany, France, Japan, Canada and many other countries have patent terms of 20 years from the first filing of the patent application. The United States is unique in its approach to the allocation of patent rights. This is unchanged by the lengthening of the U.S. patent term. In the United States, patent rights are granted to the "first to invent" rather than the universally accepted approach of the "first to file." Consequently the United States has a unique "Interference System," which it uses to determine which party was the first to invent.

The basic principles of novelty, utility and non-obviousness apply as pre-requisites to patentability in the United States. However, with regard to the determination of both novelty and non-obviousness, what constitutes prior use or public knowledge, i.e. "prior art," differs considerably from standards commonly adopted elsewhere. Although the subject matter described in a printed publication or patent will constitute prior art, whether or not it is published or patented in the United States, the same is not true of subject matter in public use or known to the public. In latter cases, only use or knowledge within the United States or its territories constitutes prior art. Many countries determine the applicability of prior art without geographic limitations.

The United States grants a one-year grace period from the time an invention is disclosed to the public to the time the patent application must be filed. In other words, as long as an application for a patent is filed not more than one year from the date the subject matter is publicly disclosed, the patent application must be filed before any disclosure is made to the public. Thus, in other countries, the inventors' freedom of use and publication of their inventions is considerably restricted. Some countries seek an intermediate level of freedom. For example, Indonesia grants a six month grace period for use or public display, but only where the use is found to be experimental and the public display is at an exhibition.

The United States requires that the mode for working the invention be disclosed as part of the patent application. The majority of countries impose no such requirement, and, therefore, an inventor may possibly "hide" the best way of using or making the patented product or process. However, this practice is antithetical to the underlying purpose of a patent system because it hinders disclosures of technological innovations. In the United States, patent applications are not published or indexed until after they are granted. Thus, third parties may not oppose the grant of a patent nor even know that an application has been filed. Other countries publish the patent applications and have procedures for third parties to object to the granting of a patent. The European Patent Office, for example, has such a procedure. Finally, the United States requires maintenance fees to be paid at three-and-a-half years, seven-and-a-half years and eleven-and-a-half years respectively after the original grant of a patent while other countries require annual maintenance fees.

4

PHARMACEUTICAL PATENTS: NEW HORIZONS IN INDIA

1. THE BACKGROUND

The ground rules set by the Government will ultimately determine the nature of the pharmaceutical industry's operations in the country: it strengths and weaknesses, its capacity for taking risks, and its willingness — or unwillingness — to do so, as well as the scope for national and multinational enterprise to commit funds, conduct research, develop, manufacture and sell. For pharmaceuticals, patents are relevant to all these aspects of industrial activity, but their impact is more complex than is often supposed. That is because pharmaceutical patents by themselves are industrially meaningless. The vast majority of pharmaceutical patents never leads to a saleable product, because most patented drug substances will fail to clear the regulatory hurdles of safety and efficacy during a lengthy and difficult development period, averaging ten years from discovery to registration. On the other hand, without patents, the incentive to innovate is lacking, because the financial risk is too high when measured against potential rewards. A therapeutically innovative new drug on a ten year pilgrimage of development may or may not lead to the market; and if it does, may still fail commercially; and even if it succeeds, would quickly be copied if it is not protected by patents.

Deemed a Luxury

In India, pharmaceutical innovation is deemed a luxury. Every nation has the right to reject the burdens of innovation in its industrial strategy, although in tomorrow's world of international trade, the refusal to protect inventions made elsewhere would probably attract penalties in other forms. But, attitudes are changing and the Government in the post-reform period has declared in public statements that it wanted to encourage original research and development, particularly in the area of new drugs for tropical diseases which is not at all adequately covered by efforts in Europe, North America or Japan. The more important thing is that India is potentially capable of innovating pharmaceutically. We have academic skills, although there are obviously some gaps in the biological and pharmacological sciences which would need special attention.

In effect, experts and observers are generally agreed that what is in short supply in India is not scientific genius, but industrial cash flow. And cash flow for pharmaceutical innovation is intimately linked with patent protection, as well as with the wider sphere of government controls and incentives. Rather than look at pharmaceutical patents in isolation, we have to see patents in the wider context of both national and multinational pharmaceutical development in India. It is pointless to argue whether patents are in themselves good or bad: there are valid reasons for either view, depending on one's fundamental aims and objectives.

A Fact of Industrial Life

What matters at this point of time is that full pharmaceutical patent protection will be a fact of industrial life in India, since the agreement on TRIPs will eventually govern the regime of patent protection. The consequences of this act need to be examined, together with the part that each of the players — Indian drug companies, the Government, and multinationals — can play in building the future under patents. At the outset, one must reject the determinist view that 'A' inevitably leads to 'B' which then unfailingly produces the end result 'C'. That the outcome is in the hands of those shaping events — in this case, Government and industrialists who can either conduct total war and produce chaos or gradually hammer out a constructive consensus.

2. RELEVANT FACTS ABOUT TRIPS

The main provisions of TRIPs - (Chart I) - insofar as these are different from the existing form of pharmaceutical protection under the Indian Patents Act 1970 — are:

* a minimum patent term of 20 years from the date of filing
* pharmaceutical products to become patentable as such

TRIPs

Main Patent Provisions:

Minimum patent term:
20 Years from filing

Pharmaceuticals:
Patentable as *Products*

Import:
Accepted as `Working' a Patent

Compulsory licensing:
Special Circumstances Only

Burden of proof (Process patents)
Reversed (Defendant's Onus)

Chart I

'BUT.......'

Pharma Product patents in India:
Only the After 10 - Year Transitional Period ⟶ Year 2005

No Pipeline Protection
For existing drugs

Chart II

* Import to be accepted as 'working' a patent
* compulsory licensing to be confined to special circumstances, such as emergency or abuse of patent rights
* reversal of the burden of proof in legal actions over process patents—this will oblige the defendant to prove that his process is non-infringing.

Evidently, this amounts to an absolutely fundamental change from the present situation where the pharmaceutical patent term is seven years; only processes (not products) are patentable; importation is not regarded as 'working' a patent; licences can be obtained within three years of patent grant, either as 'licences of right' or compulsorily on a variety of grounds (including that of 'not working' the patent); and the burden of proof in process infringement actions rests with the patentee.

The effect of these basic changes will, however, be delayed by two important concessions to developing countries without current patent cover for drug substances. India played an important part in negotiating these. These are:

Firstly, a transitional period of ten years before product cover for pharmaceuticals must be adoped.

And secondly, 'pipeline' drugs whose patents have already been published elsewhere will not qualify for product cover under TRIPs. Only drugs for which patents are first filed after TRIPs comes into effect may receive limited marketing exclusivity before end of the transitional period.

The 2004 deadline

In practice, the transitional period is running from 1995 until 2004. It gives Indian companies roughly nine years in which to adapt their strategy to the new situation. At the same time, it deprives research-based multinationals of any protection for new drugs, now in the development pipeline, whose patents have already been published anywhere in the world — even though many of these new drugs will not actually become marketable until after the turn of the millennium. Having to adapt to radical change is never easy. Nor is having to wait a decade for the implementation of an agreed change.

3. THE TRANSITIONAL DECADE

Meanwhile, the transitional decade is going to be one of extreme uncertainty for all concerned. It is one thing to sign an agreement, but quite another to agree on its interpretation and implementation. Only one prediction can be made confidently today: once the transitional clock starts ticking, things can never be the same again. The knowledge that change is on the way puts the focus on how best to adapt to its consequences. But, at present, even these consequences are seen as two contradictory scenarios of the future:

The Two Scenarios

First, the 'disaster scenario', starting with an explosion of prices for patented drugs as soon as the TRIPs agreement is ratified. Over a period, that price explosion will engulf the greater part of the pharmaceutical market, imports will soar, exports will dry up, and the Indian-owned pharmaceutical industry — which now holds between 60 and 70 per cent of the national market— will be destroyed by multinational patent power and exclusive marketing rights. Now, the alternative, the 'sunrise scenario'. This conveys an entirely different vision of the pharmaceutical future under patents. It sees the acceptance of patent cover as energising for both sides of the industry: multinational drug companies will take on new commitments to invest and expand research in India after years of clamping down or withdrawing altogether. There will be many opportunities for collaboration between Indian and multinational companies in product and process development and in co-marketing. Above all, the new environment will enable the more advanced Indian companies to make the transition from a 'copying' culture to a research-based strategy and, eventually, to a global presence.

If the disaster scenario is backward looking and based on fears about a future under patents, the sunrise scenario treats the pharmaceutical situation as dynamic and is based primarily on hopes which may or may not be realisable. Reality, however, is neither as black as the disaster scenario paints it, nor as rapid and magical as sunrise; for, the Government — not patents — will set the scene in which Indian and multinational companies will be operating. When pharmaceutical patents come into effect, these will be one new item in a wide spectrum of ground rules. Patents will affect a limited part of the total pharmaceutical market and their impact will really depend on how the other ground rules set by Government will influence investment, research, prices and profits. When can drug patents have only a limited effect on the market?

'Pharma Patents'

Limited Market Impact :

1. Terms of TRIPs Agreement
2. Moderate Pace of
   - Drug Innovation
   - Market Penetration
3. Patent Model of Indian Market (June 1993)

Chart III

There are three streams of evidence in support of this assertion: The TRIPs Agreement clearly spells out the fact that none of the drugs that are already on the market can be retrospectively protected by patents in India. Neither can drugs, that are now in the development pipeline but whose patents have already been published in other countries, ever be covered by Indian patents. (Chart III)

Waiting for 2003

What this means is that only drugs as yet unknown, whose patents are published from 1995 onwards, can achieve product cover in India. Since it takes an average ten years to take a new drug from discovery to market introduction, even 'fast-track' drugs are very unlikely to reach the Indian market with exclusive rights before the year 2003. Thereafter, the weight of patented drugs on the Indian market will depend both on the rate of innovation and on that of penetration. The impact of innovation on markets can be revolutionary in particular areas of therapy, but markets as a whole change more slowly when older drugs provide adequate therapy in many categories, as these do today. Moreover, half the nominal patent life is lost before most new drugs can be marketed, so that their effective patent life is relatively short. Once the initial wave of new product cover has worked its way through the system, there is then a balance between new patents and the expiry of old ones. In the last three decades, the pace of innovation in Europe and North America has been steady rather than rapid, with the result that patent expiry and generic access to markets have reduced the patented segment of the drug market quite dramatically. In India, there is no product cover at all for drugs today: build-up of such cover is not only deferred by the transitional period under 'TRIPs', but also tied to the pace of innovation. One way of estimating the influence of patents on market structure is to construct a national model of the Indian pharmacy market as it would have looked in 1993 if European-sytle patent protection had then been operating in India.

4. THE HEINZ MODEL

This model developed by Dr. Heinz is based on an analysis by Dr. Heinz Redwood, an international consultant on pharmaceuticals, of the top-500 pharmaceutical brands on the Indian pharmacy market in June 1993. It shows, in aggregate, the sales value of each of the 24 drug substances in the top 500 brands which were still covered by product patents in Europe in 1993, together with the year in which their patents will expire.

The first point to note is that none of the notionally patented drugs in the top 500 on the Indian market in 1993 had a European patent expiry date later than 2001. The median date of patent expiry of the 24 drug substances was in fact 1997, only four years after the date of the model. This bears out the fact that new drugs

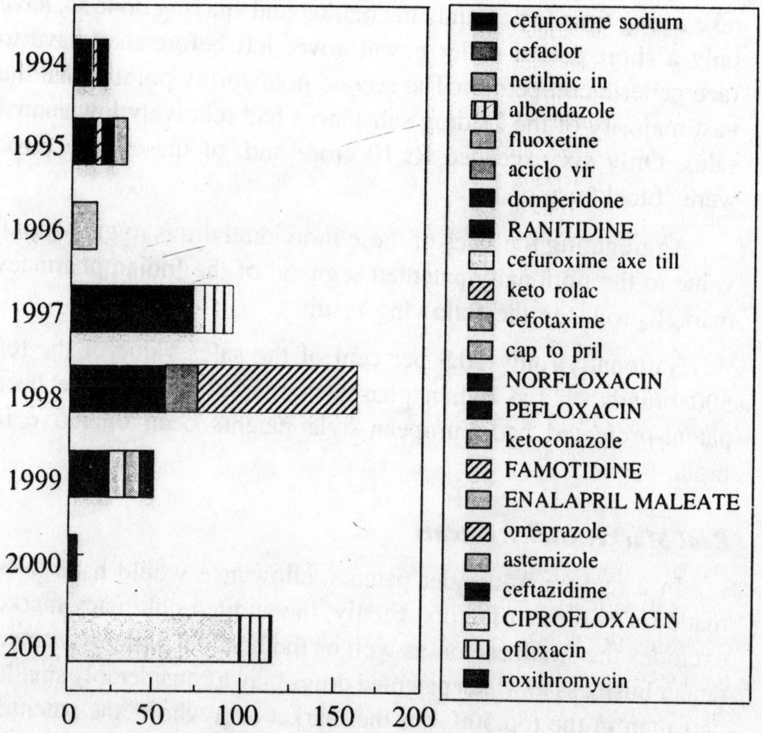

Chart IV

National `Patent Model' of Indian Pharmacy Market

`Top-500' Brands
Sales Value, Mat June 1993

	Rs.crores
Total Top-500	3,013
`Patented' Segment	328

`Patented' Share of Top-500
10.9%

Chart V

Patent Expiry Model - India 1994-2001 Prospective

Actual pharmacy sales value (Rs.crore, MAT June 1993) of drugs in Top-500 Indian brands shown against year to patent expiry in EUROPE (basic product patent) take a long time to penetrate the market and , having done so, have only a short period under patent cover left before they have to face generic competition.The second noteworthy point is that the vast majority of the 24 drug substances had relatively low annual sales. Only six exceeded Rs.10 crore and, of these, only three were 'blockbusters'.

Aggregating the sales of these individual drugs to give a total value to the notionally patented segment of the Indian pharmacy market produces the following result:

Nationally, only 10.9 per cent of the sales value of the top 500 brands on the Indian pharmacy market would have been patent-protected had European-style patents been operative in India.

Real Market Under Patents

In a real market under patents, allowance would have to be made for two other factors. Firstly, the audited pharmacy market excludes the small sector, as well as the hospital and government tender business in which patented drugs play a considerably smaller part than in the top 500. For the market as a whole, the patented segment would probably be only 7.08 per cent by value. On the other hand, the second adjustment would work in the opposite direction, because a price premium would have to be added for patented products which normally sell at higher prices. It is, after all, the purpose of patents to encourage innovation by suitably rewarding the innovator for a limited period when his efforts are successful.

It tends to be assumed that the price premium for patented drugs in India would be equivalent to the corresponding U.S.prices: hence the belief in a price explosion of spectacular force. But, according to Dr.Heinz Redwood, this price explosion is a myth; that it cannot spread across the Indian market as a result of product patenting; and that attempts by patentees to implement it for individual drugs will either have little impact on market volume or can be stopped by Government. Quite apart from the developmental limits to patent encroachment on the market, there are at least three major built-in checks and balances in India that will prevent a generalised price explosion of patented drugs.

Why Drug Prices Will Not Explode

Checks and Balances 10.9%

1. Limited Purchasing Power
2. Therapeutic Price Competition
3. Drug Price Control

Chart VI

The first two factors operate in those segments of the Indian market that are already free from price control. In addition, the Government has the use of actual and reserve powers of drug price control and can exercise its bulk purchasing power in supplying the needs of the National Health Programme. The impact of patent protection of essential drugs is perhaps the first point to be considered: of the 250 or so drug substances, which are in the 7th model list of the World Health Organisation's essential drugs, only 13 were still covered by Europe product patents in 1993; and of these, only eight were actually recommended as 'essential' and the remaining five were designated as 'complementary' drugs.

All but irrelevant

A similar analysis of the 143 essential drugs, whose prices are regulated in the national interest under India's Drugs (Prices) Control Order (DPCO 1987), reveals that only one of these drug substances is still effectively protected by product patents in Europe today. Thus, patents are all but irrelevant in the context of the drive to ensure easy access to essential drugs and generally the demands of the National Health Programme. When we come to private sector sales, limited purchasing power will check price explosions in the free-pricing segment of the Indian market. Patentees will be confronted by an unavoidable trade-off between price and volume: the higher the price, the lower the volume sold, and *vice versa.* U.S. prices with U.S. sales volumes are extremely improbable in India where the purchasing power per head of population is roughly one-twentieth of that in the USA, whilst actual per capita spending on drugs is less than one-sixtieth of U.S. expenditure.

The private sector of the Indian market would 'in effect' be largely self-regulating without the need for price control other than in exceptional circumstances, because the second restraining factor adds weight to the first: price competition between different drug substances for the same therapeutic indications is an everyday fact of the Indian pharmaceutical market. Outside the National Health Programme, the vast majority of patients pays out-of-pocket for their prescription drugs. Naturally, they are price conscious in relation to what they perceive as affordable. This explains, for example, why the quinolone antibacterials, which are not price-controlled and sell at considerably higher prices than older antibiotics, have a far lower share of antibacterial prescriptions than of market value. Indeed, during 1993, Indian quinolone prices had been sharply reduced in a free pricing environment.

Checking Price Explosions

No one would claim that market forces can produce 'perfect' pharmaceutical markets in price/volume terms; but market forces are strong enough to act as an effective check on attempted price explosions. The question asks itself: What about patented drugs for which there are no substitutes because they are therapeutically unique? The other is: Is the Indian patient to be deprived of these by patentees who prefer high prices to high volumes? No; of course not. The problem is real but it does not occur frequently. When it does, then pharmapolitical pressures come into play, and it would seem that these are much more powerful in India than in Europe or the USA — where experience has repeatedly demonstrated their potency in recent years.

For a patented drug that is not therapeutically unique, the patentee should be free to choose between high price/low volume and low price/high volume strategies. For a unique drug, the high price/low volume option is socially questionable. If the drug is also 'essential', it becomes unacceptable. The remedies start with political pressures which pharmaceutical companies ignore only at their peril. These end with statutory price control which the Government can always exercise in the form of reserve powers. That a new drug is unique does not justify the society depriving the patent holder of his intellectual property rights, nor is it a valid reason for withholding pricing freedom from therapeutically competitive drugs which almost certainly make up well over 95 per cent of the total pharmaceutical market. Uniqueness does, however, justify the use of reserve powers in the rare event that other pressures would have failed to produce a socially and politically equitable solution for health care in a situation of national importance.

The purpose of pharmaceutical patents is to promote the development of innovative drug therapy. That involves the encouragement of innovative — as distinct from imitative — research and development. For industry, this also requires a profit

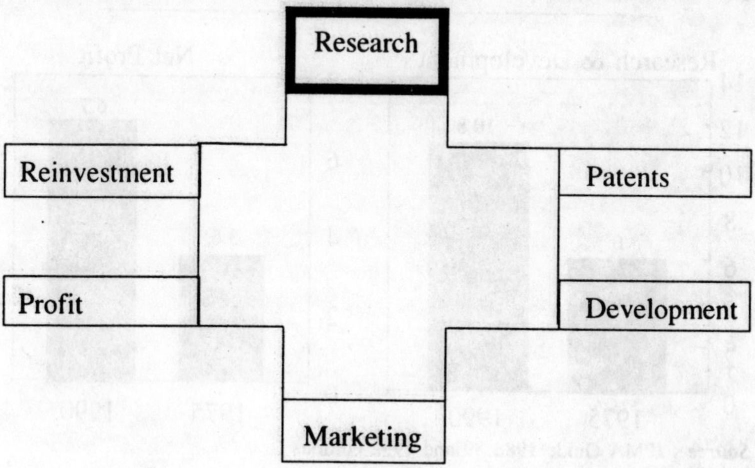

Chart VII

base that is sufficiently high and reliable to carry the risk of research and development failure before and between successful projects.

A Virtuous Circle

Research — Patents — Development — Marketing — Profit — and reinvestment in more research, thus, form what one might call a virtuous circle in the quest for improved drug therapy. If we remove any one of the links in this chain, the entire strategy falls apart.

At present, pharmaceutical R&D in India is on a low key. Actual spending is between 1 and 2 per cent of drug sales, compared with about 15 per cent in Europe and North America, and nearer 10 per cent in Japan. Patentability is a major galvanising force for pharmaceutical R&D, together with profitability. The virtuous circle ensures that the two reinforce one another. The Japanese experience demonstrates this quite clearly, and there are

Japan

Before and After Pharma Product Patents R&D Profit, % of Sales 1975, 1990

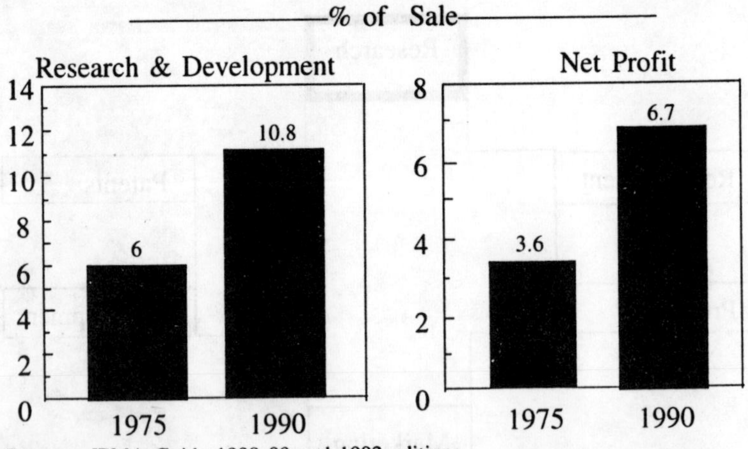

Source : JPMA Guide 1988 89 and 1992 editions

Chart VIII

certain parallels between Japan's pharmaceutical situation in the 1960s and India's in the 1990s.

Japanese Experience

Until 1976, pharmaceutical product patents were not available in Japan which was known for its prolific copying of patented drugs discovered elsewhere. It was then legal in Japan, as it is in India today. By the mid-1970s, the Japanese chemical industry had advanced technologically to a point where protection from foreign patent domination was no longer regarded as imperative. Indeed, in his *Japanese `Commentary on Patent Law'*, Kosaku Yoshifuji noted that, by then, protection was seen as damaging, because, in his words:

Japan

Before and After Pharma Product Patents % share of worldwide origination of `Major Global Drugs'

1960 - May 1992

Drug product patents accepted from 1976 in Japan
`Major Global Drugs' = marketed or `pre-registration phase' in at least 6 of the world's 7 largest markets by May 1992

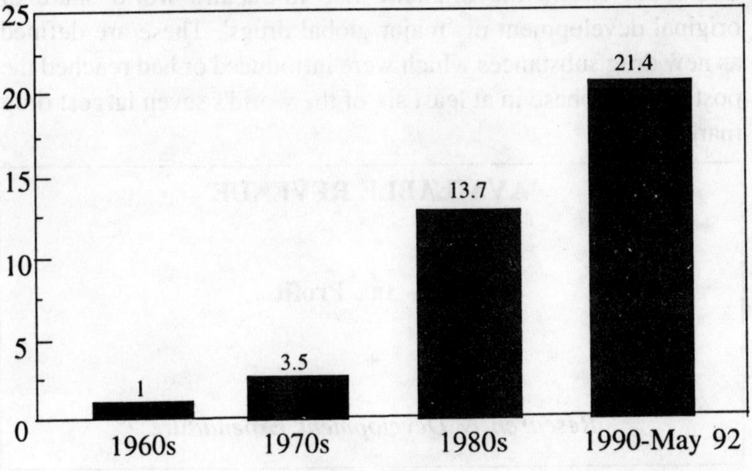

Chart IX

"the appetite for the development of original new substances etc. by Japan's researchers was being lost; they were being driven to imitation of other people's patents". Indeed, in 1974, the Commission of Inquiry into Industrial Property, which had been set up by the Japanese Government three years earlier, recommended the adoption of pharmaceutical product patents whilst observing that, "in the pharmaceutical industry one would not go as far as to say that Japan is at the European and American level in the basic research technology of such things as pharmacology". This was not, however, seen as a sufficient reason to withhold patent protection from drugs, and industry actually supported the move. There appears to be no overwhelming reason why the galvanising effect of drug plants in Japan should not also occur in India, with its strong chemical base and vast pool of scientific talent, over the next two decades.

Between 1975—the year before pharmaceutical product patents came into force — and 1990, pharmaceutical R&D in 15 major Japanese-owned companies increased from six per cent of sales to 10.8 per cent. During the same period, net profit after tax nearly doubled from 3.6 per cent to 6.7 per cent of sales. A similar 'before-and-after' analysis spanning the 32 years from 1960 until mid-1992, shows the dramatic rise in Japan's world share of original development of 'major global drugs'. These are defined as new drug substances which were introduced or had reached the post-clinical phase in at least six of the world's seven largest drug markets.

`AVAILABLE REVENUE'

Pre - tax Profit

\+

Research & Development Expenditure

Chart X

A Remarkable Transformation

Japan was virtually absent from this scene in the 1960s and played only a very minor role in the 70s. However, by the 1980s, one in every seven newly introduced 'Major Global Drugs' was of Japanese origin, and during the first two and a half years of the last decade, Japan's had achieved more than a 20 per cent world share. Of course, patents were not the only reason for this. Japanese authorities also gave strong encouragement to new drugs in their pricing regime throughout this period, though falling well short of the free market incentives that have produced the outstanding lead in the origination of major global drugs by the United States. This brings the debate to the role of profit and the concept of 'available revenue' in promoting a virtuous circle of industrial development in the pharmaceutical sphere.

'Available Revenue' (% of Sales) in the Pharma Industry

Indernational Comparisons

India	:	1992/93
Japan	:	1991/92, actual net profit, Pre-tax estimate
MNC	:	Multinationals
Patent groups	:	pharma segment 1991/92

R&D

% of Sales

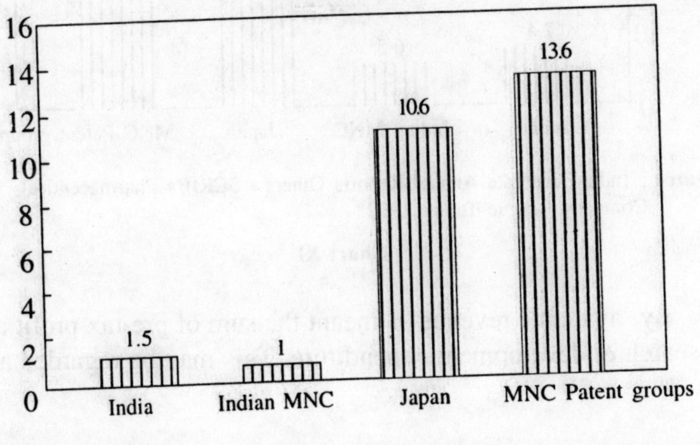

Pre-Tax profit

% of Sales

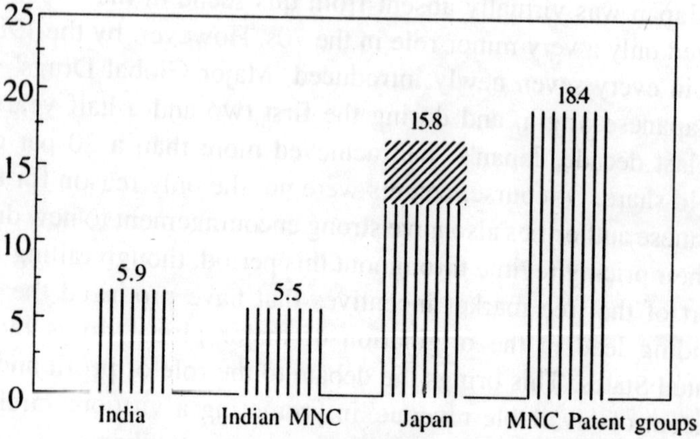

Available Revenue

(=R&D+Pre-tax Profit)

% of Sales

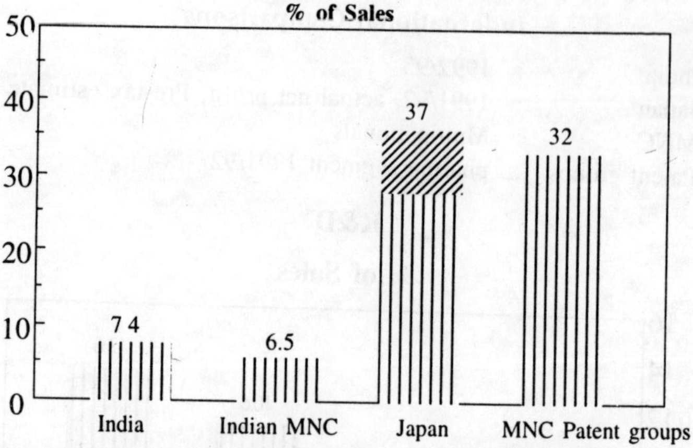

Source : India-Corporate Annual Reports Others - SCRIP's Pharmaceutical Company League Tables 1992

Chart XI

By 'available revenue' is meant the sum of pre-tax profit and research & development expenditure. This may be regarded as a pool of internally generated funds which ultimately determines what management can afford to spend on R&D without compromising the company's status as financially secure in the eyes of providers of loan finance and shareholders. 'Available revenue' is not an exact measure, because it leaves out taxation which the Government may or may not be willing to use as a further instrument to encourage research and development; but 'available revenue' as a percentage of sales is sufficiently indicative to be useful in comparing the financial pools of drug companies in India with those of multinational and Japanese companies.

On chart XI, the clusters of bars on the left and in the centre measure R&D and pre-tax profit as per cent of sales in the early 1990s. The cluster on the right is the sum of the other two. The black bar shows that 'available revenue' in a sample of Indian-owned companies in the financial year 1992/93 was 7.4 per cent of sales. The next bar shows a very similar picture for the affiliates of multinational drug companies in India: a little lower, at 6.5 per cent of sales.

Suggested Threshold
Of 'Available Revenue'
For Pharma R & D in India
15-18 per cent of Sales

Chart XII

For Japanese companies in 1991-92, the level of 'available revenue' at an estimated 20.6 per cent was roughly three times as high as that available to companies in India and the bar on the extreme right shows that the multinational parent groups of the affiliates in the Indian sample realised an 'available revenue' of 32 per cent of their global pharmaceutical sales—about five times the revenue available to companies in India.

Profit and R&D

Profit and R&D march more or less hand in hand: higher profitability generates higher R&D ratios which, in turn, often

Encouragement of Pharma R&D

(Model)

Step 1
Product Patents
Step 2
Financial Incentives
(example = tax concessions)
Step 3
Price Increase for Controlled Drugs
(to boost `Available Revenue' for R&D)
Step 4
Ending Price Control
except under Reserve Powers

Chart XIII

(but not always) lead to improved levels of profitability. What these comparisons suggest is that current levels of profitability in India are too low to stimulate a strongly positive research & development strategy among Indian or multinational drug companies in India without incurring severe risk of financial instability. That is not to suggest that profitability in India must rise to Western standards before a commitment to R&D can become a long term option in corporate strategy. Indian research and development costs are far lower. Consequently, India could in theory achieve the same results at a fraction of Euro-American costs. But, profitability still needs to be well above current levels. Evidently, Japan once again represents a half-way stage between the present situation in India and the Euro-American commitment to R&D. If 'available revenue' were to rise from the 1992-93 level of seven per cent of sales to a level much closer to Japan's 20 per cent mark—for example to between 15 and 18 per cent of sales—this should open the doors to original drug research and development in India by allowing R&D to rise to Japanese standards as a percentage of sales while letting pre-tax profits also improve above the current Indian level.

Watertight Product Patents

Watertight pharmaceutical product patents under the 'TRIPs' agreement constitute the first and indispensable step. No one is going to spend substantial funds on creative, high risk research and development in India without assured patent protection in the event of success. In the absence of patents, copying will always be the preferable and, indeed, financially the more prudent strategy. The second step is to provide a financial incentive for capital and current expenditure on R&D via taxation or in other ways.

The third step would be for the Government to allow the pharmaceutical industry to 'catch up' on the cost increases that have eroded profit in recent years as a result of high rates of inflation and rupee devaluation. By making unrecovered costs 'allowable' and in effect authorising a corresponding 'once-for-all' increase in the selling prices of controlled drugs, 'available revenue' for R&D would be materially boosted by restoring 'real' price levels in relation to 'real' costs. The fourth, and ultimately the most decisive step, would be to change the system of pharmaceutical price regulation to the one that limits control to governmental use of reserve powers. In the end, the consequences of patents under 'TRIPs' will depend on the willingness of the players to adapt to the new rules of the game, and to act constructively. Unless they do so, patent protection will be restrictive without being creative: it will put an end to 'copying' but it will not spark innovation. It will become a sterile pharma political conflict, closing doors instead of opening horizons. This could not be in anybody's real interest.

Constructive Options

There some constructive options for patents under TRIPs that are open to the three players: Indian pharmaceutical companies, multinationals in India, and Government. Indian companies could face difficult problems but, in a sense, theirs are the clearest choices. For them, the use to which the transitional decade is put will be crucial because, evidently, adaption is the name of the game. Many of the leading companies recognised this from the start and have already announced joint ventures and co-marketing agreements with multinationals in India, as well as strategic moves to develop and invest in overseas markets. The enormous advances made by Indian companies in chemical manufacturing of active drug substances under the existing regime without product patents will not be lost once patents come into force. On the contrary, the real opportunity for them lies in overseas markets where many of these drugs have now lost their patent protection or will soon lose it with the approach of patent expiry.

In rapidly growing global generic markets, high-quality/low cost operation is the key to success. India possesses both and can further improve its competitive position by expanding local production of key chemical intermediates. These are major business opportunities on a global scale, because the therapeutic life of most drug substances is far longer than its patent life. Contrary to media folklore, the volume potential of most good drugs reaches its peak after more than 15 years on the market and medical obsolescence often comes much later. Today's strong pressures of cost containment of health care in the industrialised world are reinforcing this trend and prolonging the medical life of old, established drugs. The second option for Indian companies lies in joint ventures, licensing agreements and co-marketing arrangements with multinational research-based companies in India. Several such moves have already been announced in recent years.

Government Ground Rules

The third and boldest option is for Indian companies themselves to engage in original pharmaceutical R&D. Here too, several announcements have already been made, but for a wider movement in this direction, changes in Government ground rules are necessary. Nothing could be worse in the longer term than the possible failure of these pioneer ventures to establish creative R&D in the Indian pharmaceutical industry, if scientific endeavour and the implied financial risks are not sufficiently underwritten by basic industrial profitability. Taking the three options for strategic adaptation during the transitional decade as a whole, there is no substance in the suggestion that patents will destroy the viability of Indian companies. Only unwillingness to adapt or undue delay in doing so would have that result.

Coming now to research-based multinational drug companies, these fall into two groups: those who already have Indian affiliates of their own and intend to stay in India and those who have until now deliberately written India out of their global corporate strategy, either by never investing in the country in the first place or by making a deliberate decision to withdraw. The first group of multinationals evidently are committed to India — though their degree of commitment varies considerably. The second group has no such commitment: its members are either candidates for joint ventures and arms-length agreements with Indian drug companies; or they may be open to persuasion to take a more positive view of direct investment as their perception of the investment climate in India brightens. For research-based multinationals, the way in which the 'TRIPs' agreement on pharmaceutical product patents is actually implemented in India will be one of the keys to their future policy of investment in the country.

Persuasive Factors

The pharma political situation may develop in such a way that implementation is placed in doubt — and nothing could be easier than to undermine 'TRIPs', whose text is heavily spiced with ambiguities. Given the prospects of real patent protection, on the other hand, there is every reason to believe that multinational drug companies would deepen their commitment to India. If just one such group can be persuaded to establish original R & D in India, others would soon follow. The available pool of scientificitalent, low costs and firm patent protection would be persuasive factors in producing a radical shift of strategy. For such a shift to be welcomed, two other aspects need to be considered: first the Government's affirmation that it actually wishes multinationals to intensify their involvement in India; and secondly, a sympathetic recognition of India's underlying needs by multinationals, particularly in terms of planning sales development of important new drugs in conjunction with India's co-marketing partners, and considering local production where this makes industrial sense in a large market like India.

Finally, the options for the Government in relation to pharmaceutical patent protection under TRIPs can be identified as either 'stopping short' or 'following on'. Stopping short means accepting pharmaceutical product patents on paper whilst maintaining a control system under which patentees will reap few benefits from it in practice. Following on means changing the ground rules in order to set off a chain reaction that will, first, help India's own drug industry to consign 'copying culture' to history — as Japan did more than twenty years ago; and secondly, encourage foreign pharmaceutical companies to invest in India. This, more than anything else, would be the signal that both sides of industry need in order to break with outdated concepts and move decisively towards new horizons in India.

5

INTELLECTUAL PROPERTY, PROTECTION, DIRECT INVESTMENT, AND TECHNOLOGY TRANSFER:

Germany, Japan and the United States

1. EFFECTS OF INTELLECTUAL PROPERTY PROTECTION: A SURVEY OF JAPANESE AND GERMAN FIRMS

A study released in 1995 by the International Finance Corporation of the World Bank on these issues are still relevant to us. An earlier study by the IFC indicated that the industries particularly likely to be affected by intellectual property protection included chemicals, pharmaceuticals, electrical equipment, and machinery. Since these industries tend to regard patents as relatively important, it is not surprising that they were indicated to be particularly likely to be affected by intellectual property protection. This study has its focus largely, but not entirely, on these industries. A random sample of 45 major Japanese firms (40 from the above four industries and five from the transportation equipment, metals, and food industries) and 35 major German firms (30 from the above four industries and five from the transportation equipment, metals, and food industries) was chosen. The frame was the list of 30 largest firms in each of these industries in each country. The machinery and electrical equipment firms tended to produce items related to computers and electronics, among other things. A substantial proportion of the respondents were among the top 200 R & D spenders outside the U.S. As shown in the Table 1, the response rate was relatively high (71 per cent in Japan and 51 per cent in Germany), but lower than the very high figure for the United States of America, (94%). The respondents generally were patent attorneys, specialists in the firms' international operations, and top executives. The limitations of survey data of this type are well known, but interpreted with proper caution these can be useful.

Table 1

Composition of the Sample of German, Japanese and U.S. Firms

	Chemicals and Drugs	*Machinery and Electrical (Number of Firms in Sample)*	*Others*	*Total*
Germany	7	11	2	20
Japan	16	13	3	32
United States	1	59	19	94
Number among top 200 R & D spenders outside the U.S.				
Germany	2	3	1	6
Japan	10	8	0	18

Based on List of Top 200 non-U.S. firms, based on expenditure on research and development, in *Business Week*, June 28, 1993.

Effect on FDI

In all the three countries, the percentage of firms indicating that intellectual property protection has a major effect on their foreign direct investment decisions depends greatly on the type of investments in question. As would be expected, the percentage reporting that such protection is important tends to be lower for investments in sales and distribution outlets and in rudimentary production and assembly operations than for investments in facilities to manufacture components and complete products or do research and development (Table 2). This is true in all the three countries.

Table 2

Per cent of Major German, Japanese and U.S. Firms Reporting that Strength or Weakness of Intellectual Property Protection has Strong Effects on Whether They Will make Direct Investment of Various Kinds

	Sales and distribution outlets	*Rudimentary Production and assembly facilities*	*Facilities to manufacture components*	*Facilities to manufacture complete products*	*Research and development facilities*	*Mean*
			Chemicals and Drugs			
Germany	0	17	75	86	86	53
Japan	44	53	67	80	88	66
United States	19	4	71	87	100	65
			Machinery and Electrical Equipment			
Germany	20	27	55	60	60	44
Japan	42	45	80	80	70	63
United States	19	32	54	70	79	51
			All Firms			
Germany	11	21	55	63	63	43
Japan	39	45	64	71	76	59
United States	19	34	53	67	81	51

In accordance with the earlier findings for U.S. firms, the percentage of Japanese and German firms regarding such protection as important is higher in the chemical, pharmaceutical, machinery and electrical equipment industries than in the transportation equipment, metals and food industries.

The chemical and pharmaceutical industries tend to have a larger percentage of firms regarding such protection as important than do the machinery and electrical equipment industries. This is true in all the three countries. The chemical and pharmaceutical industries are lumped together because of their many similarities and because firms frequently are engaged in both; for much the same reasons, machinery and electrical equipment are lumped together because of their many similarities and because firms frequently are engaged in both; for much the same reasons, machinery and electrical equipment are lumped together.

Small Difference

Perhaps, the most interesting finding is that, regardless of whether one considers chemical and pharmaceutical firms, machinery and electrical equipment firms or all firms in the sample, there is a remarkably small difference between Japan and Germany combined and the United States in the percentage of firms reporting that intellectual property protection was important in this regard. In chemicals and pharmaceuticals, the mean percentage for Japanese and German firms is 62 in Table 2; for U.S. firms, it is 65. In machinery and electrical equipment, the mean percentage for Japanese and German firms is 54 in Table 2; for U.S. firms, this is 51. In the entire sample in Table 2, the mean percentage for Japanese and German firms is 53; for U.S. firms, this is 51. The German and Japanese firms are combined so that the sample size is reasonably large. Of course, this does not mean that U.S. firms in some industries may not view such protection as more important than their Japanese or German counterparts, but it does indicate that the bulk of Japanese and German firms in high technology industries do regard a country's system of intellectual property protection as important when deciding whether to make direct investments there. Moreover, according to the results presented in the next three sections, Japanese and German firms, like their U.S. counterparts, often look carefully at the nature of such protection when deciding whether to transfer advanced technology to a particular country, and if so, how.

2. INTELLECTUAL PROPERTY PROTECTION AND INVESTMENT IN JOINT VENTURES

Each of the Japanese and German firms in the IFC sample was asked whether, in its view, any of the 14 countries — Argentina, Brazil, Chile, Hong Kong, India, Indonesia, Mexico, Nigeria, Philippines, Singapore, Republic of Korea, Thailand, Venezuela, and Taiwan and China — had intellectual property protection that was too weak in 1994 to allow it to invest in joint ventures (where it contributed advanced technology) with local

Table 3

Percent of Major German, and U.S. Firms Reporting that Intellectual Property Protection is too Weak to Permit Investment in Joint Ventures with Local Partners, by Industry and Host Country

	Chemicals and Drugs				*Machinery and Electrial Equipment*			
Host Country	*Germany*	*Japan*	*U.S.*	*Mean*	*Germany*	*Japan*	*U.S.*	*Mean*
Argentina	57	33	40	43	11	25	28	21
Brazil	43	27	47	39	33	38	48	40
Chile	33	44	31	36	12	25	26	21
Hong Kong	14	0	21	12	0	0	23	8
India	71	71	80	74	33	33	43	36
Indonesia	50	20	50	40	38	11	27	25
Mexico	0	0	47	16	11	20	23	18
Nigeria	57	33	64	51	50	38	31	40
Philippines	29	15	43	29	0	50	24	25
Singapore	0	0	20	7	0	0	12	4
Republic of Korea	33	0	33	22	12	31	23	22
Taiwan, China	17	7	27	17	29	46	29	35
Thailand	29	29	43	34	25	25	26	25
Venezuela	0	20	40	20	12	29	20	20
Mean	31	21	42	31	19	26	27	24

partners in that country. These countries were selected because of their size and importance, as well as the frequency with which they have been cited in connection with controversies over intellectual property protection.

In the chemical and pharmaceutical industries, at least 25 per cent of the firms in all three countries felt that intellectual property protection in India, Argentina, Brazil, Chile and Thailand was too weak to allow them to invest in such joint ventures there (Table 3). In the machinery and electrical equipment industries, this was true in Brazil, Nigeria, India, Thailand, and Taiwan, China. In both sets of industries, the feeling, on the average, was that protection was strongest in Singapore and Hong Kong. U.S. chemical and pharmaceutical firms seemed more likely than their German or Japanese counterparts (and the Germans seemed more likely than the Japanese) to regard protection in these 14 countries as too weak to permit such joint ventures; the mean percentage in Table 3 is 42 for the U.S., 31 for Germany, and 21 for Japan. In the machinery and electrical equipment industries, the Japanese seemed to be about as likely as the Americans (and both seemed more likely than the Germans) to regard protection in these 14 countries as too weak; the mean percentage is 27 for the U.S., 26 for Japan, and 19 for Germany.

Table 4

Least Squares Relationships between German, Japanese, and U.S. Measures of Perceived Intellectual Property Protection in fourteen Countries: Joint Ventures

Dependent Variable	*Independent Variable*	*Intercept*	*Slope*	*Adjusted*
	Chemicals and Drugs			
Germany	U.S.	-10.4	0.99	0.44
Japan	U.S.	-16.9	0.91	0.49
German	Japan	12.9	0.84	0.53
	Machinery and Electrical			
Germany	U.S.	-11.8	1.13	0.37
Japan	U.S.	4.2	0.82	0.17
Germany	Japan	9.3	0.37	0.05

A Positive Correlation

There generally is a positive correlation between the percentage of one country's firms that regard protection in a particular country as too weak to permit such joint ventures there and the percentage of another country's firms that feel the same way. The values of the coefficient of determination and the least-squares regression are shown in Table 4. But this correlation seems stronger among the chemical and pharmaceutical firms than among the machinery and electrical equipment firms. Indeed, in the machinery and electrical equipment industries, there is little or no correlation in this regard between Germany and Japan.

3. INTELLECTUAL PROPERTY PROTECTION AND TECHNOLOGY TRANSFER TO WHOLLY-OWNED SUBSIDIARIES

Each of the Japanese and German firms in the IFC sample

Table 5

Per cent of Major German, Japanese, and U.S. Firms Reporting that Intellectual Property Protection is Too Weak to Permit Transfers to Their Newest or Most Effective Technology to Wholly Owned Subsidiaries, by Industry and Host Country

	Chemicals and Drugs				*Machinery and Electrical Equipment*			
Host Country	*Germany*	*Japan*	*U.S.*	*Mean*	*Germany*	*Japan*	*U.S.*	*Mean*
Argentina	43	30	44	39	11	29	18	19
Brazil	43	18	50	37	22	33	32	29
Chile	33	44	47	41	0	29	24	18
Hong Kong	14	0	21	12	0	0	26	9
India	71	64	81	72	11	30	39	27
Indonesia	17	27	40	28	0	20	27	16
Mexico	0	0	31	10	11	20	22	18
Nigeria	14	50	67	44	44	38	24	35
Philippines	14	36	47	32	22	50	22	35
Singapore	0	0	12	4	0	0	10	3
Republic of Korea	17	7	31	18	11	25	25	20
Taiwan, China	17	20	19	19	11	46	38	32
Thailand	14	43	60	39	11	33	22	22
Venezuela	17	33	50	33	11	25	18	18
Mean	22	27	43	31	12	27	25	21

was also asked whether, if it had a wholly-owned subsidiary in one of these 14 countries, it would be willing to transfer its newest or most effective technology to such a subsidiary — or whether the weakness of the country's system of intellectual property protection would make such transfers very unlikely. Firms with subsidiaries (or joint ventures) in the country in question were asked this question. Firms without subsidiaries (or joint ventures) there were asked whether they would be willing to transfer such technology if they had such a subsidiary. In the chemical and pharmaceutical industries, over 25 per cent of the firms in all three countries felt that intellectual property protection in India, Chile, and Argentina was too weak to permit such transfers (Table 5). In the machinery and electrical equipment industries, over 20 per cent felt that this was the case in Nigeria, Brazil and the Philippines. In both sets of industries, on an average, Singapore and Hong Kong were regarded as having the strongest protection.

U.S. chemical and pharmaceutical firms seemed more likely than their Japanese or German counterparts (and the Japanese seemed more likely than the Germans) to regard protection in these 14 countries as too weak to permit such transfers; the mean percentage in Table 5 is 43 for the U.S., 27 for Japan, and 22 for

Table 6
Least Squares Relationships between German, Japanese, and U.S. Measures of Perceived Intellectual Property Protection in Fourteen Countries: Technology Transfer to Wholly-Owned Subsidiaries

Dependent Variable	*Independent variable*	*Intercept*	*Slope*	*Adjusted*
	Chemicals and Drugs			
Germany	U.S.	-4.	0.63	0.35
Japan	U.S.	-13.8	0.94	0.78
Germany	Japan	7.3	0.57	0.31
	Machinery and Electrical			
Germany	U.S.	6.8	0.20	-0.06
Japan	U.S.	7.2	0.80	0.12
Germany	Japan	-.7	0.50	0.32

Germany. In the machinery and electrical equipment industries, the Japanese seemed about as likely as the Americans (and both seemed more likely than the Germans) to regard protection in these 14 countries as too weak to permit such transfers; the mean percentage is 27 for Japan, 25 for the U.S. and 12 for Germany.

A positive correlation generally exists between the percentage of one country's firms that regard protection in a particular country as too weak to permit such technology transfers there and the percentage of another country's firms that feel the same way. (Table 6.) But, this correlation seems stronger among the chemical and pharmaceutical firms than among the machinery and electrical equipment firms (where, for example, there is no correlation at all between German and U.S. firms).

4. INTELLECTUAL PROPERTY PROTECTION AND LICENSING

Finally, each of the Japanese and German firms in the IFC

Table 7

Per cent of Major German, Japanese and U.S. Firms Reporting that Intellectual Property Protection is Too Weak to Permit Transfers to Their Newest or Most Effective Technology to Unrelated Firms, by Industry and Host Country

	Chemicals and Drugs				*Machinery and Electrical Equipment*			
Host Country	*Germany*	*Japan*	*U.S.*	*Mean*	*Germany*	*Japan*	*U.S.*	*Mean*
Argentina	57	44	62	54	22	29	27	26
Brazil	43	36	69	49	33	29	51	41
Chile	33	55	47	45	25	29	24	26
Hong Kong	14	7	33	18	12	11	26	16
India	100	85	81	89	38	44	44	42
Indonesia	67	43	73	61	50	22	35	36
Mexico	0	7	56	21	22	20	32	25
Nigeria	57	50	73	60	50	38	28	39
Philippines	43	38	47	43	14	50	29	31
Singapore	0	0	25	8	11	0	12	8
Republic of Korea	33	7	38	26	12	38	32	27
Taiwan, China	33	21	44	33	14	54	46	38
Thailand	57	50	73	60	12	38	30	27
Venezuela	17	44	62	41	14	25	23	21
Mean	40	35	56	43	24	31	31	29

sample was asked whether the protection of intellectual property in each of these countries was too weak to allow it to license its newest or most effective technology to unrelated firms in that country. In the chemical and pharmaceutical industries, over 40 per cent of the firms in all three countries felt that protection in India, Indonesia, Nigeria, Thailand and Argentina was too weak to permit such licensing (Table 7). In the machinery and electrical equipment industries, over 25 per cent in all the three countries felt this way about India, Brazil, and Nigeria. As usual, Singapore

Table 8

Least Squares Relationships between German, Japanese and U.S. Measures of Perceived Intellectual Property Protection in Fourteen Countries: Licensing

Dependent Variable	*Independent variable*	*Intercept*	*Slope*	*Adjusted*
		Chemicals and Drugs		
Germany	U.S.	-27.3	1.20	0.53
Japan	U.S.	-26.3	1.09	0.59
Germany	Japan	6.1	0.96	0.67
		Machinery and Electrial		
Germany	U.S.	8.4	0.48	0.05
Japan	U.S.	0.6	0.98	0.40
Germany	Japan	19.9	0.12	-0.07

Table 9

Adjusted between Three Measures of Perceived Intellectual Property Protection, Germany, Japan and the U.S.

	Germany		*Japan*		*United States*	
	Joint Ventures	*Licensing*	*Joint Ventures*	*Licensing*	*Joint Ventures*	*Licensing*
			Chemicals			
Subsidiaries	0.51	0.51	0.79	0.92	0.73	0.70
Licensing	0.83		0.91		0.72	
			Machinery and electrical			
Subsidiaries	0.21	0.08	0.91	0.86	0.54	0.78
Licensing	0.62		0.86		0.70	

and Hong Kong received the highest grades from both sets of industries, on an average.

Once again, U.S. firms in the chemical and pharmaceutical industries seemed more concerned about intellectual property protection in these 14 countries than their Japanese and German rivals; but in the machinery and electrical equipment industries, Japanese firms appeared to be as much concerned as the Americans. As shown in Table 7, the mean percentage in chemicals and pharmaceuticals is 56 for the U.S., 40 for Germany, and 35 for Japan; in machinery and electrical equipment, it is 31 for both the U.S. and Japan and 24 for Germany. There generally is a positive correlation between the percentage of one country's firms that regard protection in a particular country as too weak to permit such licensing there and the percentage of another country's firms that feel the same way (Table 8). But, as usual, this correlation seems higher among the chemical and pharmaceutical firms than among the machinery and electrical equipment firms (where the correlation between Germany and both Japan and the United States is close to zero).

5. WHY ARE SOME COUNTRIES PERCEIVED TO AFFORD STRONGER PROTECTION THAN OTHERS?

The IFC study presents three crude measures of the perceived strength or weakness of intellectual property protection: (1) the percentage of firms believing that protection there is too weak to allow them to invest in joint ventures (where they contribute advanced technology) with local partners, (2) the percentage believing that protection is too weak to warrant the transfer of their newest or most effective technology to a wholly-owned subsidiary in that country; and (3) the percentage believing that protection is too weak to permit them to license their newest or most effective technology to unrelated firms in that country. A country's standing based on one of these measures tends to be highly correlated with its standing based on another of them. As shown in Table 9, the coefficient of determination between any pair of these measures is about 0.90 in Japan, 0.70 in the U.S., and 0.50 in Germany.

In the chemical and pharmaceutical industries, as seen in Tables 4, 6, and 8, a country's standing based on the perception of U.S. firms is positively correlated with its standing based on Japanese perceptions and both are positively correlated with its standing based on German perceptions. This is true regardless of which of the above three measures is used. To understand why, one must recognise that some countries like India, Argentina, and Brazil do not issue product patents for drugs or chemicals and that other countries, while they may have laws protecting intellectual property, do little to enforce them. Such countries receive very poor grades from chemical and drug firms, regardless of whether they are based in the U.S., Japan or Germany, because of the importance of patents in these industries.

Table 10

Adjusted between Chemical and Pharmaceutical Industries' and Machinery and Electrical Industries' Measures of Perceived Intellectual Property Protection in Fourteen Major Developing Countries

	Germany	*Japan*	*United States*	*Mean*
Joint Ventures	0.34	0.02	0.37	0.24
Licensing	0.32	0.16	0.17	0.22
Subsidiaries	-0.08	0.29	0.02	0.08
Mean	0.19	0.16	0.19	0.18

In the machinery and electrical equipment industries, the correlation between a country's standing based on U.S. perceptions and its standing based on Japanese or German perceptions tends to be positive, but lower than in chemicals and pharmaceuticals. This may be related to the fact that intellectual property protection is generally regarded as less important in machinery and electrical equipment than in chemicals and pharmaceuticals (where local firms can imitate an innovator's new products relatively easily). Since differences among developing countries seem to be regarded as less pronounced and less crucial than in chemicals and pharmaceuticals, there is greater disagreement among the Americans, Japanese and Germans over the standing in this regard of particular countries.

6. DIFFERENCES IN PERCEPTIONS AMONG INDUSTRIES

In all three countries, intellectual property protection seems to be less important in transportation equipment, metals or food than in chemicals, pharmaceuticals, machinery and electrical equipment. In part, this is because competitors in industries like metals and transportation equipment frequently cannot make use of a firm's technology without many complex and expensive inputs. Regardless of whether American, Japanese or German firms are considered, there is only a relatively moderate amount of correlation between a country's standing in the eyes of the chemical and pharmaceutical industries. This is true, no matter which of the above three measures of the perceived strength or weakness of intellectual property protection is used. As shown in Table 10, the value of the adjusted coefficient of determination averages about 0.2.

To a considerable extent, this is because a country's laws often affect different industries in quite different ways. Take the case of Argentina, which denies patent protection to pharmaceutical products. Regardless of whether American, Japanese or German perceptions are considered, Argentina gets poor rating from pharmaceutical producers, whereas machinery and electrical equipment industries in all three countries seem to regard intellectual property protection in Argentina as stronger than the average among this group of 14 countries. In Table 3, the mean percentage of machinery and electrical equipment firms regarding protection in Argentina as inadequate is 21; in Table 3, it is 19; and in Table 7, it is 26. In every case, it is lower than the average for these 14 countries.

In addition, the competence and aggressiveness of local firms may be different in the chemical and pharmaceutical industries than in the machinery and electrical equipment industries. Thus, even if intellectual property laws (and their enforcement) are the same in both sets of industries, American, Japanese or German firms in industries facing local firms that are more aggressive in exploiting weak laws and enforcement may perceive protection to be weaker than American, Japanese or German firms in industries with less aggressive local firms. For example , it has been suggested that Argentina's drug firms have been much more aggressive than other parts of Argentinean industry, which may help to account for the inter-industry differences observed here in the perception of the strength or weakness of protection in Argentina.

	Chemicals and pharmaceuticals			*Machinery and electrical equipment*		
	Germany	*Japan*	*U.S.*	*Germany*	*Japan*	*U.S.*
East Asia	24	9	32	17	19	23
Latin America	27	25	41	16	27	29

The mean percentages in Table 5 are:

	Chemicals and pharmaceuticals			*Machinery and electrical equipment*		
	Germany	*Japan*	*U.S.*	*Germany*	*Japan*	*U.S.*
East Asia	13	16	30	6	21	25
Latin America	27	25	44	11	27	23

The mean percentages in Table 7 are:

	Chemicals and pharmaceuticals			*Machinery and electrical equipment*		
	Germany	*Japan*	*U.S.*	*Germany*	*Japan*	*U.S.*
East Asia	34	21	48	18	27	30
Latin America	30	37	59	23	28	31

7. DIFFERENCES IN PERCEPTIONS AMONG U.S., JAPANESE AND GERMAN FIRMS

In the chemical and pharmaceutical industries, U.S. firms seem substantially more likely than their Japanese counterparts to regard protection in these 14 countries as too weak to permit joint ventures which entail the contribution of advanced technology, transfer of such technology to wholly-owned subsidiaries there or licensing of such technology to unrelated firms there. But, in the machinery and electrical equipment industries, there is essentially no difference between U.S. and Japanese firms in this regard. In part, this may be because, while the major U.S. chemical and pharmaceutical firms are world technological leaders, their Japanese rivals are still not quite as strong technologically. Thus, U.S. firms might be expected to require stronger protection before exposing or transferring their most advanced technology. On the other hand, in many types of machinery and electrical equipment, Japanese firms are often regarded as at least as strong technologically as their U.S. rivals; so it would not be surprising if their requirements, attitudes and perceptions were similar.

German chemical and drug firms, which have long been noted for their technological strength, generally seem to be midway between the U.S. and Japanese firms in this regard. In machinery and electrical equipment, on the other hand, German firms seem less likely than their U.S. and Japanese counterparts to regard protection in these 14 countries as too weak to permit joint ventures, where they contribute advanced technology, transfers of such technology to wholly-owned subsidiaries there or licensing of such technology to unrelated firms there. If the rate of innovation in machinery and electrical equipment has tended to be lower in Germany than in the U.S. and Japan, this might help to explain these findings.

East Asia, where growth has been rapid, has been compared with other areas like Latin America. In both the chemical and drug industries and the machinery and electrical equipment industries, the percentage of firms regarding intellectual property protection as too weak to warrant direct investment or technology transfer in the East Asian countries considered by the IFC study tends to be lower than in the Latin American countries. This is true, regardless of whether the perceptions of the U.S., Japanese or German firms are used. If we compare the five Latin American countries (Argentina, Brazil, Chile, Mexico and Venezuela) with the six East Asian countries (Hong Kong, Indonesia, Singapore,

Republic of Korea, Thailand, and Taiwan, China), the mean percentages in Table 3 are:

Turning to individual countries, it is worth noting that in both sets of industries, German and Japanese firms seem less concerned than U.S. firms about intellectual property protection in Mexico, Hong Kong and Singapore. In the case of Mexico, this may be because the German and Japanese data pertain to 1994 whereas the U.S. data pertain to 1991.

8. INTELLECTUAL PROPERTY PROTECTION AND FOREIGN DIRECT INVESTMENT: A SIMPLE ECONOMETRIC MODEL

Having extended the coverage of the surveys to include Japanese and German firms, the IFC study turned to the construction of a simple econometric model to test whether the perceived strength or weakness of intellectual property protection in a country influenced the amount of foreign direct investment received by this country. An attempt was made to estimate the relationship between a variety of independent variables, on the one hand, and the amount of foreign direct investment, on the other. Then, holding other independent variables constant, the effect of the perceived strength or weakness of intellectual property protection in a country on how much foreign direct investment it received was evaluated.

Because data concerning Japanese and German foreign direct investment were not available for all these 14 countries, the tests were confined to U.S. experience. The dependent variable was: I_{it}, defined as U.S. capital outflow in millions of dollars in the ith country in year t. As a measure of the perceived weakness of intellectual property protection in the ith country, the IFC used Gi, the average of (1) the mean percentage of U.S. firms regarding protection in the ith country as too weak to permit them to invest in joint ventures where they contribute advanced technology and (2) the mean percentage of U.S. firms regarding protection in the ith country as too weak to allow them to transfer advanced technology to wholly-owned subsidiaries there. The percentage for each industry was weighted equally. The data on licensing are excluded because they seem less relevant to foreign direct investment than the components of G_i, but if they were included, the results would have changed very little.

The following model is proposed in the IFC study:

$$I_{it}=0o+0_1G_i+0_2k_i+0_3M_i+0_4F_i+0_5S_i+0_6O_i+0_7d_{1t}+0_8d_{2t}+0_9d_{3t}+e_{it} \quad (1)$$

Ki is a measure of the size of market in the ith country. This measure is based on the ith country's GDP. Where GDP in year - 1, rather than ki, is used, the results are essentially the same.

Table 11

Least-Squares Estimates of Coefficients in Equation (1), When All and Various Subsets of Variables are Included, 1990-93

Coefficient	*All Variables*	*Subset 1*	*Subset 2*	*Subset 3*
0_o	-781	-704	-271	-362
	(-1.92)	(-1.74)	(-1.16)	(-1.71)
0_1	-21.3**	-21.3**	-22.7**	-19.7**
	(-2.45)	(-2.41)	(-2.57)	(-2.40)
0_2	172***	172***	113***	105***
	(3.30)	(3.25)	(3.93)	(3.84)
0_3	595**	595**	568**	571**
	(2.96)	(2.92)	(2.78)	(2.80)
0_4	108***	108***	111***	101***
	(4.90)	(4.82)	(4.93)	(5.17)
0_5	-66.7	-66.7	-28.8	—
	(-1.60)	(-1.57)	(-0.92)	
0_6	57.2	57.2	—	—
	(1.33)	(1.31)		
0_7	241	—	—	—
	(1.87)			
0_8	56.9	—	—	—
	(0.44)			
0_9	11.1	—	—	—
	(0.09)			
R^{-2}	0.54	0.52	0.51	0.52

*** Significant at .001 level (one-tailed test except for 0_o, 0_6, 0_7, 0_8, and 0_9).

** Significant at .01 level (one-tailed test except for 0_o, 0_6, 0_7, 0_8, 0_9).

Table 12
Least-Squares Estimates of Coefficients in Equation (1), When All and Various Subsets of Variables are Included, 1991-93.

Coefficient	*All Variables*	*Subset 1*	*Subset 2*	*Subset 3*
0_0	-991	-899	-370	-479
	(-1.99)	(-1.80)	(-1.28)	(-1.83)
0_1	-26.0*	-26.0*	-27.8*	-24.1*
	(-2.42)	(-2.38)	(-2.54)	(-2.38)
0_2	212***	212***	141***	131***
	(3.30)	(3.25)	(3.95)	(3.88)
0_3	443*	443*	410	413
	(1.79)	(1.76)	(1.62)	(1.64)
0_4	133***	133***	136***	124***
	(4.87)	(4.79)	(4.89)	(5.14)
0_5	-80.8	-80.8	-34.5	—
	(-1.56)	(-1.54)	(-0.89)	
0_6	69.8	69.8	—	—
	(1.32)	(1.30		
0_7	230	—	—	—
	(1.67)			
0_8	45.9	—	—	—
	(0.33)			
R^{-2}	0.55	0.54	0.53	0.53

*** Significant at .001 level (one-tailed test except for 0_0, 0_6, 0_7, and 0_8).
** Significant at .01 level (one-tailed test except for 0_0,0_6,0_7, and 0_8).
* Significant at .05 level (one-tailed test except for 0_0,0_6,0_7, and 0_8).

Mi is a dummy variable equalling 1 for Mexico and zero otherwise, fi is the level (stock) of foreign direct investment prior to year t in the ith country. Si is a measure of the degree of industrialisation in the ith country, (This measure, based on manufacturing and mining as a per cent of gross domestic product,) and Oi is a measure of the openness (freedom from import restrictions, price controls profit repatriation controls, and the like) of the ith country's economy. This measure is based on nine measures of government intervention — import restrictions, export requirements, local content requirements, price controls, profit repatriation controls, exchange controls, foreign equity limitations for existing and new investment and the risk of expropriation. t=1990, 1991, 1992 or 1993, dit is a dummy variable which equals 1 if t=1993 and zero otherwise, d_{2t} is a dummy variable which equals 1 if t=1992 and zero otherwise, and d_{3t} is a dummy variable which equals 1 if t=1991 and zero otherwise.

The Rationale

The rationale for including, besides Gi, each of the above independent variables in equation (1) seems straightforward. Since direct investment would be expected to be directly related to the size of a country's market, the study includes Ki. Because of Mexico's location next to the United States, the existence of many special programmes (like the maquiladora programme) to encourage U.S. direct investment in Mexico and the process leading up to NAFTA, the IFC study includes M_i. Due to the agglomeration effects, it includes Fi ,which would be expected to have a positive effect on I_{it}. Because the percentage of manufacturing or mining in GDP has been shown in earlier studies to influence the amount of foreign direct investment in a country, it includes Si. Since the openness of an economy obviously can affect I_{it}, it includes Oi.

Least squares estimates of the O's in equation (1) are contained in the first column of Table 11. The estimate of 1 is negative and statistically significant, which is in accord with the hypothesis that the volume of U.S. direct investment in manufacturing in a country tends to be inversely related to the weakness of protection there. The estimates of all of the regression coefficients have the expected sign. Omitting the time dummies (d_{it}, d_{2t}, and d_{3t}), which are not statistically significant, the results, contained in the second column of Table 11, show that the estimate of O1 continues to be negative and statistically significant. Further, if Oi and Si (neither of which has a statistically significant effect) are omitted, the results, contained in the third and fourth columns of Table 11, show that the estimate of O1 is relatively unaffected. If the 1990 data are dropped and if only 1991-93 data are included, the estimate of O1 (shown in Table 12) is higher, which would be expected since the data regarding Gi pertain to 1991. Given that the perceived levels of protection pertain to 1991 and that the effects on investment may occur with a lag, one might expect that Gi would have a more definite and pronounced effect on Iit in 1991-93 than in 1990-93. A comparison of Tables 11 and 12 indicates that this is true.

To sum up, a simple econometric model can explain about 50 per cent of the variation among these 14 developing countries and over time during 1990-93 in the amount of U.S. foreign direct investment. The key explanatory variables are the size of a country's market, the stock of prior foreign direct investment in this country, a dummy variable for Mexico and a measure of the weakness of intellectual property protection in the country. Holding other factors constant, if the percentage of firms regarding protection in a particular country as inadequate falls by 10 points, U.S. foreign direct investment there seems to increase by about $ 200 million per year. Regardless of which of a number of variants of this model is adopted, this estimate varies relatively little. However, any estimate of this sort should be treated with great caution because of data limitations and possible specification errors.

9. SUMMARY AND CONCLUSIONS

1. The bulk of the Japanese and German firms in the IFC sample report that the strength or weakness of intellectual property protection has an important effect on some, but not all, types of foreign investment decisions. For example, in chemicals and pharmaceuticals, over 80 per cent said that this factor was important with regard to investments in R & D facilities; but only about 20 per cent said that it was important with regard to sales and distribution outlets.

2. Regardless of whether one considers chemicals and pharmaceuticals, machinery and electrical equipment or all firms in the sample, there is a remarkable, though small, difference between Japan and Germany combined and the United States in the percentage of firms reporting that intellectual

property protection was important in their foreign direct investment decisions.

3. In chemicals and pharmaceuticals, at least 25 per cent of the firms in all three countries (Japan, Germany and the U.S.) felt that protection in India, Nigeria, Argentina, Brazil, Chile and Thailand was too weak to allow them to invest there in joint ventures where they contributed advanced technology. In machinery and electrical equipment, this was true in Brazil, Nigeria, India, Thailand and Taiwan China.

Protection too Weak

4. In chemicals and pharmaceuticals, over 25 per cent of the firms in the three countries felt that protection in India, Chile, and Argentina was too weak to permit them to transfer their newest or most effective technology to a wholly-owned subsidiary there. In machinery and electrical equipment, over 20 per cent in all three countries felt that this was the case in Nigeria, Brazil and the Philippines.
5. In chemicals and pharmaceuticals, over 40 per cent of the firms in all three countries felt that protection in India, Indonesia, Nigeria, Thailand and Argentina was too weak to allow them to license their newest or most effective technology to unrelated firms in these countries. In machinery and electrical equipment, over 25 per cent in all three countries felt that way about India, Brazil and Nigeria.
6. Both the chemical and pharmaceutical firms and the machinery and electrical equipment firms in all three countries tended to regard Singapore and Hong Kong as having the highest level of protection, among the 14 major countries considered in the FCI study. Japanese and German firms seemed to give them ratings marks in that respect than did U.S. firms.

7. In chemicals and pharmaceuticals, the perceptions of U.S., Japanese and German firms were more highly correlated with one another than in machinery and electrical equipment because differences among developing countries in protection often seemed more pronounced and more crucial in chemicals and pharmaceuticals than in machinery and electrical equipment.

A Modest Correlation

8. In respect of Japanese, German or U.S. firms, there is only a modest correlation between the perceived strength or weakness of protection in a country, in the chemical and pharmaceutical firms, and the perceived strength or weakness of protection in the same country, according to the machinery and electrical equipment segment. This is due in part to the fact that a country's laws often affect different industries in different ways and the competence and aggressiveness of a country's firms may differ from industry to industry.
9. In chemicals and pharmaceuticals, U.S. firms, seem substantially more likely than their Japanese counterparts to regard protection in these 14 countries as too weak to permit direct investment and the transfer of their most advanced technology, whereas in machinery and electrical equipment, there is essentially no difference between U.S. and Japanese firms in this regard. In part, this may reflect Japan's being a technological leader in many areas of machinery and electrical equipment, but not quite as strong in chemicals and pharmaceuticals.
10. A simple econometric model can explain about 50 per cent of the variation among these 14 developing countries and over time (during 1990-93) in the amount of U.S. foreign direct investment. The key explanatory variables are the size of a country's market, the stock of prior foreign direct investment in this country, a dummy variable for Mexico and a measure of the weakness of intellectual property protection in the country.

11. Holding other factors constant, if the percentage of firms regarding protection in a particular country as inadequate falls by 10 points, U.S. foreign direct investment there seems to increase by about $200 million per year. Regardless of which of a number of variations of this model is adopted, this estimate varies relatively little. However, any estimate of this sort should be treated with great caution because of data limitations and possible specification errors.
12. In conclusion, the IFC study indicates that the strength or weakness of a country's system of intellectual property protection seems to have a substantial effect in relatively high technology industries like chemicals, pharmaceuticals, machinery, and electrical equipment on the kinds of technology transferred to that country and the amount of direct investment in that country by Japanese and German firms. This finding is entirely consistent with an earlier study regarding U.S. firms, part of which has been refined and extended in the econometric analysis presented in the 1995 study.

10. APPENDIX

This appendix provides direct quotations from the responses of a sample of executives to the questions the IFC research team set. It begins with some Japanese and German firms that say that intellectual property protection is one of the important factors influencing technology transfer and investment decisions. Then come the views of some other Japanese and German firms that say that intellectual property protection is not important for such decisions. Finally, are given the views of a sample of U.S. firms regarding the differences, if any, between Japanese and German firms, and U.S. firms, in their concern over intellectual property protection.

Most of the firms contacted by the team seemed to regard intellectual property rights protection to be an important factor, but only one of a number of such factors, influencing technology transfer and investment decisions. For example, the chief patent attorney at a major Japanese chemicals firm declared as follows:

> "While the system (IPRs) necessary for the protection of intellectual property (IP) rights in developing countries is undergoing (a) gradual improvement, in comparison with that existent in countries such as Japan, the United States and Europe, this is still quite inadequate in terms of protection enforcement; protection should be improved and further fortified, and if and when such improvement is accomplished, technology transfer and direct investment would become definitely easier to implement.
>
> Our practice has been to effect such technology transfer and direct investment normally after determining how good the IP protection in the country in question is. In case the IP protection available is not sufficient, the disadvantages that may possibly be sustained would be the following:
>
> In a technology transfer case, the property value of the technology transferred would decline (for instance, if the IPRs protection available is not strong enough, the value of technology may not be retained even in case of exclusive licences.). When it comes to direct investment, difficulty would entail in keeping the superiority of the business based on that technology as well as in assuring return of the investment actually made. Furthermore, in both technology transfer and direct investment, the burden required for proper maintenance of confidentiality would be very large too.
>
> To us it is a major concern that IPRs protection should be properly attained in any country for technology transfer and direct investment, and we have been doing our best to meet that objective."

No Hi-Tech Transfer

An executive of a major Japanese chemical and pharmaceutical company responded as follows:

"Particularly, in case of transferring technology to developing countries in which the system of patent and trade secret protection is not built up enough or is weak, it is rather difficult for us to transfer high technology as compared with our competitors' technology to such countries. Therefore, in such cases we will often transfer second or third grade technology to them.

Accordingly, the transfer of the top grade technology is possible only to the subsidiaries on the following three terms and conditions:

1) the majority of which stocks we own.
2) to which we may dispatch key persons and
3) which may fully control technology of production disclosed and/or transferred by us.

However, even in this case we have difficulty in controlling a "trade secret".

As stated above, we are not willing to transfer top grade technology to such developing countries as being weak on their system of patent and trade secret protection.

Therefore, as an inevitable consequence, the amount of investment by us becomes small and we are obliged to expand our investment little by little while taking in the situation in such countries."

A top executive of a German pharmaceutical firm responded as follows:

"The strength or weakness of a developing country's system of IPRs has a substantial effect on the kinds of technology my firm will transfer. We are not prepared to transfer high technology into a country in which IPRs is not protected and in which we will lose control of it.

The strength or weakness of a country's system of IPRs is not the only criterion of our decision where my company will make direct investment but it is certainly one of the decisive factors. If we have the choice between two countries having nearly the same political and economic framework, we would certainly prefer the country with the more reliable IPRs system."

The general manager of international operations of a major Japanese electrical equipment producer made his position explicit::

"If the country does not have an adequate system or practice to protect intellectual property rights, our technology transfer to the country will be limited and we protect our rights in the following way. We will ensure, in the technology transfer agreement, that important or core technology will not be transferred without adequate consideration. For example, necessary parts will be supplied from our factory.

In the case of software, our agreement on transfer of technology specifically provides for the obligation of the transferee to protect such intellectual rights. Also, considering the difficulty of protecting the rights, we will restrict the kind of information transferred and ensure that sufficient consideration will be collected."

The general manager of the overseas department of a Japanese computer manufacturer reported:

"We may refrain from transferring our technology to the country where the intellectual property protection system is weak. However, the weakness of the country's system of intellectual property protection has no substantial effect on our investment in that country, as far as our intellectual property is not included in that investment."

Discouraging Business Desire

An executive of a large Japanese pharmaceutical firm pointed out:

"Generally speaking, the weakness of a developing country's system of intellectual property protection discourages our business desire in the market."

The director of the intellectual property department of a large Japanese chemical firm declared:

"We cannot help hesitating to transfer our technology to developing countries if the trade secret of high technology cannot be protected in those countries. Although laws and regulations for protecting trade secrets are being arranged recently in developing countries, it is difficult to transfer high technology to those countries where it is not widely recognised as social justice to respect intellectual property rights.

Our company has been investing directly in many overseas joint venture companies, but this has been mainly for manufacturing purposes. Concerning transfer of high technology, we are still hesitating as stated above."

The manager of planning and coordination of a huge Japanese electronics firm made a further point:

"A Japanese company receives royalties for a limited period when it transfers technology. In due course, though, the recipient integrates the technology. The Japanese company may then experience the so-called "boomerang effect." This aspect must be considered before a technology transfer occurs."

While most of the executives whom the IFC research team contacted felt that intellectual property protection is important, a substantial minority did not share this view. The top executives at a major German chemical firm stated:

"Both transfer of technology as such and the value of transferred technology itself are determined not by the quality of patent protection in the developing country concerned. The most important determining factors are the commercial status of the potential licence, the geographical position of the market and, in particular, the interests of this company in the respective region.

These aspects are ultimately decisive in determining investments in these countries. As to which country of a geographical region where investments are to be made further, an important parameter is the financial expenditure for the existing required work force or how well they are qualified to perform the tasks intended.

As you can infer from our remarks, the decision for or against a developing country is determined primarily by commercial aspects. Questions regarding patent laws are not in any way decisive."

Not a major factor

The manager of corporate planning of a major Japanese food company said:

"While we are concerned about the level of intellectual property protection when we intend to transfer our technology to developing countries or invest in them, it is not a substantial factor by which we make decisions where we should do so or not. Rather, such general market situations as level of per capita GDP and market shares of competitors, the prospects of particular enterprises and the existence of credible partners are regarded as more important factors for technology transfer and direct investment."

The general manager of a leading Japanese electronics firm stated:

"The strength or weakness of a developing country's system of intellectual property protection does not have a substantial effect on the kinds of technology that we will transfer to that country.

The strength or weakness of a developing country's system of intellectual property protection does not have a substantial effect on the composition and extent of our direct investment in that country."

The manager of intellectual property at a major Japanese computer firm said:

"Intellectual property protection systems of developing countries are not sufficiently effective to protect the electronic technology of this firm from being used without any right granted by this firm. If required and compelled by economic reasons, this firm will invest in developing countries, even if their intellectual property protection systems are not sufficiently strong."

The director of patents of a leading Japanese pharmaceutical firm declared:

"Investment is decided in view of many other factors than intellectual property protection, e.g. political stability, availability of educated workers, tax system, etc."

Perceptions of U.S. Firms

A sample of U.S. executives in the chemical industry (where intellectual property protection is regarded as particularly important) were contacted to determine their views concerning the differences, if any, between Japanese and German firms, and U.S. firms, with regard to the importance of intellectual property protection in technology transfer and investment decisions. Most seemed to emphasise the similarities rather than the differences.

One chemical company executive commented:

"The issue of intellectual property protection covers two areas: whether a developing country has adequate intellectual property laws, and given such legislation, whether the country enforces its laws appropriately to encourage direct investment by companies residing in developed countries. Germany and Japan are similar to the U.S. in having concerns over this issue related to developing countries. At a meeting in Beijing in 1994, several Japanese companies expressed their concern about direct investment in China, including consumer products, unless that country's government would take a stronger position on enforcement of the newly established legislation (within the last 5 years). The recent problems with China revolved around violation of existing laws in trademark protection. The major German companies are as concerned as U.S. companies (our experience is more with chemical and biotechnology operations) concerning this issue. In conclusion, given the two countries in question, I feel that both countries are similar to the U.S. concerning the strength of the intellectual property system and its influence on technology transfer and direct investment."

The director of international marketing at another major U.S. chemical company said:

> "I think they are all equally concerned and, if anything, Japanese and German firms may be more stringent in their desire for protection."

A leading patent attorney at one of the U.S. chemical giants stated:

> "I know from my contact with Japanese and Europeans working on high minimum standards of protection of intellectual property in the GATT that their companies are concerned about protecting their intellectual property".

Beyond IPRs

The chief patent counsel of another major chemical producer said:

> "As you know, many factors in addition to the viability of the intellectual property system affect differences in technology transfer/investment policies between German and Japanese firms and U.S. firms. These factors included export control regulations, financing availability, technology owner's business strategy and liability concerns. My opinion is that these factors far outshadow any differ-

> ences caused by the viability of the intellectual property system of the developing country, and in fact, cause any perceived differences, especially in the chemical industry.
>
> While unquestionably the viability of a developing country's intellectual property system influences whether, and if so, what technology will be transferred, my experience in the chemical industry is that this factor alone does not materially distinguish a U.S. firm from one in Japan or Germany."

However, not all of the U.S. chemical executives felt that the Japanese and German firms were concerned in the same way as U.S. firms about intellectual property protection. A patent attorney at one major chemical firm said that German and Japanese firms relied more heavily than U.S. firms on controlling information sent to subsidiaries in developing countries by putting German or Japanese personnel, rather than personnel from the host country, in key positions. Also, he said that Japanese and German firms are more likely to conform to the local business climate and custom, rather than act strictly in accord with the customs at home. It underscored the tentativeness of these remarks, which he said were based only on anecdotal evidence. Obviously, they should be treated with appropriate caution the IFC study noted.

6

PRAGMATISM SHOULD PREVAIL

Gene Patenting

Agracetus, a small agricultural biotechnology company in Wisconsin in the United States had filed in November 1987, without any fuss or fanfare, an application with the Patent Office in Calcutta. It was, for all practical purposes, a copy of the application it filed a year earlier in the U.S. In April 1991, Agracetus, which later became a subsidiary of the U.S. chemical group, W.R. Grace & Co., received the U.S. patent it had sought and a few months later, in July that year, the Indian patent as well.

That event duly sparked a row, which ended only with the Centre revoking in October 1995 the patent which most believed should never have been granted in the first place. The Indian Patent Office had granted Agracetus rights over cotton plants and seeds carrying foreign genes introduced using the bacterium, agrobacterium tumefaciens. The Indian Patent Act does not explicity forbid patenting of living matter. But, two clauses in the section on "what are not inventions" effectively exclude any kind of gene patenting. The first disallows patents for "a method of agriculture or horticulture." The second, a sweeping exclusionary clause, would not permit patents for "any process for the medicinal, surgical, curative, prophylactic or other treatment of human beings or any process for a similar treatment of animals or plants to render them free of disease or to increase their economic value or that of their products."

This regime, obviously, has to change, as we noted in the introduction. Having signed the revised General Agreement on Tariffs and Trade, Indian patent laws have to be modified to bring these in line with the TRIPs requirements. There are, however, exclusion clauses in the TRIPs agreement, which India can use to its benefit if it chooses to, though even here the moot question is if too much protection should be sought. Gene patenting affects two sectors of vital concern to India: agriculture and health. Indian research efforts in these areas are in a nascent stage and are far from being on the same scale as in the U.S. and the European countries. The latter are the most advanced in gene-related research and have been granting fairly broad patents. If India were to grant similar patents, it would block many important avenues of research.

Japanese example

While amending the patents framework, India is free to follow Japan's example. Japan's patents have tended to be very narrowly defined and companies can often circumvent patents held by competitors with only very slight modifications of a product or process, but should India use the exclusion clauses in TRIPs to limit severely the scope of gene patents which it will grant?. Naturally occurring or trivially modified micro organisms, gene sequences, cellular or sub-cellular materials, cell lines and the like, however, can be treated as discoveries and not patentable. Genetically modified micro organisms should, however, be allowed patent protection, provided there has been substantial human intervention in altering its genetic make up and also if a valuable product has been created. But, in such cases, the patent should be solely for the trait or use claimed.

Gene patents, thus, could be specifically for what is described in the patent application. For example, in the two cotton patents Agracetus was granted in the U.S. — the first of which was granted in India as well — the application was described as a method of introducing foreign genes into cotton using the bacterium, agrobacterium tumefaciens. The foreign gene would be inserted into the cotton cells by two plasmids (circular strips of DNA), which were described in detail, in the agrobacterium. One could say that the patent should have been strictly for the use of those two plasmids. In the first patent, Agracetus also claimed rights over all cotton plants and seeds, which carried a foreign gene that was inserted using agrobacterium tumefaciens, irrespective of which plasmids were used. In the subsequent patent filed in the U.S., Agracetus got rights over all genetically engineered cotton varieties, no matter how the foreign gene had been introduced. (On appeal, both these patents were revoked by the U.S. Patent Office in December 1995.) India is free to explore the possibility of going still further. In gene-related process patents such as the two agracetus patents referred to above, patents could be granted only for the genes specified in the patent application. In retrospect, the Agracetus patents would then not have permitted the insertion of any foreign gene using those two plasmids, but would have been limited to specific genes.

No Patenting of Plants

Considering the importance of agriculture, no patenting of plants should be permitted. TRIPs requires that there should be legal protection for plant varieties. India, thus, has to have a Plant Varieties Act for the purpose. The U.S. and Europe, which already have separate legislation for protecting plant varieties, also permit patenting of plants. Patents offer greater protection, compared to the plant varieties legislation, to its property right holders: the protection period is longer, there are no special exemptions for farmers and unlicensed use of protected varieties for the development of new varieties is also not allowed. In the light of this, it is being recognised that the only form of intellectual property protection for plants, even those which are genetically engineered, should be the proposed Plant Varieties Act.

Voluntary organisations and research institutions, no doubt, have an important watchdog role when gene patenting becomes possible in India. The initiative on the Agracetus patent in India was taken by the Rural Advanced Foundation International (RAFI) based in Canada. RAFI keeps a close track of biotechnology patents being applied for and granted throughout the world. It challenged the broad European patent for soybean given to Agracetus. Indian research groups will have to perform a similar role within the country.

To amend the Indian Patent Act in such a way that, while conforming to the GATT requirements, it is able to protect national interests as far as justified in the global context of free trade is a complex task. It will in any case be necessary to lay down detailed guidelines on what would be patentable in India. Then there will be less chance of patent examiners and law courts being guided by Western precedents in areas such as gene patenting where the West has a considerable body of patent law and India has none. GATT requires India to bring its patent laws in conformity with TRIPs by 2000 although the introduction of product patents can be delayed till 2005. A sense of urgency is easily warranted.

IF YOU ARE A MANAGER WHY DON'T YOU TICKLE YOUR BRAIN WITH QUESTIONS SUCH AS THESE?

1. What is the role of the WTO-monitored mechanism to protect intellectual property rights?
2. Why should India provide for such a mechanism?
3. What are the essential aspects of the TRIPs agreement?
4. What benefit can India derive from the agreement along with other developing countries?
5. What do you understand by intellectual property?
6. What is copyright?
7. What are the essential elements of patents?
8. Explain the progress towards protection for intellectual property.
9. Explain in brief the U.S. Patent system.
10. What is the level of pharmaceutical patents in India?
11. Explain the provisions of the TRIPs agreement for pharmaceuticals.
12. Is our pharmaceutical industry likely to gain or lose?
13. Will drug prices go up or down?
14. Explain the progress made by Japan in pharmaceutical patents.
15. The IFC survey shows the effects of intellectual property protection. What are the likely implications for India?
16. Will direct foreign investment and technology transfer grow or fall with the protection of intellectual property?
17. In gene patenting, what precautions should India take?

THE BASE MATERIAL FOR THE STUDY

1. *The Global Trade Act*, WTO.
2. *Global Trade: The Challenge and Opportunity* by K.S. Ramachandran.
3. The sector reports on the new trade regime by the Indian Institute of Foreign Trade.
4. *Pharmaceutical Patents: New Horizons in India*, by Dr. Heinz Redwood.
5. *The IFC Study on Intellectual Property Protection*, Direct Investment and Technology Transfer, 1995.

PART III

MACRO & MICRO ISSUES OF LIBERALISATION

1

THE MARKET PLACE

1. EFFECTIVE DEMAND, EFFECTIVE PRODUCT

No product emerges just like that. It has to be developed and promoted. The Gods might have created the earth and the sky but the market place is man's handiwork and remains so. How does one define a product? Not everything can be called a product, which essentially demands a manufacturing activity. But, this itself won't do in a competitive environment. For a product to be called one, it must be saleable; rather it must get sold. The one that remains on the shelf as an inventory has no right to call itself a product. One can say this of an also-ran as well.

This may seem scandalous to conventional writers on management-related issues, but then it makes no sense to give descriptions that are just notional. Just as demand has to be effective to make an impact on the market, a product must have a substantial demand for it to be called by that name. It is not enough for a company to exist in name; it must be doing something worthwhile. This, indeed, is the essence of corporate planning. To make a product what it should be, the manufacturer has to acquire a brand and, not only that, a positioning advantage as well. These are no less important than quality. As for quality, this has to be broadcast, not too loudly, only subtly. No prospective buyer would want to be bullied or shouted at. He or she wants to be persuaded. This should explain why aggressive promotional campaigns have failed in the past, not just here but also globally.

Description of Product

If Colgate reigns over all other brands of toothpaste it is because the persuasion has been done so very well that its superiority over its possible rivals is widely accepted. Very few people have any doubts over that. This is precisely what the market demands. Something which sells only residually does not merit the description of product. If the manufacturer winds up the show, and this is going to make no difference to the market then the product with which the unit was associated virtually dismisses itself. Keynes made a great contribution to economics by highlighting the phenomenon of effective demand. The literature on management would get enriched with serious doubts being voiced over the correctness of the description of product being indiscriminately applied.

This would be justified by the fact that no also-rans can really survive the pressures of a competitive market. Granted that there are sick units galore and till sometime ago the Government was — if not always quickly — nationalising private sector companies that could not cope with the challenges of producing and selling, yet generally in a competitive environment sick units will be either liquidated or will merge with the stronger ones. May, be, if political priorities had not intervened earlier — from the Sixties to the early Nineties — to lay down the rules, there would have been no sick units as such and one among the Government's priorities would not have been their revival or rehabilitation — a process that soon made a mockery of economic management. Again, if the Government had not sworn by the dominance of public sector, the latter would not have been broadly identified with sickness.

The Ground Rules

It is clear that ground rules must be prescribed for what can qualify as a product. A ten per cent share of the market must be one of these. Profit is also an essential criterion. A producer's balance sheet must not be in the red if what he turns out is to be treated as a product. May be, as Keynes did with demand, one can think of qualifying the product as an effective product. When managers the world over are going gaga with what is known as the virtual product, there can be no conceptual objection to an effective product.

In fact, a virtual product can emerge only from an effective product, not a dud one. Let us remember this. This is what the market economics tells us. But then, who is listening? Indian management students and managers are only keen to hear *gurus* — preferably *firangis* — and may have no ears for writers indulging in what they might readily perceive the suggested qualification for a product as an exercise in conceptual gimmickry. Yet, when Keynes refused to look at demand that was not effective and was only notional, everyone applauded, and with reason. When somebody talks of a virtual product again we hear loud applause. After all, this stands for one which is there even before the consumer has thought of it. So why can't we debate on an effective product — that is real, not dud.

But for Keynes, economists would have continued to swear by the wisdom of Alfred Marshall, and we all owe it to him the recognition that demand has to be effective to be relevant. Likewise, management has got revolutionised with the ideas of Peter Drucker and Tom Peters. Over the years, with concepts like the virtual corporation and product, there has been a dramatic change in the perceptions of writers on management. India has its own management *gurus*, but somehow teaching of management still remains drab and the annual conference of management schools regularly rues the poor-to-indifferent quality of management teaching in the country. The understanding of management can do with a lot of exposure to fresh ideas, and concepts must emerge from developments in the market place and from how one product succeeds and another flops.

Effective Supply

Just as market price is determined by effective demand and effective supply — ironically, Keynes did not bother too much about the supply side and did not think that supply like demand also had to be effective — the product must be good to sell before it can make an impact in the market place. Managers must focus on making what they produce — whether it be a good or service — an effective player in the market before contemplating a shift to the other stage, the virtual phase, which is really the ultimate.

But then, the producer of an also ran cannot even dream of coming up with a product which calls for the highest level of corporate skills, and managers must know the consumer's preferences and must be very sure that what they have come up with is just what the consumer has been craving for. Finally, no manufacturer of a product or provider of service really needs a concept for him to succeed. A sensible market player knows what he needs for success. Essentially, he must have a good feel of the market for him to know what will sell and what will not. Good market research advocates itself. But, such research must be really top class. There can be no compromise with quality. The target audience must be tapped and the researcher must make sure that he has done this. It is the responsibility of the company to monitor the research to ensure that the consumer is not taken for granted.

2. CORPORATE IDEALS VS REALITIES

Multinational Corporations, positioned as they are, may have reason to be concerned about who is ruling which country, though this should not be seen as a legitimate justification for active interference. Yet, some of them have an ugly record of destabilising Third World governments. At least, in one Latin American country the overthrow of a radical political regime sometime ago was traced to the powerful MNC hand. The question asks itself: should the management of an MNC — or for that matter a big domestic industrial house — involve, along with several things, deciding which party or political force should be in power where? American MNCs are as much involved in local as in Third World politics. There are Indian companies which do extend — even explicit — support to certain parties. Recently, it was rumoured that a corporate had a hand in the removal of a key official in the Union Finance Ministery.

Reference had been made during the 1996 poll to a certain industrial house backing a number of candidates of a particular political party in West Bengal. As for MNCs doing business in India, quite a few of them had earlier openly declared themselves in favour of the Congress for fear that reform might suffer a reversal if it got voted out. The FIIs got into the act also and came up with all manner of poll forecasts. The 1998 poll was characterised by such kite flying. This was the story of the next election to the Lok Sabha as well.

Should a CEO and his advisers have a strategy for governments as well? While lobbying for concessions and favourable policy/administrative prescriptions is definitely part of corporate decision-making, can this legitimately extend to influencing the fate of governments? Politicians need funds and elections mean a lot of dough — to receive and to spend — and the nexus between politicians and businessmen develops all too easily and is sustained. It serves both. That we can see, but is this how the cause of true professionalism should be served?

Not Quid Pro Quo

Should a political party or leader compromise with issues and ideology simply because substantial financial support has come from a particular industrial house? It just cannot be that issues do not matter and that a government is only concerned about a *quid pro quo* with a section of the business community. During long years of economic radicalism which declared an antipathy to private enterprise, the Congress under Mrs. Indira Gandhi was the main beneficiary of business funds. Those who provided the dough must have got something from the Government but not certainly in policy formulation. There are, of course, exceptions, and one industrial house with a lot of clout is known to get liberal fiscal concessions as well as projects despite changing political regimes.

The MNCs would want to protect and improve upon their business but not all of them would be prepared to emulate the Latin American act of destabilising a duly elected government because it did not suit their interests. One should say this of Indian companies as well. A sensible CEO knows where the buck should stop. For the company to thrive, some political patronage is necessary and acquiring this will, thus, find its way into the corporate strategy but this will be at the margin as Dr. Helen Hughes, the reputed Australian economist, would have put it — though she used the expression in respect of foreign investment for development

Essentially, an enterprise would prosper or flop because of the inner strength or weakness, and not the kind of support it receives from a government. For, ultimately, it is not the stability or continuity of a particular political regime which sets the agenda for corporate prosperity.

Indeed, corporate dynamism is best demonstrated when companies perform best against severe odds. Tom Peters was not joking when he wrote of thriving on chaos. He meant what he said, and he had in mind the best of CEOs, those who flourished no matter what the environment was. A difficult and uncompromising political regime does not necessarily mean the end of the world for a CEO and his team who have got their strategy right. Alternatively, even the most supportive regime can do nothing for a corporate management that has not got its performing tactics right. When you add up everything, professional excellence stands out and political and administrative support plays only a peripheral role.

While lobbying is necessary to avert gross injustice or favoured treatment being meted out to a rival, this, at best, is only one of the instruments that a CEO who knows his drill will want to have at his disposal. He will prefer instead to rely on the product or service to sell itself on merit. But, not all managements are moved by the ideal way of winning business and letting merit dictate. When one company woos an influential political leader, another decides to follow suit. It is not quite like keeping up with the Joneses but the two are not too different. The basic principle is the same: because one person does something, not doing the same thing is certainly bad for another. The corporate sector is moved by the fear that not lobbying hard enough will have grave repercussions on business opportunities.

Seat of Power

It is easy for outsiders and management *gurus* to discourse on professionalism, but then if those in the hot seat are convinced that they cannot be too professional if they want to be in the business, you cannot really blame them. The customer is an unknown quantity and that long before a product reaches the consumer so many things have to be done. There are umpteen clearances to get and in this, proximity to the seat of power not only helps move the wheels but is even crucial.

No wonder, corporate bodies want to give donations to political parties in cash rather than by cheque as would be warranted by considerations of promoting probity in public life. Payment by cheque establishes support for a certain political party or leader, while spending in cash leaves no traces. Politicians are free to make a pretence of transparency but they are known to hold grudges and the corporate sector can more than burn its fingers if it makes a big donation to the wrong party — wrong in the sense that it falters, and badly, at the hustings.

In a way, the professionalism of industrial houses depends on this attribute spreading among politicians. For a start, the political elite must accept the inevitability of businessmen having to woo leaders of different parties and must stop behaving like spoilt children — "no lollypop, I will hate you!" The Americans are not incorruptible but nobody has heard of any company operating in the United States being harassed because of its known and established links with a particular party. There is some maturity there, which we must start emulating. No Republican administration, whether at the federal or state level, will think of not obliging a manufacturer merely because the latter was a supporter of the Democratic party. This is true of the Democrats as well. While lobbies do work overtime in Capitol Hill, rarely are orders won or denied because of political alignments. Fifty years after Independence such balance is still missing in this country. Both the politicians and captains of industry are to blame for this, though the former must take more of the blame as they set the norms for everyone having tc deal with them. The mice, obviously, cannot preach to the cat; rather, the cat must decide not to torment the mice.

3. CHATTERING CLASSES VS MASSES

The chattering classes, meaning the elite, do not like politics. They won't vote. Going to the polling booth is deemed an unworthy act and they will skip this and use any pretext for going anywhere other than places where votes are cast. But, they will surely rue the indifference of the populace to the electoral process next morning, when the media reports of low-to-indifferent voting, ignoring quite easily their own deliberate failure to exercise their right to franchise. Rajni Kothari was not exaggerating when he once wrote of the elite entertaining itself in air-conditioned drawing rooms and discoursing on the benefits likely to accrue to society if only the poor were not around. How many people who travel only in cars and planes know the pains of travel by second class train compartments and in buses in the metropolises? With several people in the country in no position to afford a square meal a day, nobody can wish away all the dirt and filth. If human excreta is all there on a city's roads, it is just unavoidable.

Elite Attitudes

Slums are, no doubt, dirty and foul-smelling but they provide shelter to millions of people who cannot otherwise survive in heartless cities. The elite thinks that slums are eyesores. In posh drawing-rooms, over glasses of scotch whiskey, men who are properly suited and booted discuss often the risks of proliferating slums. They will look down from their luxury apartments and point their fingers at slums in the vicinity. Wherever you go, there are slums and dirty people — this is their daily refrain. Little do they realise that but for the slums they will get nobody to drive their limousines or cook their meals. That during the outbreak of plague in the recent past the fear that these people would be the carriers is by no means irrelevant to this debate.

In a dynamic world, today's slum children can become tomorrow's super gods. Film star Govinda was picked up right from one of Bombay's slums and cricketer Vinod Kambli once belonged to the slum world. Some of today's corporate barons came possibly from the slums. The one who adored the Prime Minister's Gaddi after the 1991 poll prided himself on being the son of the soil. Mr. Narasimha Rao also spoke of his poor origins while chiding, during his election campaign, the erstwhile Maharaja who was a ministerial colleague until the hawala scandal caught up with him.

Thus, poverty is not something to be ashamed of, but it is not also something to be boasted of. It is all right for successful people, who have left their years of poverty well behind them, to remember nostalgically the past. But, ask any man or woman fighting for the next meal, you will get only harsh words about their living conditions by way of an answer; no wonder, since being poor is very cruel, both in economic and social terms. It is only with a lot of help — willingly provided — that there will be a ray of hope for those living under conditions of destitution. Even then, progress comes only slowly to them while it does very fast and easily to people who start with a silver spoon or even foot (as the U.S. media recently described the advantages of belonging to dynasties) in their mouths. The road is really hard for people who are socio-economically depressed. Yet, progress is not always denied to people without means. Often, those who are up in life today are the ones who had started at the bottom of the ladder, may be a score years ago. Challenges make them do things better. Mrs. Margaret Thatcher—the iron lady of Britain — was a grocer's daughter and Reagan was a petty actor to start with.

Threat from Parvenus

In this fiercely competitive corporate world, those who go by the description of barons do not come up just like that. They have to fight very hard to reach the top and even harder to maintain their ascendence. They may be flying their own aircraft either for holidaying or going to their factories. But, some 20 years ago, they might have walked barefoot or used their bicycles. From rags to riches is a way of life, not just a dramatic story line. This happens everyday. As for the reverse process, even though the rich do not always get reduced to rags, there are cases of yesterday's pioneers of industry losing out to brats with no particular lineage to boast of. Some industrial groups have, no doubt, survived the onslaught of *parvenus* and even flourished, but some others have yielded ground to the newcomers. There are several products that have gone into the wilderness simply unable to withstand the pressure mounted by better and stronger competitors. This is no place for the complacent and sleepy rich. The elite better be careful, least its empire comes crashing down like a pack of cards. There is nothing like permanent poverty or perpetual affluence. The rich may not like the riff-raff coming up in life and flaunting its new-found strength, but then nobody can object to its progress.

Most Chief Ministers of today were men of no consequence some 30 years ago. The emergence of Mr. P V Narasimha Rao on the national scene had demonstrated that dynasty did not enjoy the clout that it had fifteen years ago. Generally, in politics there is nothing like inheritance. This is ceasing to be a big factor in the corporate world also.

Mr. Deve Gowda was also a *mannina maga* (son of the soil), who became the nation's chief executive, and there are several with the same humble origins in other — though lesser — positions of authority. Partly, this is because of democracy but an equally good reason would be that the people in question were able to grasp the opportunities that even did not come their way. Stalin's origins were quite lowly, so was Hitler's. But, both came to control the destinies of two major nations and to influence those of other countries as well. Napoleon was a *parvenu* but he became the French emperor. That he had to settle finally for ignominy can hardly be cited against poor people's capacity to climb to the top. After all, Charles I of England was executed by Cromwell, whose blood was red, not blue. That England could never forget that brutal end to the king hardly helped erase that part of history related to the monarch with a divine right to rule ending his life on the executioner's block.

Price of Oblivion

Corporate magnates do not quite face the same fate, but they do pay the price of oblivion for their inability to cope with the changing times. Not all the industrial sickness in the country is manipulated to allow the promoters to make their gains and go for greener pastures. Often, when a unit winds up, the owners also get into serious financial problems. For all the boom in brands, there is on the other side the sad story of brands that the consumers did not want. Just as successful politicians get reduced to less than also-rans because of changed circumstances — this happened even to Mrs. Margaret Thatcher — today's corporate barons may, some years hence, bite the dust if their competitive skills have got blunted.

2

FISCAL POLICY: PRUDENCE VS PRESSURES

1. LET GOVERNMENT BORROW CHEAP

When there is a talk of deepening financial sector reforms, the tendency is to forget that the accord between RBI and the Union Finance Ministry is a key aspect, and, even more so, that reform — meaning that part of it concerning reduction of Centre's fiscal deficit — would be taking the right course only when there is a total retreat on the phase-out of ad hoc treasury bills. Yes, fiscal management presently is getting constrained largely because of the limits placed on RBI lending to the Centre on concessional terms. The Centre will, no doubt, be tempted to over-spend when there are no limits on access to cheap Reserve Bank credit, but then the fiscal impact of such over-spending is not likely to be more than that of the enhanced interest burden arising out of the borrowing from the market at substantially higher rates in lieu of central bank accommodation.

In the wake of the RBI moving towards reduction in interest rates generally, the Central Government's interest burden is still going to get reduced only by a small margin and, to that extent, the pressure on fiscal managers is going to ease only slightly. Thus, a retreat from a regime of high and market-determined returns is justified in respect of the Government sector's financial needs. Even at the risk of encouraging profligacy on the part of the Central as well as state governments, it would make sense to return to a fiscal arrangement where the Centre is able to tap the RBI significantly through the traditional ad hoc treasury bills. It has been argued, and with reason, that ad hocs, quite sometime ago, ceased to be ad hocs, but when the need is for the Central Government to borrow cheap and, in the process, also let others tap the market on easy terms, this reasoning should not be ignored.

Easing the Debt Trap

When the Centre taps the market less, interest rates can only move down, not up. The debt trap — a situation where fresh borrowings are needed merely to meet the needs of debt servicing — has greater chances of getting weakened through a reduced interest burden for the Centre and states than when the burden is rising thanks to market-related interest rates and the Centre is having to tap the market often at an exhorbitant cost rather than the RBI at a mere four plus per cent interest as it was before the accord on limited recourse to ad hocs came into force.

The logic of low or modest inflation rates getting reflected in interest rates of a comparable magnitude is acceptable generally, but this has not been in evidence in the Indian context of a moderate movement in the wholesale price index. At less than six per cent as of september 2000 the rise in the index is by no means considerable and there is no case for lending rates being over 15 per cent. The link between inflation and interest rates is on the premise that when the rate of inflation is high and rising, will be the real rate of interest can be high and rising as well since the real rate will, in any case, be lower. The higher the rate of inflation the lower will be the real rate of interest and this justifies a high and rising nominal rate of interest. Conversely, when the rate of inflation is down and rising, a reasonable real rate of interest would demand a substantial fall in the nominal rate of interest. But, this cannot be effected independent of the supply of money, specifically lendable funds, and even more so the demand for credit. In fact, when the latter is larger in relation to supply, unless there is a substantial release of funds into the money market, the demand factor will be more assertive. In such a situation, the link between inflation and rate of interest becomes merely notional.

No theory or concept has a universal and perpetual application. What holds good elsewhere does not necessarily hold good here. Even where the concept has been proved right in one country or place in one context may fail to pass the test in another context in the same country or place. Interest rates can be administered and can otherwise be influenced, but inflation cannot be administered. While interest rates can be held down by diktat, inflationary forces do not accept official orders but move on their own. While supply management can work, it takes its time to exercise an impact on prices at the market place. There is no such lag in respect of administered interest rates.

As long as the Central Government meets its needs outside the market and on terms that deliberately hold down the cost of borrowing, market rates of interest can generally be expected to be under control. Indeed, it was only when the Government and RBI ventured to reform a critical segment of financial sector activity — the manner of Central Government borrowing — that the largest financier of the Government commercial banks—began to hold the entire government sector (Centre and states) to ransom — demanding and getting a return that in their perception the market demanded. Once the banks set the terms, the needy borrowers had no option but to accept them.

True reform does demand an end to the administered interest rate regime, but critical to holding the fiscal deficit in check is Central Government borrowing at a modest cost. Given the disturbing trend in the Centre's interest burden, the latter must take precedence over the former. While it may seem farfetched to say that the slow down in the manufacturing sector during the fiscal year 2000-01 was precipitated only by the Centre tapping the market, that too on the latter's terms, yet the ground realities point to the adverse effect of restrictions being placed on Centre's borrowing from RBI by way of low issue of cost ad hocs.

SLR must stay up

Against the backdrop of what all has followed the September 1994 accord between RBI and the Union Finance Ministry, the SLR must also stay up. While nobody can seriously advocate a massive securities scandal as it erupted in 1991-92—which itself most people, particularly the Union Finance Minister of the time, blamed on the low yields of Government securities—banks would be better off overall with an interest rate regime that is moderate rather than anarchic.

Banks must begin to operate with a narrow spread consistent with what their counterparts abroad do. This is a measure of globalisation that demands more urgent attention than an end to the administered interest rate regime. The fact that a bank known for its conservatism — the Indian Bank — had been run in a most callous manner just when it should have taken advantage of the high interest rate regime and prospered should support a return to the pre-September 1994 regime.

2. FISCAL DEFICIT AND POVERTY

Economists are always worried about the size of the Government's fiscal deficit. They see in a large fiscal gap a strong inflationary content. Inflation containment virtually means holding down the growth in the Government's deficit spending. There is no doubt that any government, whether of an economic superpower or an LDC, has to live within its means. The laws of prudence apply to all countries irrespective of their economic status. There can be no compromise over this and it does not need the IMF to emphasise this.

But, unfortunately, economists are often overplaying the fiscal deficit card. What matters to them are the figures — the bare arithemetic — and not how the money that governments mobilise is used. Efficiency takes the backseat and the self-proclaimed fiscal experts think — and proclaim to the world — that if anything has to be done by any government, this is to narrow the fiscal gap. The consequences of fiscal containment or stabilisation, as the IMF and World Bank describe it, do not matter. When there is so much of poverty around, governments should have — where they do not have it, they must find it through an extra effort at mobilisation — the wherewithal to take care of poverty alleviation. Yet, in the name of restraining growth in fiscal deficit, what usually gets done is a pruning of expenditure on social welfare. Ironically, when governments respond to the pressures of poverty reduction by letting the deficit rise, they are accused of being populist. Agreed that governments — not just those of Third World countries — do have a penchant for populist measures, yet the fact remains that in a situation of serious resource constraints the only course left to responsive political regimes for attending to the problems of the poor is to allow the deficit rise. Without taking recourse to this, it is often not possible to do anything substantial towards poverty reduction. But, once this happens, what follows is that the poor is quickly made the casualty when somebody or the other — this does not have to be the IMF — complains about a lack of control over the deficit.

Not a Convenient Excuse

Nobody is suggesting that fiscal discipline should not be a priority, but economists and the IMF should not make this a convenient excuse for neglect of the poor. The downtrodden in the community need caring and it reflects a gross insensitivity towards the millions below the poverty line for anyone to advocate a pruning of government expenditure on the social sector, but this is what we have. Yet, if waste is a factor in Government spending this is not to be attributed to the fact that the Government is having to dish out some dough on programmes of poverty reduction. We are not talking welfare economics here, but just good economic governance. After all, under liberalisation, a large segment of poor people means inadequacy of effective demand, which limits the stimulus to economic growth.

Economics, particularly fiscal economics, should not be delinked from the wider goal of poverty alleviation. That poor have problems surviving must concern governments and it does not call for populist sentiment to make poverty alleviation possible. Agreed that the record generally of political regimes is hardly reassuring on this score and starting from Mrs. Indira Gandhi successive political regimes have made efforts towards poverty reduction an instrument of populism, yet, a situation has now come about where any strategy to help the poor is seen to be populist and politicians run the risk of being accused of being motivated by self-interest whenever they do something for the poor.

The idea is not to legitimise rabid populism, but only to underscore the perception among economists that anything by way of poverty alleviation is necessarily populist and thereby irrational. That the poor cannot do without a strong helping hand is generally ignored and any programme to uplift the deprived sections of the community quickly invites criticism. While fiscal discipline is important this must be achieved through good management of resources. Inflation control is quite as important and here the strategy should be a sound mix of demand and supply management — not demand management alone. When too much stress is placed on the latter, fiscal restraint takes precedence over other aspects of economic governance. This hurts the poor ultimately since welfare spending is seen to be economically unjustified. When funds are misused in the name of power development and the cost of a project in an equally important infrastructural area shoots up by a substantial margin, this does not attract the same adverse attention as when some crores of rupees are disbursed for a *rozgar yojana* and a slippage is reported.

Wake up Time for Economists

Year after year, projects in the so-called priority areas run into rough weather and the Department of Programme Implementation meticulously lists the details, but fiscal economists wake up only when a Prime Minister announces from the ramparts of the Red Fort a programme of poverty alleviation. When Dr. Manmohan Singh deliberately eschewed giving the process of fiscal stabilisation a humane face, he was applauded for sticking to the reform agenda. But, once he made a provision for social welfare spending in response to demands that the reform programme should not hurt the poor, his popularity rating among economists suffered.

Good management of the nation's finances depends partly on avoidance of waste of any kind and partly on efficient utilisation of the assets already existing. It is much more than arithmetic. While figures will always add up, when physical performance is slack nothing can really compensate for it. A massive failure in one programme or project cannot be cancelled out by a limited success elsewhere. The perception is that when performance is abysmal in one key area of the economy the remedy lics in cutting the outlay on an unrelated area. It is because of the legitimacy given to this perception that fiscal management overall is lackadaisical. The deplorable thing is that the Government does not even know the essence of fiscal sanity.

The magnitude of poverty does not justify slackness and this book is hardly pleading for slackness being endorsed, although people who are really concerned about the lot of the poor and downtrodden would advocate a policy of going slow on fiscal restraint if ultimately this can help the poor through enhanced social welfare spending. But then, the poor should not be asked to pay the price for the mistakes and inadequacies of politicians and bureaucrats. If there is ineptness or inefficiency in economic management, this is not the fault of those who cannot afford a square meal a day. Those who are inept or inefficient must look for other scapegoats than people who are barely surviving.

3. TIME FOR A NATIONAL POLICY

Budget is only one aspect of fiscal policy, perhaps not the most crucial one as many people think. It is largely an exercise in arithmetic — if we leave out the policy pronouncements that the Finance Minister makes and the signals that he sends out — one that also turns out to be wrong most of the time. Indeed, if we examine the revised estimates for several years, we would want to repudiate the figures part of the budget.

If there is any sanctity in budget making, this arises from the changes that the Finance Minister makes in tax rates. In a way, this is the crux of the budgetary effort, rather than the figures. Under reform, this part of fiscal policy must get sharpened. In fact, this is how economic activity must be influenced. While no Finance Minister can get away without pursuing a tax policy for revenue's sake, the cuts and hikes in tax rates and the introduction and withdrawal of taxes with a goal that is wider than revenue collection are what the budget should focus on, particularly with an economy that is liberalising. The late Dr. Gautam Mathur, quite some time ago, had recommended what he called the disparity tax to discourage investments that were of low priority and encourage those of high priority.

The changes in tax policy that are made under liberalisation should have Dr. Mathur's recommendation as the basis. Discrimination between sectors and sections must be the basic thrust of tax policy. Here, I must return to budgeting under United Front rule and with good reason. The circumstances bearing on fiscal policy then are by no means irrelevant to 2000-2001. Some evidence of deliberate discrimination was available in the 1996-97 budget. For instance, Mr. Chidambaram favoured income taxpayers in lower slabs and deliberately avoided extending the hike in standard deduction and reduction in the rate of tax to other taxpayers. The restriction on use of post cards — and the requirement that a much more expensive alternative should be taken recourse to for quiz and other programmes — was also a small step towards fiscal discrimination. The end of the zero tax regime put a stop to a system that had deteriorated from one of discrimination to that of indiscrimination. But, these had only a limited economic end and were hardly designed to enhance the competitiveness of the economy overall, which should, indeed, be the main thrust of fiscal policy. These had nothing in common with the principle behind the disparity tax. Rather, seen against the background of coalition politics, the two measures cited were essentially a fiscal effort to buy peace within the coalition and without.

Reasoning behind MAT

The investment allowance, tax incentives and depreciation benefits are part of a fiscal scheme to promote certain areas of activity, but these have over time resulted in a situation where some of the best performing companies — in terms of profits — did not pay any corporate tax. One may argue that the introduction of the minimum alternative tax was not quite the remedy to this anomaly. But then, if the government had not provided a package of incentives industrial development would have suffered. One can even say that the imposition of a minimum tax on companies that otherwise would not have to pay any tax at all might even have a discouraging effect on investment and industrial growth. It was, obviously, very difficult for the finance minister concerned to anticipate the emergence of zero tax companies over a period.

While Mr. Chidambaram had acted decisively to end the anomaly, one wondered if this was not motivated by the politically perceived need to signal to the Leftists that the budget would not offer anything on a platter to the capitalists. When fiscal intervention in the form of a minimum tax came, it was intended to hurt. Yet, when we consider four years later that the fiscal impact was only 12 per cent or thereabout of profits, there was still an incentive. Discrimination remains. The only thing is that unlike in the past companies have to pay a tax within a regime of incentives.

Fiscal policy is only partly an exercise in revenue mobilisation, though with reform the Government has a social commitment to honour. Liberalisation is intended to hurt, and this calls for a special thrust on social welfare. The Government, therefore, must have resources to take care of the poor who are neglected by the reform process and those who are hurt by measures to boost the economy's competitiveness overall. Populism has a role in the fiscal policy to that extent, but it is the responsibility of the finance minister to ensure that scarce funds are not squandered away and the pressure of populism does not become the tail that wags the dog. There is always the danger of this happening in a democracy, particularly one where the Government is one of an uneasy coalition. Especially when he was being blamed for pursuing the Congress party's goals, Mr. Chidambaram was under pressure to throw prudence to the winds, in respect of areas where the disgruntled elements in the coalition had a vested interest.No wonder, the Finance Minister had chosen to go slow on insurance reform, disinvestment of Government equity in the public sector and on exit policy. The public sector, thus, was denied a meaningful agenda consistent with the pressures of liberalisation. In respect of insurance, five years after an export committee declared itself on various aspects of reform, the U F Government proclaimed that there was no hurry for reform, without clarifying that because the Leftists did not want it nothing could be done.

Fiscal Policy Compulsions

Fiscal policy can — and should — never the distanced from political as well as social compulsions. No finance minister is independent of the Government and this functionary has to meet the goals that the Government has set for itself. There have been instances globally of finance ministers quitting in protest over aspects of fiscal policy. Where the central banks are strong, the finance minister is under tremendous pressure and there are cases of this functionary having to quit precisely because of not being able to take orders from the central bank. In India, this problem is not there but there are others which the finance minister has to take in his stride.

Perhaps, the time has come for formulation of fiscal policy being entrusted to a select committee of Parliament rather than to the finance minister of a particular government. In the United States, budgeting involves two parties, the government as well as opposition. Ultimately what emerges is a consensus. When hung parliaments and coalition governments are emerging, it is better to make the formulation of fiscal policy the responsibility of parliament. Fiscal policy must reflect national concerns, not the pulls and pressures facing a government. With an elusive majority in Parliament, the Rao Government should not have, legitimately, prepared budgets on the basis of its priorities and compulsions. Likewise, the Deve Gowda Ministry had no legitimacy — which contrived numbers didn't give — for presenting a budget that Mr. Chidambaram declared as reflecting the United Front's common minimum programme. This was the time when the major political parties had to think seriously of a national fiscal policy and a national budget. Circumstances have not changed dramaticaly since then. Mr. Yashawnt Singh as Finance under NDA is not differently placed from Mr. Chidambaram, the improved numbers in the Lok Sabha notwithstanding. There are pressures that he can do nothing about.

4. FROM INCENTIVES TO SUBSIDIES

Ideally, the budget is required to look beyond the arithmetic of receipts and expenditure. Yet, just as the figures are often rendered meaningless, policy pronouncements also get reduced to irrelevance. The 1996-97 Union Budget saved itself a possible criticism later that its declaration of intent proved to be an exercise in rhetorics, by ducking major issues of reform, though this could not, obviously, be the provocation for that. The obvious one was that the constituents of the ruling combine could not agree on the basics of reform. The leftists did not want hikes in administered prices and cuts in subsidies as well as jobs. They also did not want any reform of the public sector — which ruled out both exit policy and disinvestment leading to privatisation. If this was the story of United Front the partners of NDA are not any more supportive of the harder aspects of reform.

When Dr. Manmohan Singh could not successfully grapple with these parts of reform, one could not legitimately blame Mr. Chidambaram or Mr. Yashwant Sinha for steering clear of them. But then, without addressing itself to the unfinished part of reform no budget from 1996-97 to 2000-01 merited the description as an exercise in continuation of the reform effort. If there was any continuity, this lay in the inability to push the reform agenda through, something that did not merit kudos. All governments have problems. There is never anything like a government being able to honour all its commitments — whether populistic or rational. It needs clarifying that populism does not always get translated into policy and administrative action. Often, promises and commitments that help garner votes fail to get translated into policy and administrative measures.

After all, everything has to be tested at the market place. This is why grandiose schemes do not often get off the ground. It is not just that politicians yield to bureaucrats. Rather, those who have come to power have to go through a procedure that those who aspire for it do not have to. Granted that rules are often broken to accommodate irregularities and scandals surface everywhere at the drop of a hat as it were, yet scandals are still more the exception than the rules. Just as not all populist proposals do not get into the statute book or the policy and administrative frame, rational and well thought-out proposals fail to get the nod, though for contrary reasons.

The stock market has moaned for a long period not because reform was ignored but because of perceived worries over the sutare of the economy. During 1996-97 the provocation was MAT U Companies which because of a mix of concessions and reliefs had not been paying any tax — in the face of an impressive track and profit record — had to pay just over 12 per cent of profits as tax. Agreed that when no tax is paid on profits of Rs.300-400 crore, this level of minimum tax will deprive the companies about Rs.30-40 crore annually, still one did not have to flaunt his Marxist credentials to justify imposition of a tax liability on undertakings that make substantial profits and escape taxation altogether. Yet, the minimum tax does not declare that the regime of relief and concessions provided with a certain purpose is irrelevant. While reform justifies fiscal as well other incentives to boost competition, the commitment to reform demands that these should not deteriorate into subsidies. There is a distinction between incentives and subsidies and the latter have no place in a reforming economy. It is the responsibility of any government — coalition or otherwise — to prevent such a deterioration.

But, the budget, for 1996-97 as well as those for other post-reform years have otherwise ducked the issue of subsidy reduction. Rather, these loudly repudiated that part of the reform process by enhancing the subsidy. While a case can always be made for taxing the zero tax companies heavily and providing larger subsidies to the farm sector, the correct approach would be the reverse — provide added encouragement to industry and phase out the support mechanism in respect of agriculture. The 1997-98 budget was widely perceived to be a dream budget, but turned out to be a damp squib. It was saved by the VDIS, 1997 garnering Rs. 10,500 crore. For their part, the budgets for 1998-99, 1999-2000 and 2000-01 have hardly been spectacular in their impact on reform as well as fiscal management. The respective finance ministers have just about managed to keep their heads above water in terms of fiscal arithmetic. They could not go beyond that arithmatical priority.

3

RUNNING THE ECONOMY

1. NOT IDEOLOGY, BUT SELF-INTEREST

Governments are moved by several forces, within and without. This is true of all of them, and irrespective of their character. The only difference between a dictatorial and a truly democratic government is that while in respect of the former the impetus comes largely from the one who heads it or those close to him/her, in case of the latter, the pull and push come from interests that are perceived by the ruling elite to wield a lot of influence. It is not unusual for governments under a democratic system to be pushed or pulled by political forces that either help create new pockets of influence or are able to capitalise on the strength of those that are already there.

There is really nothing like a truly independent government, one that is able to go entirely on its own steam. Even where the provocation is provided by a difficult environment or combination of factors, once the response to the latter comes in the form of policies and administrative measures, political forces and non-political lobbies take over. For instance, over the past few years, in different Third World countries reform or liberalisation has emerged as a major driving force for economic policy under pressure of a difficult economic situation, largely relating to BoP pressures. But, once reform became the watchword, more than the inner strength or the process itself what helped push the reform measures deeper was the self-interest of some powerful sections.

Just as in the past regulation was used by certain forces or interests to give themselves a stranglehold over the economy, under deregulation often the same forces or interests have assumed the role of forcing reform forward.

Not dialectics but facts

This is not an exercise in dialectics but a statement of facts. No wonder, those who were part of the regulation and control bandwagon have been quick to get into the other bandwagon of reform and decontrol in India. Ideology does play some part but in politics ideology is generally overtaken by pragmatism — or if you think that this is simplistic or soft, let us call it self-interest. Under long years of communism, it would be foolhardy to think that the system was consolidated only by the strength of ideology. In truth, it was not. What really helped consolidate the hold of communism was that several powerful people and institutions gained from its spread and it was in their interest to make the communist system all pervasive.

This is not to make fun of the communist ideologists but to stress the obvious. More than ideology what ultimately mattered was the the self-interest of those who were advancing it. Tight regulation and State control gave them a substantial clout and, effectively, they needed communism much more than the other way round. When Mr. Mikhail Gorbachev went about advocating *perestroika* and *glasnost*, the apostles of statism had to turn towards the free market for their own survival. If, in the past, the inefficiency that was explicit in State dominance gave them a lot of authority, this they began to enjoy under the changed dispensation on the strength of *glasnost* and *perestroika*. Obviously, ideology did not really matter; what did was the fact that the source of power had changed and they had to shift their sights and nobody was so foolish as to defy the change and face the consequence of powerlessness. Who knows, the mafia that is holding the Russian free market to ransom is controlled by the very people, who, before Mr. Gorbachev applied the broomstick to the cobweb that had gathered, had flourished on the strength of communism.

This happened in distant China and elsewhere in the social bloc. The confirmed Maoists were the ones who started and consolidated the modernisation programme. Mr. Deng was, no doubt, repudiating the essence of Maoism when he in 1978 had put China on the path of free market or reform, but, mind you, he had been a staunch Maoist until then. Even in countries under autocratic regimes it was never the decision of one or a few that settled which way the economy should go. Mr. Deng would not have ended the long phase of statism without the support of influential sections in the Communist party and their self-interest. Mr. Gorbachev and Mr. Deng alike were able to put their respective nations towards a remarkable economic transformation only because of the backing of other people, who quickly recognised that there were considerable benefits for them in the changed economic environment.

From fellow travellers to reformists

Likewise, in reforming India, all those who were making gains from all the controls and regulations are doing precisely that under liberalisation. If erstwhile fellow travellers and those that found a lot to object to earlier to the post-1991 reform measures are now in the reform bandwagon, one obvious reason is that this transformation is perceived to be in the interests of those people who were in the forefront of the opposition to reform then and have now changed their colours.

If controls were selectively loosened to help the favoured people, now the benefits of reform are being directed again to those close to the corridors of power. If irregularities were committed under cover of regulation then, presently these are deemed quite natural with liberalisation, though the protection that controls earlier offered to scamsters is not there presently. Ironically, some economists believe that the economic reform phase had started even when Mrs. Indira Gandhi was around. There was selective loosening of controls no doubt, but these were only cosmetic when compared to the kind of changes that have taken place since the middle of 1991. Mrs. Indira Gandhi generally never wavered from the path of State regulation, and as for Mr. Rajiv Gandhi nothing much happened in the sphere of economic liberalisation. In either case, controls worked over time to protect those at the helm.

Nobody knew of any scam when Mrs. Indira Gandhi was in power and the only thing that her detractors could pounce on was the Shah Commission report, that too only when she was out of power. Nothing surfaced and the kind of judicial activism that we have been witnessing in recent years could not have even been visualised in her time. The Allahabad High Court ruling against her paled into insignificance when compared to the inactivity that otherewise prevailed. In regard to Mr. Rajiv Gandhi also, the Bofors probe was sought to be scuttled by a member of the judiciary. Compare a certain judgement during the Emergency with the directive much later to CBI on the bribes alleged to have been paid to certain MPs and the recent indictment of the Central Government leading to the ouster of the Union Law Minister, there has been a dramatic change. Indeed, one might say that Mr. Narasimha Rao might have escaped adverse attention on all the scandals where his involvement was widely assumed if only he had to his advantage the facilities that were open to his predecessors.

However, to say that now probity is in sharp focus or that the Indian nation is getting more democratic would be downright foolish, though one can attribute the fact that a former Prime Minister can be put under a lot of pressure to the essential spirit of reform process — decontrol. It is hardly incidental that when India is liberalising there are also some signs of the rule of law asserting itself against the erstwhile high and mighty.

2. EXPLOITATION, PARTLY BY CHOICE

Ideally, economics should not be all about exploitation and should also be concerned about justice, not just economic but also social. Yet, even without liberalisation and reform, you will find that in economics the focus is on exploitation largely—exploitation of one's needs and another's resources or potential. An episode of *Star Trek* emphasises this tellingly. There are two communities, one of which needs regular supplies of narcotic in the mistaken belief that the drug is life saving, a cure for plague. The other is the one which provides the supply. Indeed, it does nothing other than to produce and sell the drug. It has no other economic activity. *Star Trek* deals with a very distant future, 500 years away. The scenario should not be so primitive as this, but then, this is the storyline.

Yet, what this episode underlines is broadly relevant to the past, present and future. One's need is another's compulsion. This is how the economic system operates. There are refinements on either side but the basic fact of inter-dependence remains. One may want to say that the buyer is the exploited one and the supplier the exploiter. But, this perception is not quite correct.

Dumping Ground

Coming to multilateral arrangements, the complaint of developing countries is that they are exploited by the rich nations. Under long years of colonialism, this did occur, but what is taking place today should not be confused with what all went under colonialism. The Third World has long been the dumping ground for technology that became outdated in the developed economies. While barriers were erected against imports from developing countries, producers in the rich nations had the clout in terms of capacity as well as marketing to push what they turned out on the markets of developing countries. But, this was not the same as the exploitation that took place in the colonial era of the distant past. We must make this distinction lest we confuse the recent scenario and the one that is emerging with what prevailed earlier.

This is not to say that no exploitation is taking place under growing global liberalisation — no arm-twisting — but to warn against glossing over the growing inter-dependence among different countries. The multinational corporations need business and do not mind compromising on several issues to secure orders. Take for instance the pressure that the US corporate giants some time ego brought on the US Government in respect of the latter's threat to impose trade sanctions on China under WTO provisions. President Clinton then needed to play up to southern textile lobby with the presidential election to follow, but he also had to cope with the compulsion that the big US corporates had a lot of stake in China. The latter also warned that it would do business with the rivals of suppliers from the US. After all, Americans are not the only ones in the fray. There are several others. Even in India, a determined state government could dictate to Enron. While there was a fear earlier that the flow of foreign investment to India would suffer because of the renegotiation with Enron this has been belied. If foreign investors are not responding as enthusiastically as expected to India's opening up, this has less to do with the counter arm-twisting that some state governments have resorted to than the glaring bottlenecks that are there and the administrative failure to tackle these effectively.

Arm-twisting

What emerges is that arm-twisting can also be done by the prospective buyers. Vietnam does this regardless of its gross under-development. Though it is described as an emerging tiger, this is an exaggeration. To that extent, its capacity to dictate to MNCs is significant and should not be dismissed lightly. Thus, effectively it demonstrates that exploitation is open to a supplier as much to a prospective buyer. This is hardly new economics. This has always been the economics of the free market and this remains. Thus, if a Third World government is taken for a ride, such exploitation has less to do with the clout of MNCs than the failure of the government of the host country to set the agenda for the multinational corporations.

One knows enough of the colonial era to say with assurance that exploitation did not come solely because of the power of colonisers. While might did play a part, the fact that the natives did not join hands to resist the colonisers also had a role. This is an observation that is quite relevant to the present when one government in Maharashtra surrendered and gave everything on a platter to Enron and its successor did not waste any time in overruling the agreement reached earlier. In British India, the only way the nation's economic sovereignty could have been safeguarded was by way of an assertiveness of various rulers, which itself would have demanded all of them standing together as one. The British consolidated their exploitation mainly because no ruler looked beyond his own ambitions and personal interests. Even now, Indian states do not have to tell an MNC to go by their dictates. Effectively, exploitation is partly by choice and only partly by compulsion.

Understanding the situation

Third World governments and *swadeshi*-wallahs must recognise this. The sooner they do this the better it would be for the quality of policy-making and decision-taking. On regional and international fora we will have less of empty rhetoric and more of healthy discussion if those who are leading the campaign against the perceived threats from advanced countries in terms of policy impediments and administrative barriers begin to view exploitation differently. The debate over *swadeshi* vs *videshi* will be more to the purpose if exploitation is properly understood and defined.

While such an understanding should not — unless the government is inept — lead to indiscrimination on the direction of foreign investment and MNC support should be forthcoming more for hard areas of investment and less for quick gestation investments, what is to the point is that the approach to MNCs would become a balanced one — that is neither one of appeasement nor total distrust. Even the *phoren* craze will weaken with such an approach, knowing that this craze is a reflection of the feeling that goods that come from the Western countries are necessarily good in quality.

The feeling of superiority in quality is the genesis of exploitation. This must be understood. Just as the old Indian rulers were quick to respect the British might and paved the way for their exploitation of the Indian nation, under liberalisation, Indian consumers are clearing the decks for MNC exploitation of the domestic market — at the expense of indigenous suppliers — on the basis of the assumed superiority of Western goods. But, once it is accepted that exploitation works both ways and prospective buyers can also put pressure on willing suppliers, the blind acceptance of the superior quality of Western goods should disappear.

4

SHIFTING FEDERAL EQUATIONS

When the nation for a time had a Prime Minister who could not look beyond his home state, not much could be said of its economic integration. Mr. Deve Gowda, however, in retrospect need not feel bad about the fact that his elevation to the nation's top most post had failed to give him a national perception. After all, for the late Mr. Charan Singh, Uttar Pradesh was Bharat. With such a noble precedent, Mr. Gowda could have Karnataka as Bharat. Yet, in this age of globalisation, it is odd that we have leaders who cannot look beyond sub-regions. But then, this is Bharat. With liberalisation, the Indian nation should have become a single economic entity, but ironically the process would appear to have encouraged greater decentralisation, especially with foreign investors being wooed by state governments and the former themselves ignoring the Centre and reaching out to those in power in different states.

The United States Ambassador to India, some years ago, was sending a powerful signal against the nation's economic unity when he was happy to be seen world-wide milking the cow of the Bihar Chief Minister. That was not intended to be a PR exercise but an act that symbolised the shift of economic power from the Centre to the states. While New Delhi does control the purse-strings, decision making is getting decentralised. States may still complain that they have to move Delhi for this and that, but the fact is that with liberalisation — although the reform process in terms of fiscal discipline and cutting the bureaucratic red-tape may not have filtered down to the states — what could not be achieved in the 45 years that preceded the initiation of economic reform — making the economic system less unitary and more federal — is beginning to take place in some measure. In a way, this aspect of the reform effort is giving the constitutional amendments for strengthening the Panchayati Raj institutions the backing that was possibly unintended and unexpected.

In Conflict with Reform

Yet, a crucial element of reform — giving the Indian economy a globally competitive edge — would suffer with states asserting themselves against the Centre and fighting battles among themselves rather than joining forces with New Delhi for fighting the multinational corporations. Decentralisation is *per se* in conflict with reform. Let there be no doubt about this. While the Indian economy badly needs a common market, this will not even be a goal when states have sales tax wars and vie with one another in giving MNCs favourable terms, in the process letting the global corporate giants exploit the competition among the different states and ultimately get for themselves a deal that would make the economy overall less — and not more — competitive, as it should be under reform. What Enron was initially allowed to do in respect of power project costs and tariffs can easily become the general rule with one state government trying to score over another.

While the European Community is closing all inter-member barriers and pushing itself as one massive economic entity and members of ASEAN are forging closer economic integration, here we are trying to become more and more insular. While as a sound political goal, decentralisation does make sense, efforts in this direction should not be allowed to impede the emergence of India as a major global economic player. While political power must be exercised more and more at the grass roots level, this should not weaken the strength of the Indian economy vis-a-vis the rest of the world. Surely, Indian goods and services cannot become competitive in global terms with preferential sales tax rates at the state level for producers within and other reliefs and concessions to entrepreneurs given indiscriminately as part of a wooing exercise.

Everything for the best players

Competitiveness demands the best players getting the best advantages and the best locations. While small must be encouraged, ultimately it is not smallness *per se* which can flourish but the strength behind smallness. Unity in diversity makes for a good political principle but should get shot down if advanced as an economic premise. Unity must lie in unity, if the goal is to advance the cause of India as a global economic player. The Panchayati Raj institutions must play a bigger role in political as well as economic administration, but this must be supportive and catalystic in respect of economic development and not detrimental, which it will surely become if the local bosses are more keen to demonstrate what harm they can do to economic decision making than set themselves earnestly to the task of promoting India's global competitiveness.

This is not intended as an essay against decentralisation and Panchayati Raj institutions and the constitutional amendments but for responsible decentralisation. Unfortunately, a Prime Minister who carries his regional and sub-regional battles to his gaddi at the Centre does not quite send the most re-assuring signals about what decentralisation will do in the coming years. Again, the regional satraps who are only anxious to get their pound of flesh in lieu of their support to the coalition Government at the Centre and to the Prime Minister are not the best champions of decentralisation that would give the Indian economy the strength it needs *vis-a-vis* its competitors multilaterally.

Closing ranks

Agreed that there are economic divisions even within the European Community and ASEAN is hardly a regional common market and the Government of United States has several regional and sub-regional pressure groups to contend with, still the fact is that they are all closing their ranks through regional trade blocs to meet the challenges and capitalise on the opportunities thrown up by the new global trade accord. But here, in the name of decentralisation — and oddly enough, also liberalisation — the states are determined to weaken India as an international economic force. While over-centralisation can kill initiative at the local levels, a measure of centralisation is necessary to avoid a situation where MNCs are able to play one state against another.

For the global players, India must not only seem but be a strong economic entity which cannot be trifled with. Coalition governments of the Centre sustained by emerging regional forces must particularly realise this, no matter what their political future is. While the kind of aberrations that went in the name of Central guidance to economic reform must be avoided, the anarchy that is explicit in too much decentralisation is hardly the better option.

Nobody is saying that state governments and local bodies should not have greater fiscal powers, but this is not to be confused with the wider issue of making India an economic power to reckon with globally. A loose federation might not have hurt the economic integration of a nation *vis-a-vis* others in the global arena before, but not any longer. The Centre must largely speak for the Indian nation and formulate the economic policies. It must set the ground rules for investment, whether it is by foreign companies or their domestic counterparts. The states must not view this as an act of weakening further their influence. The stronger the Centre the stronger will the states be.

5

THE GAMES THAT POLITICIANS PLAY

1. BLAMING IT ON PAST SINNERS

A government, wherever it is, has problems doing its job. One regime can conveniently blame another — the predecessor or the one before it — for the complexity of the challenges it faces. But then, doing this is not going to make its task any easier. One must recall the strident observations of Mr. R. Venkataraman as Union Finance Minister in his first budget under Mrs. Indira Gandhi in 1980 about the Janata Government. Eleven years later, Dr. Manmohan Singh emulated that when he came up with the first of his five successive budgets. But, knowing that the Congress has generally dominated the national scene, there has only been limited scope for such tactics at the Central level. The relative instability in the states, has, in contrast, offered greater scope, although blaming someone hardly provides the basis either for sound policymaking or effective administration. No regime can show itself to be incompetent to cope with the burden that its predecessor has left. In fact, a mature leadership would want to boast of an ability to turn a bad legacy into a platform for impressive progress. A situation that one regime inherits, left to itself, would more or less set its own agenda. Unless the new government has the capacity to alter the macro scenario to its advantage and is also able to demonstrate this quickly, it will soon have an impossible task on its hands.

There is always room for honest differences for other mortals, but for politicians there is often nothing like an honest difference. What matters is expediency. This, indeed, is what most guides them. Election manifestos are moved by perceived compulsions, though these are appropriately camouflaged by lofty commitments to social uplift. The heavens are promised to the voter so that the politicians can rule the earth. Quite some time ago, the Rudolphs wrote of the demand and command forces in the Indian political economy. Some of their observations are relevant to the present context, although most political leaders may not have bothered to browse over their outstanding work, *Lakshmi: India's Political Economy*.

What emerged from the book was that both command and demand influences mattered in India under long years of Mr. Nehru and later when Mrs. Indira Gandhi was at the helm. Command policies represent the actions of rulers on their own in pursuit of long-term goals and demand policies constitute the latter's response to short-term objectives and to the pressure of the populace. While the authors of the book saw the two as two different phenomena, if we look at them closely we can see that they are only two sides of the same coin, though we must obviously allow for the difference in gestation periods of the measures taken. For, no leader would act unless moved by what he or she perceives to be a winning factor and this perception applies irrespective of the time frame and the motive.

Wooing the Constituency

Wooing the constituency, in its wider sense, is what the politician is concerned about. Most voters hardly ever get to see their representatives in the legislature from close quarters once they are safely ensconced in Parliament or the state assembly. Thus, when we say constituency it denotes the populace in general, of a state or the nation. Ultimately, what is known to win votes is a catchy slogan, though whether it is enough to keep a regime in place for the full term of five years is ultimately a game of numbers. Who plays this game better than others is the one who will be able to form a government — one that will last. Mr. Rao succeeded—but at a price—in this game better than anyone had done before or may perhaps do in the coming years, though in retrospect judging by the virtual rout of the Congress in the 1996 poll, he could not possibly have crossed the first hurdle of being invited to form a government on his own.

Mrs. Indira Gandhi could not cope with the power of the syndicate and spent an uncomfortable time when the party's stalwarts formed the Congress(O). She could only fret and fume but the partymen who chose to stick to the syndicate could not be bought over. A general election, backed by a lot of political rhetoric as well as strategy — in the shape of nationalisation of 14 leading commercial banks of the time and the enactment of MRTP Act — was needed to consolidate her position.

But only a few years later, despite her massive popularity because of India's support for the Bangladesh war of independence in 1971, she could not cope with the growing clout of the Opposition. There were some members of the Opposition, who had no hesitation in calling her Durga after the 1971 war but the same people had had enough of her ways of governance well before the emergency was thrust on an unwilling nation. In the months that preceded the declaration of internal emergency, nothing worked for her. The *garibi hatao* programme, which the Rudolphs rightly called a demand measure, effectively had no takers. A big mandate and a strong representation for the Congress in the Lok Sabha were not enough to see Mrs. Indira Gandhi through the five year period with comfort. Though she lasted the full term, a major part of it was either spent in trying — in vain — to ward off the Opposition challenge or taking the nation through, possibly, its darkest period since Independence.

Keeping Government Stable

In contrast, despite so many scandals and the selective political use of a particular scandal, Mr. Narasimha Rao kept his government intact. He was blamed for having resorted to horse-trading and bribery and a faces a unique conviction for that and for not letting the government fall in the house of Parliament as Mr. Morarji Desai and Mr. V P Singh had done earlier. Nobody can ask for legitimising horse-trading, but then, one supposes, this is a lesser evil than either the declaration of an internal emergency or the other alternative of having governments for very short periods. The Italians, in recent years, have recognised the wisdom of stable governments and India cannot, obviously, accept a hung parliament and elections every year or even sooner as being the best for democracy.

Granted that corruption and misuse of authority should not get fostered in the name of stability, yet it is quite irresponsible to argue for frequent changes of political regimes as a necessary demonstration of the democratic character of Indian polity. What makes a good — even exhilarating — copy for a newspaper column can hardly make for a good strategy for governance. At the outset, a reference was made to regimes having to look beyond their legacies. When we have unstable governments, the temptation would be greater for governments blaming their predecessors for their problems. By the time they begin to look at their own agenda they would not be there any more, a scenario that good governance cannot accept. Only up to a point do frequent changes in political regimes reflect the democratic spirit. While voters must be free to be divided equally among different political parties, their real maturity lies in choosing a regime that will both last and work and not barely survive and devote the period of survial to simply find fault with the one that preceded it.

Come election time, everyone goes berserk. For the Election Commission everything by way of administrative action is against the model code of conduct. Which means that the administration wherever it is must come to a standstill. The earlier CEC declared that he was not Jesus but Moses. The Christians must have been delighted, so should have been the Jews, for different reasons obviously. This important constitutional functionary can be both if he wants to, but the fact is that in the name of a fair and free poll he is not letting even critical administrative decisions being taken. For instance, cotton exports, of course, have political overtones but for a state government to move the concerned High Court on the matter and for the latter to direct the Centre to act advances the cause of good poll conduct to the extreme point where nothing else matters. The result is that the nation is in a state of anarchy on matters other than those of poll conduct.

Defining flexibility

The present CEC, very much like his predecessor, can call himself Moses and say that he is not Jesus but this is an option that is not open to a responsible government which, rather, cannot settle for being either or neither and sometimes it has to be everything and sometimes nothing. It can never say that it will be this but not that. After all, flexibility is the hallmark of sound governance. Governments have to be several things simultaneously to be able to perform well and when the situation so demands, its maturity should reflect itself even in a form of self-denial. They cannot be too rigid at any point of time, though as for flexibility this should never be extended to a point where it turns into scandalous. Flexibility is not `anything goes'. There has to be respect for probity and for norms of conduct.

No administrator or political leader can say that corruption is only an aspect of flexibility. Money has to pass hands if sensible decisions have to be taken — this cannot be the watchword of any government, though under five years of Mr. Narasimha Rao rule *sub chalta hai* had become the main plank of decision making. There have been scandals galore, and no sector was free of corruption. The Petroleum Minister had given LPG dealerships to,his friends and relatives and those of his ministerial colleagues not excluding the Prime Minister himself. Another member of the Rao team decided peremptorily that she could give house allotments to any one that she chose because that was her ministerial responsibility. When someone holds charge of a ministry that deals with sugar, it does not necessarily mean that several crores of rupees should be earned by way of cuts or kick-backs from a particular decision or that deals should be entered into that would give the minister a lot of dough. No Government runs by itself. It demands a commitment, a strong one at that. The politicians and officials who are part of it must share this as a matter of course, not by fits and starts. Commitment means professionalism, which leaves no room for corruption. No murky deals will be negotiated and there will be no `saints' to be consulted on who should be appointed where and who should not get the nod.

But, this is a lofty ideal when you see the record of the present and the not-so-distant past. A minister sees himself only as a politician and uses his decision-making authority largely for political ends. In whatever a minister does or doesn't there is politics. No wonder, a supposedly commercial transaction carries a kick-back that will go into either the party's or the minister's personal coffer. This explains why when companies can give donations to political parties and for political purposes their managements are reluctant to use the legitimate course of making payments by cheque and prefer the cash route, which reveals neither the donor nor the donee. In a way, a previous dialogue between political leaders and leaders of industry at the CII annual session was wasted because of the political ambience that left no room for transparency and above-the-board dealings. Everything had to be done covertly, not openly. We may all bemoan how democracy has reduced itself but where is the remedy?

Coming back to the Election Commission, agreed that it has to ensure that the poll process does not get vitiated but polls are not everything. Granted that the Commission has to assert itself because the administration cannot be trusted to exercise propriety, yet when a government cannot conduct itself properly for nearly five years, how can it be forced to put on the best face for a brief period when the Election Commission's writ runs? The solution does not lie in extending the latter's writ to the non-poll period as well. That would be tantamount to creating a super institution, a kind of Frankenstein. The nation must seek a less damaging remedy, but then will its political elite provide this?

2. SPARE A THOUGHT

Passing judgments is perhaps the easiest thing to do. No wonder, everyone does this, and as a matter of course. When you say judgement you normally have in mind the courts, but the fact is that we all do this. The media does this day in and day out, politicians do this and so does anyone who can express a view. In economics, as in politics, judgements are supposed to be based on facts but then facts can be twisted consistent with the user's needs or compulsions.

One is innocent unless proved guilty — this is the basis of the rule of law. But what remedy is there to character assassination? The moment there is a probe or a case filed in a court, your credentials are in tatters. So many junior government officials are condemned to social ostracism for years because of suspicion. Their innocence remains in dispute — and doubt — for long and one must be in their shoes to feel the trauma. The *hawala* disclosures drew a lot of flak because Mr. Narasimha Rao was seen to use them selectively and to give himself a tactical advantage on the eve of the 1996 elections. But, nameless — faceless — employees of government departments get hauled up in different places for petty offences. They are suspended from service and their family life destroyed. The SBI cashier, the late Mr. Malhotra, was just one of so many people who literally went through torture because of an unkind system. We are no more civilised than what we were centuries ago, and all because of the rule of law. Mere suspicion was enough then to cut off someone's head and this will do today to reduce someone to a living corpse.

Character assassination

Character assassination hurts more than an untimely death or a loss of limb. It is a living death. The politicians who were named or unnamed in the Jain diary were, no doubt, condemned before their involvement in an irregular transaction could be established. But, they could raise their voice against the then Prime Minister and accuse him of corruption. What can the inconsequential official in the dock for taking a fiver as a bribe do? There is no redress available to him.

This is not to justify taking of bribes or to demand that no notice should be taken of corruption in government offices. The registrar's office in different places is seen as a source of corruption. The Karnataka Government had mooted use of franking machines in the offices of sub-registrars to eliminate stamp vendors and deed writers functioning on the premises. But, when registration of property carries a fixed price and everyone knows this — ironically, there are reports of even serving IAS and IPS officers having to pay the customary charges for registering property outside their areas of posting — this is not going to be of any great help.

It took a long, long while for the Government to decide in favour of action against Mr. Chandraswami, whom a former Prime Minister called a saint. Mr. Harshad Mehta, the kingpin of the securities scandal, is still to be fixed for all the irregularities that he masterminded, although a number of officials of the institutions which went out of their way to oblige him are suffering the consequences of their indiscretions. The former chairman of the Housing Bank had earlier committed suicide and a former senior official of SBI was cleared only with his death although his part in the scam was less than marginal.

We can all get exercised by the way CBI either moves or chooses not to in respect of selected individuals, provided the ones singled out for leniency are high and mighty. But, we don't spare a thought for the small bribe taker, the person whose upper limit is perhaps Rs.100. In the securities scandal, not all officials who colluded with Mr. Harshad Mehta are known to have acquired substantial assets. While they all bent the rules to oblige the big bull, CBI has not found evidence of large bribes in respect of several of them.

The *hawala* disclosures paled into insignificance when compared with the kind of sums that Mr. Harshad Mehta and others like him had made at the expense of certain banks and other financial institutions. The sugar import scandal also involved amounts that the Jain diary did not reveal. In the Bofors gun deal, the kick-back was considerable. It cannot be that ministers and senior officials should only take crores as bribes or kick-backs and also that nothing would be done against such irregularities.

Voters, the Judges

When it comes to politicians, their judges are seen to be the voters, who will give their verdict. If a corrupt leader gets past the hustings, nothing can be held against him. No wonder, people with a criminal record get elected to the legislature and even become ministers. But, how many sub-registrars caught with their pants down can get away as most politicians — lowly or highly placed — can? Politicians are a class by themselves and unlike you and me they will never have to undergo the trauma that clerks and peons and police constables must be prepared for when they take a fiver and tenner and are caught in the act.

Small men remain small men, unless there is a strong political connection, which makes all the difference between a person who counts for nothing and one who carries weight. Although the different political parties were at one time making a lot of fuss about keeping *hawala*-tainted people in hibernation, this is not to be taken seriously. The Jain diary was not the ultimate in political corruption. It was a mistake to think so, though everybody had done that. Those whose names had found their way into the diary were not the most corrupt among politicians nor can one say that those who had escaped mention did not know what corruption was.

While it would be wrong to suggest that politics runs only on corruption, it must be acknowledged that corruption has a role in political activity and politicians are the ones who help this to flourish. They are the ones who don't suffer the consequences of discovery unlike so many inconsequential members of the administrative system. The file pushers, wherever they are, are always in danger of being caught in the act of taking some money and paying the price for it, unless they have a political godfather to offer protection. This one cannot say of any politician, whether it be the small town operator or his national counterpart. The American and British have no qualms about washing their linen in public but here in India the national media generally eschews reporting on a politician's under- world connections or activities, the revelation of which links would have truly devastating consequences in the case of lesser mortals. The US and British media have no inhibitions about disclosures about the supposedly high and mighty as long as these are well founded. But here, only the local press knowingly risks exposing the misdemeanors of politicians and there have been instances of poorly paid members of the fourth estate and their dear ones getting badly hurt for their involvement in such exposures.

It does not follow that the vernacular press should keep off the politicians or that the ill paid stringers who do investigative stories of the other life of politicians should switch over to the kind of stuff that their big brothers in the metropolises dish out and get paid handsomely for their limited labours. Rather, there is a case for the big newspapers to be more outspoken about personal indiscretions or excesses by politicians, cutting across parties, not just in editorials but in newspaper reports as well. If the *Washington Post* in the United States could go to town with reports about the first citizen's other life, what objection can there be to a change in reporting schedule in respect of the big Indian newspapers? For the Press Council what is perfectly reasonable for the Americans cannot be immoral or unethical for the Indians, not certainly in this age of liberalisation when everything that is American sells like hot cakes.

3. POSITIONING YES, WHAT ABOUT THE PRODUCT?

Globally, this is the age of virtual products, the ones which exist even before the producer and the consumer have thought of them. The virtual revolution that is taking place, with the Japanese well in front, means implicitly cultivating the consumer before the product is out. Super-imposed on the Indian political scenario of recent years, one can say that BJP is the only party which, like the Japanese manufacturers, has been consistently virtualising its product. One can even say that the party's tacticians have understood the nuances of virtualisation as well as, may be, even better than the Japanese companies!

As for other parties, they earlier tried to understand the basics of positioning and, to some extent, even develop a product that the voter would take. But, their efforts were well short of virtualisation. As for Mr. V P Singh, in Mandal card he had developed a product that could sell — that it didn't for his own party but did for others is not another matter and emphasised his positioning failure.

The forward-backward linkages make good economic sense. No doubt, politicians readily assume that what is good — not just defensible — politics is necessarily good economics, but the obvious economic merit of such a linkage is enough to win it political acceptability.

Success or failure

In the corporate world, positioning of a product is what is seen to matter most in its promotion. Politicians also do this, without knowing anything about the theory of positioning. Yet, positioning is a key aspect of political success or failure. Governments can fall because of wrong positioning and dark horses emerge winners at the hustings due to good positioning. Positioning concerns the market place and politicians also have to deal with the market place. It is immaterial that their market place is perceived to differ from what the producers and suppliers of various goods and services have to concern themselves with. Indeed, if you look at things closely, you will realise that the market place is broadly the same for politicians and producers of goods and services, depending on the kind of consumers that the latter are targeting. Just as a better-positioned producer sells his ware better, the political party that has positioned itself wisely does well at the hustings.

Social backwardness has, since Mr. V P Singh adopted the Mandal plank, emerged as an effective platform for positioning. The success of BSP emphasises this. Yet, the giant strides the BJP has taken since the 1980 election show that social backwardness is not everything. It is not a one way street. It is an irony that while Mr. V.P. Singh had sought to use the Mandal card only to benefit the Janata Dal, the BSP and the Samajwadi Party have made considerable gains in election after election from the reservations of jobs and educational opportunities made on the basis of the Mandal formula, even though the Janata Dal itself has got reduced to a force of no political consequence.

BJP's virtualisation efforts have taken a different dimension after the party was able to form a coalition Government at the Centre in two successive elections. The party has tactically given up its earlier agenda—particularly the construction of the Ram Temple — and also given itself a reformist image in contrast to its old *Swadeshi* leanings. The signal sent out that the leadership is keen to extend the party's appeal to the minority communities is a further aspect of its positioning. Considered especially against the backdrop of Mr. Atal Bihari Vajpayee's observations in the United States suggestive of BJP's continued commitment to what its critics have long been calling the hidden agenda, this public posturing as a secular and progressive political force is even more impressive. This is not quite a game of deception and what really emerges is the leadership's maturity.

6

WINDING UP

A book such as this can hardly conclude itself. For, the issues raised will continue to be relevant for several years. These will have to be widely debated and policies and administrative measures will necessarily reflect at least some of them. Policymakers and strategists in the business community will have to address these matters. I have tried to set the agenda for the immediate future and can only hope that this will receive considerable attention among those who have a critical role in the development of the economy on a liberal basis.

Attitudes primarily have to change and liberalisation in this respect has to be pervasive touching nearly all sections of the community. Rhetoric is only one aspect and high level exchanges with governments of United States and other developed countries are also not the ultimate in reform. Opening up has to push itself and policies and administrative initiatives can only play some role. The assurance that characterised the old framework of controls and regulations—that the statute, the rule book and enforcing bureaucracy and related institutions will take care of the goals—cannot work in respect of a deregulated environment and it would be grossly unrealistic to assume that the decisions taken—whatever these are and at whatever level—will take care of themselves. The impetus to development has to come from different players, who may not always be the decision makers.

Corporate planning, IPRs and issues of liberalisation, as I have discussed these in the foregoing pages, are areas that provide immense scope for ingenuity and this is precisely what I would expect. My endeavours would have succeeded if this ignenuity grows in every sector of the economy and among diverse players. Yet, I must caution against this being confused with the attitude of anything goes that was characteristic of the initial years of reform.

INDEX